The Sound of Silence

The Sound of Silence

Indigenous Perspectives on the Historical Archaeology of Colonialism

Edited by
Tiina Äikäs and Anna-Kaisa Salmi

berghahn
NEW YORK · OXFORD
www.berghahnbooks.com

First published in 2019 by
Berghahn Books
www.berghahnbooks.com

Library of Congress Cataloging-in-Publication Data
A C.I.P. cataloging record is available from the Library of Congress
Library of Congress Cataloging in Publication Control Number:
2019015100

British Library Cataloguing in Publication Data
A catalogue record for this book is available from the British Library

ISBN 978-1-78920-329-5 hardback
ISBN 978-1-80073-921-5 paperback
ISBN 978-1-78920-330-1 ebook

https://doi.org/10.3167/9781789203295

Contents

Chapter 5

Chapter 6

Chapter 7

Chapter 8

Afterword

Illustrations

Figures

Tables

Introduction
In Search of Indigenous Voices in the Historical Archaeology of Colonial Encounters

Tiina Äikäs and Anna-Kaisa Salmi

Colonial Encounters and Indigenous Lifeways

Colonial encounters between Indigenous peoples and European state powers are overarching themes in the historical archaeology of the modern era, and postcolonial historical archaeology has repeatedly emphasized the complex two-way nature of colonial encounters (e.g., Ferris, Harrison, and Wilcox 2014; Oliver 2013; Hillerdal, Karlström, and Ojala 2017, 9–10). Even though colonialism is mostly about unequal human relations (Gosden 2004), it is clear that these are two-way relations. The colonizers and the colonized both shape the other, and there is an ongoing negotiation of identities, shared spaces, and material culture (e.g., Ferris et al. 2014; Oliver 2013; Hillerdal et al. 2017, 9–10). Indigenous people are therefore fully engaged with colonial encounters and with the changes in material culture in relation to those encounters (Hart, Oland, and Frink 2012, 4). Moreover, colonial interactions include many kinds of processes, such as assimilation, cultural revivalism, and transnationalism (Oliver and Edwald 2016). Ethnic identities in colonial societies are culturally contingent, fluid, and multiple: according to Oliver and Edwald (2016), they are slow and complex legacies of interaction. Seeing colonialism in this way, as a context rather than as a "defining moment" for Indigenous peoples, helps us see colonial encounters as long-term processes on the continuum of Indigenous histories (Silliman 2005; Hart et al. 2012, 5).

This volume has been conceptualized around the role of material culture in the transformation of Indigenous cultures in colonial contact, with an aim to include both emic and etic interpretations and compare Indigenous cultures around the world. Indigenous peoples are culturally distinctive groups whose history is often affected by colonial encounters. While the meaning of "Indigenous" varies nationally and regionally, there are recurring themes in their current and historical trajectories (although the views of different Indigenous groups on those trajectories may differ): rhetorics of sovereignty, narratives of pluriethnic autonomy, and debates over environmental stewardship (Tsing 2007). Following the writings of Katherine Hayes (2015) and Craig N. Cipolla (2017), we see the concept of indigeneity as inseparable from the historical and political context and as a reaction and resistance to European colonialism. As Hillerdal et al. put it: "Concepts of identity and indigeneity are relational, and can be viewed as positions, as marking difference and power in political reality as well as theoretical debate ... [they] challenge simplified categorizations of 'Us' and 'Them', and emphasize the complexity of the relations between indigenous and non-indigenous pasts and presents" (2017, 1).

The examples in this volume come from different parts of the world. They include both overseas colonialism and cases from northern Europe where nation states have exercised colonialism on Sámi. We concur with Hart et al. (2012) that by taking a global perspective, our aim is not to homogenize or reduce the diverse ways in which Indigenous people reacted to colonialism. As the local examples in this book demonstrate, different Indigenous groups had different ways to cope with, resist, and oppose colonialism and to include and transform material markers of colonial contact in their daily lives. A comparative perspective of these case studies offers the opportunity to explore the similarities and differences in the processes behind cultural contacts, change, and renewal. With this volume, we hope to find common trajectories in Indigenous colonial histories and to explore new ways of understanding cultural contact, hybridization, and power relations between Indigenous peoples and colonial powers from the Indigenous point of view. In this introductory chapter, we focus especially on three common threads that are discussed in this volume and that highlight the importance of Indigenous perspectives in historical archaeology. First, we will discuss Indigenous peoples' creative reappropriation of colonizer-produced material things. We will also highlight that colonialism and cultural appropriation are ongoing processes that still need to be mitigated when dealing with Indigenous material culture. Finally, we will discuss the potentials and limitations of historical archaeology in representing Indigenous voices.

Changing Meanings of Material Culture in Colonial Contexts

The meanings and uses of material culture change over time. These changes are co-dependent and create new meanings for material culture. The meanings attached to objects and places change during their life cycle through social interaction (Appadurai 1986; Gosden and Marshall 1999; Meskell 2004). Already in 1995, Kent G. Lightfood and Antoinette Martinez noted that colonial-Indigenous interaction can play a critical role in cultural transformations—how people modify, create, and syncretize material objects in culture contact situations (Lightfoot and Martinez 1995, 475). The usual approach has been to investigate how colonialism changes Indigenous cultures under the premise that changes in the cultural practices of the colonizers are innovative adaptations, whereas changes in the cultural practices of the colonized are losses of identity (Beaudoin 2017, 47). Moreover, European observers often interpret the new Indigenous use of European objects as misuse (Cipolla 2017).

The understanding of how foreign objects were used in their new Indigenous contexts has been deepened by archaeological research (e.g., Cipolla 2017; Silliman 2005, 2009). Cipolla asks how colonial objects became entangled in their new contexts and how this new set of material relations affected Indigenous identities (2017, 6–10). He concludes that Indigenous groups incorporated foreign objects in their cultural practices in a variety of ways, sometimes replacing "traditional" material culture with foreign objects, sometimes complementing existing practices with new material culture (2017, 21). Along similar lines, Ritva Kylli et al. (Chapter 5) argue that Scandinavian foodstuffs such as butter, flour, bread, and spirits were incorporated into Sámi foodways from early on, the Sámi being actively interested in these products.

According to Creese (2017, 60), "[a] person's decisions about how to engage with foreign things, however apparently traditional or novel, were always creative and multifaceted acts of social reproduction." An example of the changing meanings of material culture are objects that moved from a domestic context to a ritual one. Meghan C. L. Howey (2017, 167) describes the Indigenous consumption of European-made kettles in the northeastern region of the US during the sixteenth and seventeenth centuries. In early colonial encounters, Indigenous groups did not use kettles for cooking in the European way, but instead their main function was as grave goods. The kettles were therefore incorporated in symbolically, ceremonially, and socially charged activities and they were likely to be seen as objects ascribed with *manit*, an animating spirit. Inga-Maria Mulk and Tim Bayliss-Smith (Chapter 2) also demonstrate how ritual practices could change in colonial contacts but at the same time remain resilient to attempts of Christianization.

Material culture also played a role in the interactions that took place between colonizers and Indigenous workers in colonial spaces. Stephen Silliman (2010) has highlighted the role of Indigenous workers laboring in distinctly colonial spaces. He argues that it is extremely complicated to differentiate Indigenous material culture from that of the colonizers because artifacts and spaces in such settings are used by multiple groups of people and their meanings and functions are often ambiguous (Silliman 2010, 29–32). Along similar lines, Risto Nurmi (Chapter 4) discusses the material culture of Sámi laborers in Early Modern mining communities. His chapter demonstrates that although there are objects and cultural practices that can be identified as "Sámi," most of the material culture was in fact shared by people of different ethnicities. Sámi material culture has played an important role in the daily activities and food culture of the mining communities. Moreover, the Sámi were actively and voluntarily involved in these communities.

The focus on the meanings and roles of material culture in colonial encounters is connected to archaeology's current occupation with "new materialism" where the agencies of things and material culture are reassessed. It now widely acknowledged that things and the material world have an active role in shaping human understanding and experience of the world. There is a network of relations between different actants, which can be human or nonhuman. (Latour 2005; Olsen 2010; Hodder 2012) Material culture also has agency in colonial encounters. Material culture can actively participate in and shape power relations between groups of people in a colonial context, as demonstrated by Madeline Fowler, Amy Roberts, and Lester-Irabinna Rigney (Chapter 1). In their case study, control over the Indigenous people by the English was acted out in "bell hegemony" where church bells structured the daily lives of people. William A. White III and Brandi E. Bethke (Chapter 6) offer an example of how material culture has agency in today's world in the way the precontact landscapes contribute to the Blackfeet's sense of history and continuity.

Ongoing Colonialism and Cultural Appropriation

Colonialism is not just about territorial claims, economic strategies, and racial ideologies; it also involves the appropriation of material culture (Naum and Nordin 2013). In many ways, Indigenous people still consider themselves colonized (Lawrence 2004). Colonial history has consequences

today, as can be seen, for example, in the conflicts concerning the exploitation of natural resources and land ownership (Ojala and Nordin 2015). In
addition, colonial legacy concerning Indigenous material culture is also
evident in contemporary discourses concerning matters such as the right
to Indigenous cultural heritage, repatriation (e.g., Nordin and Ojala 2015),
and the cultural appropriation of Indigenous material culture. In Finland,
news headlines repeatedly report the misuse of Sámi material culture.
Beauty queens and athletes dress in mock versions of Sámi clothing (*gákti*)
and advertisers use symbols from Sámi culture (Figures 0.1 and 0.2).
Members of the Sámi community see this kind of cultural appropriation
as highly disrespectful. For the Sámi, *gákti* connects its wearer to family,
shared history, and a place of origin and enables cultural creativity, but
the Finns who have worn Sámi dress have used a mock version that presents an insulting, simplified, and stereotypical picture of Sámi culture.
In addition, Sámi material culture and history are distorted in advertise-
ments, which may show a woman wearing a traditional man's hat or
Sámi shamans (*noaidi*) conducting their rituals in a dark and dirty tent
(*lavvu*).[1] The Sámi see the abuse of their material culture as a continuation
of colonial traditions. (Mikkonen 2016; Näkkäläjärvi 2016; Seitsonen 2018,
149; cf. Nakatani 2015; Kramvig and Flemmen 2018.)

Figure 0.1. Fake Sámi dress (left) and authentic Sámi clothing (*gákti*) (right).
(Image courtesy of the Finnish Broadcasting Company Yle. Photograph by Vesa
Toppari.)

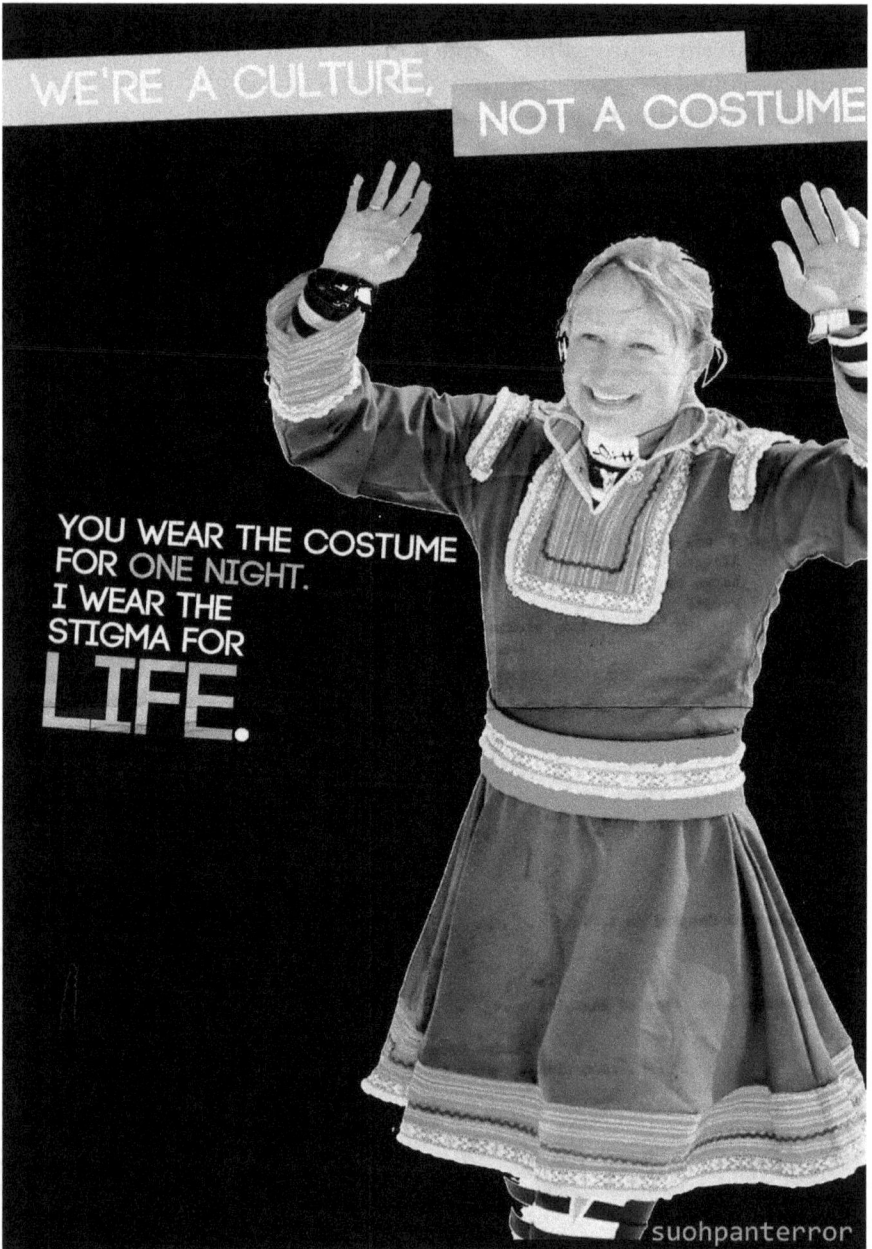

Figure 0.2. The improper use of Sámi dress has raised strong feelings and been commented on in art works by Suohpanterror. (Image courtesy of Suohpanterror.)

Mock Sámi dress has also been seen in art. In 2016, the Kiasma Museum of Contemporary Art in Finland exhibited the artwork *Grind* by video artist Jenni Hiltunen. The video is said to be a playful take on the dancehall culture with its provocative costumes, suggestive poses, roles, and blatant sexuality,[2] but its display of female buttocks dressed in male Sámi clothing aroused criticism of both the artist and the museum, which was seen to have symbolically given its blessing to the exploitation of Indigenous cultures (Paltto 2016).

In Chapter 7, Katherine Hayes discusses cultural appropriation though the case study of Sam Durant's sculpture *Scaffold* (2012) at the Walker Art Center Hayes in Minneapolis. She argues that art can be seen as cultural appropriation and that historical narratives can lose some of their meanings when told by non-Natives. Here, as in the case of Hiltunen's video, the artist does not fully grasp the nuances of historical traumas. But art can also be used to raise awareness (Edelman 1995). For example, a group of Sámi artists called Suohpanterror uses their art to take a stand on ethnopolitics, criticizing, among other things, the above-mentioned abuse of Sámi clothing (Hautala-Hirvioja 2015) (Figure 0.2).

Reinterpretations of Sources in Search of Indigenous Voices

A unifying theme across many of the chapters in this volume is the attempt to find Indigenous voices through a careful reinterpretation of archaeological and historical sources. Questions about what constitutes an Indigenous voice, how to hear it, and how to interpret it have been sources of debate in anthropology, archaeology, and postcolonial studies for decades (e.g., Spivak 1988; Hall 1999; Hart et al. 2012; Weidman 2014; Cipolla 2017). A voice, as a metaphor, has been associated with individuality, agency, and authority in Euro-American modernity. However, voices are culturally constructed and hence variable (Weidman 2014). Historical records have usually been created by elite members of the society and represent various elite opinions, voices, and strategies. On the other hand, subaltern groups, such as slaves, ethnic and sexual minorities, certain social groups, and Indigenous peoples often have no voice in historical documents (Spivak 1988). It is clear that any researcher trying to give a voice to subaltern groups of the past, whether through historical records or material culture, must be careful not to impose her own opinion on the group of people she is studying (Spivak 1988; Liebmann 2008). Indeed, Spivak (1988) is even skeptical of the idea that subaltern voices can be found by rereading historical documents.

Historical archaeology has a long legacy of using material culture as a means of finding alternative interpretations and subaltern voices of the past (Hall 1999; Hart et al. 2012; Cipolla 2017). Unlike historical documents, however, material culture was used and left behind by all social groups, including Indigenous people (Liebmann 2008). Therefore, in principle, there is a material record left behind by Indigenous people, although their voices may be absent from historical documents. Still, it has to be remembered that the material culture is interpreted by archaeologists, who can only claim to speak about, but not for, the Indigenous people in question (Liebmann 2008). Moreover, it is crucial to understand that the Indigenous peoples of the present do have a voice (Källen 2015).

Several chapters in this volume combine different sources, such as archaeological and historical data, oral histories, and current Indigenous voices to find ways to speak about Indigenous history and cultural heritage. LisaMarie Malischke (Chapter 3) combines historical and archaeological data from Fort Saint Pierre, Mississippi. By rereading historical sources from an ethnohistorical perspective, she gains a better understanding of the reversed power dynamics between the Indigenous groups and the French.

In Chapter 5, Ritva Kylli et al. take into reconsideration a body of historical sources that has previously been used to construct narratives about the primitiveness of the Sámi food culture and the Sámi in general. By carefully rereading these sources and using archaeological data to support their ideas, Kylli et al. find that the Sámi food culture was hybridized with Scandinavian and Finnish food cultures from early on. The Sámi also had agency and initiative in incorporating new foodstuffs into their foodways. Most importantly, Kylli et al. show how historical data that has previously been interpreted as evidence of Sámi primitiveness can be reread, when supported by archaeological data, to reveal how the Sámi actively shaped their material culture by using their own needs and strategies as a point of departure.

William A. White III and Brandi E. Bethke (Chapter 6) reinterpret the history of the Cut Bank Boarding School in Montana in search of Blackfeet voices. The Cut Bank Boarding School was situated in the precontact landscape with its memories of Blackfeet presence and resilience from earlier centuries. Such boarding schools were established to destruct the culture and enculturate Native peoples, and their histories are often told through the framework of the Boarding School administration. . However, White and Bethke search for the Blackfeet narrative of the history of the Cut Bank Boarding School, based on archaeological data, oral histories, and archival sources. They are able to show how the Blackfeet people are actively reclaiming and reinterpreting the landscape that they have continually used for centuries.

Rather than claiming to speak in the voice of the Indigenous group in question, the chapters in this volume present multi-angled perspectives of colonial encounters and seek to challenge old colonial narratives about the relationships between the colonizers and the colonized. The interpretations given in the chapters are just that, interpretations, presented by researchers who carefully position themselves and critically examine their ability to speak of the Indigenous perspective. Despite these challenges and reservations, the chapters in this volume show that through critical multi-source approaches, new insights into Indigenous experiences in the past can be gained. Combining material culture with historical sources, oral histories, archival sources, and current debates, the authors tease out more nuanced understandings of colonial encounters, especially the perspectives of Indigenous peoples on those encounters. The greatest contribution of this volume, then, is not the discovery of "authentic" Indigenous voices in the material or archival records, but that a more nuanced understanding of colonial histories needs to be acknowledged and sought through multiple sources.

Conclusion: New Insights and Indigenous Voices from Local Approaches

An expanding body of literature on historical archaeologies from different parts of the world has deepened our understanding of the variety of colonial encounters. Colonial encounters in places like Scandinavia, Africa, Australia, Oceania, and southeast Asia are increasingly addressed by archaeologists (e.g., Reid and Lane 2004; Paterson 2011; Naum and Nordin 2013; Flexner 2014; Cruz Berrocal and Tsang 2017). This is an important development because it allows us to emphasize local histories and interpretations over Eurocentric ones and provides alternative stories and interpretations of colonial histories, which have been as varied as the peoples taking part in them. Along the same lines, Indigenous archaeologies from different parts of the world have the potential to highlight how Indigenous peoples around the world have negotiated their relationships with colonial powers.

This volume, representing various ethnic groups from different parts of the world, shows that while colonial histories share a number of characteristics—such as unequal power relations, changing meanings of material culture, and cultural appropriation—the responses and solutions of the Indigenous communities coming into contact with colonial powers were clearly local and individual. They were also dependent on the historical context and the goals, means, and ideologies of the colonizers.

A unifying theme across this volume is that specific archaeological finds and spaces can seldom be labeled as "Indigenous" or "colonizer" material culture. Interactions between different groups in colonial societies were often close-knit. Material culture and spaces were shared by different groups. Indigenous groups adopted the colonizer's material culture and made it their own, and vice versa. The premise of several chapters in this volume was to look at the encounters between (at least) two ethnic groups in a colonial setting. However, the chapters clearly show that the use, ownership, and interpretation of material culture in colonial societies are complex issues. The agency and creativity of Indigenous peoples in transforming and negotiating (material) cultural practices in colonial settings was something that emerged from all chapters in this volume. Indigenous peoples as well as colonizers created their own solutions and cultural practices, independently or codependently. Sometimes the relations between groups were forced and fraught with tensions, sometimes they were driven by mutual interest and benefit.

In the context of Indigenous people consuming colonizers' things, this materiality was often, but not always, shaped by power and tension between the local culture and the colonizing state. The interplay of colonial power, Indigenous agency, and materiality is dependent on the nature of the colonial relationship and the strategies and choices of the people involved. In our mind, the most interesting thing about materiality in contexts of colonization is not necessarily that it differs from materiality in other contexts (because culture and materiality are always in the process of borrowing, changing, adapting), but that it can tell alternative stories about processes of colonization and the everyday lives people lead in places of colonial encounter.

Telling alternative stories is also at the heart of the second theme that emerges from this volume, the search for Indigenous voices in the past material and other records. We feel that the contributions in this volume are valuable not because they have found the way to channel "authentic" Indigenous voices from the past, but because they demonstrate that we can get closer to a multi-angled understanding of past colonial encounters by using multiple sources, such as archaeological record, historical record, oral histories, and current debates.

Finally, the chapters show that traces and tensions of colonial encounters are still present when the material culture of Indigenous peoples is displayed, used, and discussed. Cases of cultural appropriation have raised questions about who is allowed to use, modify, and mimic

Indigenous material culture and how this may be done. Thus, archaeology has a vital role to play in deepening our understanding of the histories and meanings behind the use of Indigenous material culture.

Tiina Äikäs is a postdoctoral researcher in archaeology at the University of Oulu and Docent in Archaeology at the University of Helsinki. She specializes in Sámi archaeology with a special interest in Sámi sacred places and their use from the Iron Age to contemporary times. She has also written about contemporary meanings and uses of heritage, and postcolonial archaeology.

Anna-Kaisa Salmi is Associate Professor and Academy Research Fellow in Archaeology at the University of Oulu. With a specialization in zooarchaeology, her research focuses on human-animal relationships, reindeer domestication, and foodways in northern Fennoscandia. She has a special interest in the ways people interact and live with animals, and the roles animals play in human societies and histories. Her current research concentrates on human-reindeer relationships and reindeer domestication.

Notes

1. http://www.dailymail.co.uk/video/travel/video-1213752/100-Days-Polar-Magic-unique-expedition-Finland.html (last accessed 26 April 2019).
2. https://vimeo.com/44392653 (last accessed 26 April 2019).

References

Appadurai, Arjun. 1986. *The Social Life of Things: Commodities in Cultural Perspective.* Cambridge: Cambridge University Press.

Beaudoin, Matthew A. 2017. "A Tale of Two Settlements: Consumption and the Historical Archaeology of Natives and Newcomers in the 19th-century Great Lakes Region." In *Foreign Objects: Rethinking Indigenous Consumption in American Archaeology*, ed. Craig N. Cipolla, 44–56. Tucson: University of Arizona Press.

Cipolla, Craig N. 2017. "Introduction: Indigenous People and Foreign Objects. Rethinking Consumption in American Archaeology." In *Foreign Objects: Rethinking Indigenous Consumption in American Archaeology*, ed. Craig N. Cipolla, 3–25. Tucson: University of Arizona Press.

Creese, John L. 2017. "Beyond Representation: Indigenous Economies of Affect in the Northeast Woodlands." In *Foreign Objects: Rethinking Indigenous*

Consumption in American Archaeology, ed. Craig N. Cipolla, 59–79. Tucson: University of Arizona Press.

Cruz Berrocal, María, and Cheng-hwa Tsang, eds. 2017. *Historical Archaeology of Early Modern Colonialism in Asia-Pacific*. Gainesville: University Press of Florida.

Edelman, Murray. 1995. *From Art to Politics: How Artistic Creations Shape Political Conceptions*. Chicago and London: University of Chicago Press.

Ferris, Neal, Rodney Harrison, and Michael V. Wilcox, eds. 2014. *Rethinking Colonial Pasts through Archaeology*. Oxford: Oxford University Press.

Flexner, James F. 2014. "Historical Archaeology, Contact, and Colonialism in Oceania." *Journal of Archaeological Research* 22(1): 43–87.

Gosden, Chris. 2004. *Archaeology and Colonialism: Cultural Contact From 5000 BC to the Present*. Cambridge: Cambridge University Press.

Gosden, Chris, and Yvonne Marshall. 1999. "The Cultural Biography of Objects." *World Archaeology* 31(2): 169–78.

Hall, Martin. 1999. "Subaltern Voices? Finding the Spaces between Things and Words." In *Historical Archaeology: Back from the Edge*, ed. P. Funari, S. Jones, and M. Hall, 193–202. New York: Routledge.

Hart, Siobhan M., Maxine Oland, and Liam Frink. 2012. "Finding Transitions: Global Pathways to Decolonizing Indigenous Histories in Archaeology." In *Decolonizing Indigenous Histories: Exploring Prehistoric/Colonial Transitions in Archaeology*, ed. Maxine Oland, Siobhan M. Hart, and Liam Frink, 1–15. Tucson: University of Arizona Press.

Hautala-Hirvioja, Tuija Helena. 2015. "Reflections of the Past: A Meeting between Sámi Cultural Heritage and Contemporary Finnish Sámi." In *Relate North: Art, Heritage & Identity*, ed. Timo Jokela and Glen Coutts, 78–97. Rovaniemi: Lapland University Press.

Hayes, Katherine. 2015. "Indigeneity and Diaspora: Colonialism and the Classification of Displacement." In *Rethinking Colonialism: Comparative Archaeological Approaches*, ed. Craig N. Cipolla and Katherine Howlett Hayes, 54–75. Gainesville: University Press of Florida.

Hillerdal, Charlotta, Anna Karlström, and Carl-Gösta Ojala. 2017. "Introduction." In *Archaeologies of "Us" and "Them": Debating History, Heritage and Indigeneity*, ed. Charlotta Hillerdal, Anna Karlström, and Carl-Gösta Ojala, 1–13. Milton Park, Abingdon, Oxon: Routledge.

Hodder, Ian. 2012. *Entangled: An Archaeology of the Relationships between Humans and Things*. Chichester: Wiley.

Howey, Meghan C. L. 2017. "Sympathetic Magic and Indigenous Consumption of Kettles during Early Colonial Encounter in the Northeast." In *Foreign Objects: Rethinking Indigenous Consumption in American Archaeology*, ed. Craig N. Cipolla, 162–83. Tucson: University of Arizona Press.

Källen, Anna. 2015. "Postcolonial Theory and Sámi Archaeology: A Commentary." *Arctic Anthropology* 52(2): 81–86.

Kramvig, Britt, and Anne Britt Flemmen. 2018. "Turbulent Indigenous Objects: Controversies around Cultural Appropriation and Recognition of Difference." *Journal of Material Culture*. DOI: 10.1177/1359183518782719.

Latour, Bruno. 2005. *Reassembling the Social: An Introduction to Actor-Network-Theory*. Oxford: Oxford University Press.

Lawrence, Bonita. 2004. *"Real" Indians and Others: Mixed-blood Urban Native Peoples and Indigenous Nationhood*. Lincoln: University of Nebraska Press.

Liebmann, Matthew. 2008. "Introduction: The Intersections of Archaeology and Postcolonial Studies." In *Archaeology and the Postcolonial Critique*, ed. Matthew Liebmann and Uzma Z. Rizvi, 1–20. Lanham: AltaMira Press.

Lightfoot, Kent G., and Antoinette Martinez. 1995. "Frontiers and Boundaries in Archaeological Perspective." *Annual Review in Anthropology* 24: 471–92.

Meskell, Lynn. 2004. *Object Worlds in Ancient Egypt: Material Biographies Past and Present*. Oxford and New York: Berg.

Mikkonen, Nadja. 2016. "Kyse on oikeudesta maahan, kieleen ja kulttuuriin." *YLE uutiset* 19 September 2016. Retrieved 27 March 2019 from https://yle.fi/uutiset/3-9135075.

Nakatani, Ayami. 2015. "Dressing Miss World with Balinese Brocades: The 'Fashionalization' and 'Heritagization' of Handwoven Textiles in Indonesia." *Textile* 13(1): 30–49.

Näkkäläjärvi, Pirita. 2016. "Näkökulma: Närkästyneet saamelaiset otsikoissa." *YLE uutiset* 16 May 2016. Retrieved 27 March 2019 from https://yle.fi/uutiset/osasto/sapmi/nakokulma_narkastyneet_saamelaiset_otsikoissa/8877876.

Naum, Magdalena, and Jonas M. Nordin. 2013. "Introduction: Situating Scandinavian Colonialism." In *Scandinavian Colonialism and the Rise of Modernity: Small Time Agents in a Global Arena*, ed. Magdalena Naum and Jonas M. Nordin, 3–16. New York: Springer.

Nordin, Jonas, and Carl-Gösta Ojala. 2015. "Collecting Sápmi: Early Modern Collecting of Sámi Material Culture." *Nordisk Museologi* 2: 114–22.

Ojala, Carl-Gösta, and Jonas M. Nordin. 2015. "Mining Sápmi: Colonial Histories, Sámi Archaeology, and the Exploitation of Natural Resources in Northern Sweden." *Arctic Anthropology* 52(2): 6–21.

Oliver, Jeff. 2013. "Reflections on Resistance: Agency, Identity and Being Indigenous in Colonial British Columbia." In *Historical Archaeologies of Cognition: Explorations into Faith, Hope and Charity*, ed. James Symonds, Anna Badcock, and Jeff Oliver, 98–116. Sheffield: Equinox Publishing.

Oliver, Jeff, and Ágústa Edwald. 2016. "Between Islands of Ethnicity and Shared Landscapes: Rethinking Settler Society, Cultural Landscapes and the Study of the Canadian West." *Cultural Geographies* 23(2): 199–219.

Olsen, Bjørnar. 2010. *In Defense of Things: Archaeology and the Ontology of Objects*. Lanham: Rowman & Littlefield Publishers.

Paltto, Anni-Saara. 2016. "Kiasmaa arvostellaan feikkisaamenpukuvideon ostamisesta." *YLE uutiset* 10 May 2016. Retrieved 27 March from https://yle.fi/uutiset/3-8869765.

Paterson, Alistair G. 2011. "Considering Colonialism and Capitalism in Australian Historical Archaeology: Two Case Studies of Culture Contact from the Pastoral Domain." In *The Archaeology of Capitalism in Colonial Contexts*, ed. Sarah K. Croucher and Lindsay Weiss, 243–67. New York: Springer.

Reid, Andrew, and Paul J. Lane, eds. 2004. *African Historical Archaeologies*. New York: Springer.

Seitsonen, Oula. 2018. *Digging Hitler's Arctic War. Archaeologies and Heritage of the Second World War German Military Presence in Finnish Lapland*. PhD diss., University of Helsinki.

Silliman, Stephen W. 2005. "Culture Contact or Colonialism? Challenges in the Archaeology of Native North America." *American Antiquity* 70(1): 55–74.

———. 2009. "Change and Continuity, Practice and Memory: Native American Persistence in Colonial New England." *American Antiquity* 74(2): 211–30.

———. 2010. "Indigenous Traces in Colonial Spaces: Archaeologies of Ambiguity, Origin, and Practice." *Journal of Social Archaeology* 10(1): 28–58.

Spivak, Gayatri Chakravorty. 1988. "Can the Subaltern Speak?" In *Marxism and the Interpretation of Culture*, ed. C. Nelson and L. Grossberg, 271–313. Basingstoke: Macmillan Education.

Tsing, Anna. 2007. "Indigenous Voice." In *Indigenous Experience Today*, ed. Marisol de la Cadena and Orin Starn, 33–67. London: Bloomsbury.

Weidman, Amanda. 2014. "Anthropology and Voice." *Annual Review of Anthropology* 43: 37–51.

Chapter 1

The Sounds of Colonization

An Examination of Bells at Point Pearce Aboriginal
Mission Station/Burgiyana, South Australia

_____

Madeline Fowler, Amy Roberts, and Lester-Irabinna Rigney

Introduction

The role of the church bell in European Christian traditions is well
theorized and deeply embedded in the Code of Canon Law (Peters
2001)—its ringing was a common way to call the community together
for all purposes including the sacred and spiritual. While there is a vast
archive on the missionary movement in Aboriginal Australia, the role
European bells played in Australian colonialism remains undertheorized
despite their widespread prominence. By investigating the contribution
of missionary bells in the production of colonial knowledge on Yorke
Peninsula/Guuranda,[1] this chapter examines the hegemonic power
exerted in rural and remote Aboriginal communities.

The archaeological exploration of Australia's Aboriginal missions,
while slow to develop, has seen an expansion in research quantity and
breadth in recent years (see Lydon and Ash 2010). This work, when
considered in conjunction with important Indigenous perspectives, as
well as contributions from cognate disciplines, has revealed the inher-
ent complexity involved in understanding the diverse experiences and
emotions that these colonial, and yet simultaneously very Indigenous,
spaces have produced and continue to generate. In this chapter, we add
to the multifarious investigations of missions through an examination
of an archaeology of sound. In this regard, we use the bells from Point

Pearce Aboriginal Mission/Burgiyana, South Australia, as a new means to explore: expressions of colonial power; the role of the material world in culture contact, maritime connections, and maritime cultural landscapes; and agency and resistance through spatial and sonic means.

As detailed below, at least two of the bells that rang out on the mission were salvaged from local shipwrecks. Keating (1979) has argued that one of the earliest sounds of Australia's European invaders, as heard by Indigenous peoples, was also likely a ship's bell. Thus, this oft surviving item of maritime material culture features significantly in the soundscape of Australia's colonial past.

Who Are the Narungga?

Moravian missionary, Reverend Julius Kühn, founded Point Pearce Aboriginal Mission/Burgiyana on 2 February 1868 on South Australia's Yorke Peninsula/Guuranda, in the territory of the Narungga people (Figure 1.1) (Wood and Westell 1998, 5).[2] Narungga territory encompasses the whole peninsula and is inclusive of the sea and a small archipelago of islands. Given the constant proximity to the coast, Narungga people had—and continue to maintain—a deep connection to their sea country (see summary in Roberts et al. 2016). The boundaries of the Point Pearce Aboriginal Community today include the Point Pearce/Burgiyana Peninsula and Wardang Island/Waraldi (also Wara-dharldhi). The mission used Wardang Island/Waraldi for grazing purposes from 1877 (Wanganeen 1987, 55).

Prior to the mission's establishment, the earliest interactions between Narungga and non-Indigenous peoples began with whalers and sealers in the 1830s, followed shortly afterwards by surveyors and pastoralists (Mattingley and Hampton 1988, 195; Ball 1992, 36; Krichauff 2008, 51). Although established in 1868, many Narungga people did not initially confine themselves to the mission, with a number of individuals and families remaining mobile through the latter part of the nineteenth century (Wanganeen 1987, 25; Wood and Westell 1998, 5). Other Aboriginal people from beyond Yorke Peninsula/Guuranda also moved to Point Pearce Aboriginal Mission/Burgiyana as a result of colonization. For example, in 1894, after the closure of Poonindie Mission, Aboriginal peoples from the Eyre Peninsula joined Narungga residents, and an influx of Aboriginal peoples from Point McLeay/Raukkan Mission arrived in the early 1900s (Wood and Westell 1998, 8, 22; Krichauff 2013, 70). Mobility is a key theme in the colonial control of Indigenous peoples, a topic to which we will return later in this chapter.

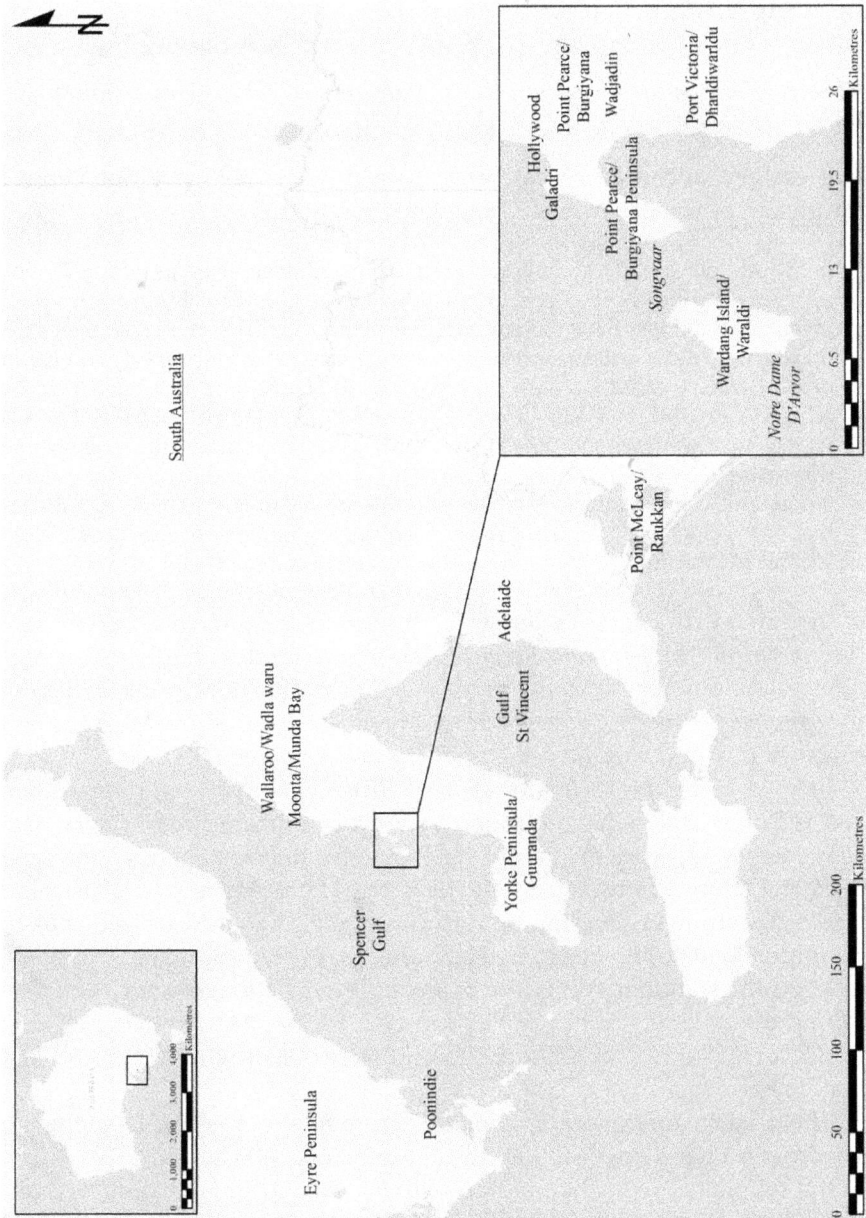

Figure 1.1. Location of Yorke Peninsula/Guuranda and other key places mentioned in the text. (Map created by the authors.)

Intangible Impacts of Bells

"The Bell Rings for Prayers": Early Missionary Bells, Conversion, and the Civilizing Agenda

The earliest documented reference to a mission bell at Point Pearce/ Burgiyana originates from 1870, when Kühn wrote:

> In the schoolroom I hold daily morning and evening services, as well as Divine services on Sundays, and give instruction daily, and let the children have their meals. At 6 o'clock the bell is sounded for rising. The boys must take their turn for fetching water and the girls prepare breakfast. All must properly comb and brush themselves, or they get no breakfast. Breakfast at 6.30, after which the school is cleaned, and I hand a few provisions to some old and sick natives. At 9 o'clock we have morning service, and school continues until 12.30, when dinner is prepared. In the afternoon school is resumed, and then the boys fetch wood and water, the girls being employed with cooking, washing, and mending. At 6 o'clock we have tea, and at 7 there is evening service, after the children are put to bed, and the older ones retire at 9 o'clock. (Archibald 1915, 14)

McArthur (1876, 1), in a letter to the editor in the *Yorke's Peninsula Advertiser and Miners' and Farmers' Journal*, reiterates the focus on religious activities in the daily routine at Point Pearce/Burgiyana during this period, writing, "On week days, immediately after breakfast the bell rings for prayers, and the same after tea in the evening."

In 1893, Higgins (1893, 43) records: "[n]ear the main building a large bell is hung. This peals out vigorously every morning at 6 o'clock as a signal to get up; work begins at 8." After a visit to Point Pearce/Burgiyana in 1900, Octopus (a pseudonym) (1900, 6) of Port Pirie (South Australia) wrote, "A stranger, hearing the oft ringing bell, would be curious as to its import." Octopus (1900, 6) elaborates with the following: "In some respects the station reminds one of an old English village, with its curfew calling the villagers to prayers and to bed. It calls the dwellers at 7 a.m. to rise; at 9.30 a.m. (for children) to school; at 7 p.m. to prayers; and at 9 p.m. to bed."

These early references to a bell/s, prior to the mission changing to government hands, reveal that this material item was a prominent aspect of the religious life of the mission with a focus on prayers and services. Indeed, given Kühn's heritage this should not be surprising, as the official Moravian view prioritized the gospel and communal cohesion over civilizing agendas (see Lydon 2009, 106; Lydon and Ash 2010, 6). However, as is evident above, work and labor also feature in the routines of Kühn and his successors. The missionary encounter thus sought to interrupt

Indigenous practices thereby changing relations of power and order. Work and labor become the key ingredients to create what Comaroff and Comaroff (1991) called a "hybrid culture," which served to civilize the "other." Referred to as the "civilization/Christianization debate," these contrasting agendas are arguably "grounded in a Cartesian mind-body dualism" (see Lydon and Ash 2010, 6–7). Below we consider further why Aboriginal people at Point Pearce/Burgiyana were subjected, through coercion, choice, or otherwise, to European notions of time and labor as dictated by the sonic regimen produced by the bell/s.

As noted above, the mission population during its early years (particularly during Kühn's tenure) was not strictly confined (as people would increasingly become in later years—see below). While this situation allowed for much more agency and mobility, it must be borne in mind that converts, sick children, orphans, and the children of ill-equipped parents predominantly formed the population during this time (see Krichauff 2011, 167). Indeed, what we know of the cross-cultural interactions between Narungga and Kühn reveals much complexity (although we are mostly reliant on Kühn's own records).

Krichauff's (2011) historical analysis of the period presents a confusing picture—on the one hand pointing to gained trust but on the other to the Narungga people's uncertainty of changing power relations—both in relation to Kühn's authority but also of course in the face of ever-increasing European colonization of their land and waters which, in particular, induced reliance on alternative sources of food. As argued by van Dommelen and Rowlands (2012, 22), the study of material culture in colonial situations allows us to more thoroughly consider the "impact of the material surroundings on people's daily life in terms of both actions and perceptions" (also see Buscaglia 2017, 648). Focusing on a bell's very materiality and function leads us to contemplate more deeply the actions of Narungga people. Indeed, during this early period, for able-bodied Narungga people choosing to take up residency at the mission (a land and seascape of deep cultural significance) and partaking or working periodically to receive food and other goods in no way equated to an implicit or long-term agreement to live one's life following the tolling of a bell. Considering the ultimate demography of Point Pearce/Burgiyana, however, leads to an interpretation of the mission as refuge for many in the face of invasion, which allowed missionaries to inculcate their own values about time and work. Comaroff and Comaroff (1986, 14–15) argued: "Christianity first took root in the fissures of the local polity, initially attracting the marginal and powerless; yet the mission by its very presence, engaged all ... in an inescapable dialogue on its own terms, even if they rejected the message"—a dialogue that led to an objectification of time which was "seen as a resource to be put to work in the interests of moral and material accumulation." The imposition of a European soundscape at Point Pearce/Burgiyana via the bell was thus powerful and encompassing.

While we do not know the origin of the original mission bell/s some images survive (see Figure 1.2); the provenance of later bells is more defined and provides an expanded maritime interpretive context. As will be evident below, work also features more prominently in daily routines over time revealing a changing didactic environment that became increasingly carceral in comparison to the early period — reminding us of the "multiple roles of missions" (Lydon and Ash 2010, 5).

"All Inmates Shall Rise": Controlling Time and Space

In 1911 the State Government introduced The Aborigines Act. The opening statement of the Act reads: "An Act to make provision for the better Protection and Control of the Aboriginal and Half-caste Inhabitants of the State of South Australia" [caps in original]. Mattingley and Hampton (1988, 43) argued that while the Act was a "belated attempt to protect Nunga [Aboriginal] people from ... Goonya [European] society" it

Figure 1.2. The mission bell during the time of construction of the superintendent's house (image likely pre-1874, see Archibald 1915). (Image reproduced with permission from Wanganeen 1987, 32.)

emphasized control and segregation and "ratified institutionalization as a way of life and confirmed the status of Nunga's as 'inmates' whose affairs and families were to be controlled in almost every respect." The trend towards segregation and state institutionalization continued with the 1913 Royal Commission into Aboriginal Affairs which resulted in the State Government taking over the mission in 1915.[3]

The "Rules for the Management and Government" of Point Pearce/ Burgiyana during this period reflect these broader societal (European Australian) attitudes. Below we include an excerpt of these rules which were also enforced by the bell (as evidenced from oral histories relating to this period and beyond—see below):

> 10. All inmates shall rise not later than 6.45 a.m. from September 30 to March 31, and not later than 7.15 a.m. from March 31 to September 30.

> 11. Work shall commence at 8 a.m. and continue until 6 p.m. from September 30 to March 21, and till 5 p.m. from March 31 to September 30, an interval of 1 hour being allowed for dinner. Saturday from 1 p.m. will be half holiday.

> 12. All inmates, and also all Officers employed on the station, shall attend Divine Service on Sundays at 11 a.m. and 7 p.m. All children shall attend Sunday-school at 2.30 p.m. (Archibald 1915, 34)

"Everything at Point Pearce Seemed to Be Ruled by the Bell": Lived Experiences and Bell Hegemony

The experience of "bell hegemony" and sonic control exerted as a result of these rules, as expressed in oral histories, is unmistakable. Olga Fudge (née Wilson, born 1897 [Mattingley 2017]), who was an Aboriginal resident at Point Pearce/Burgiyana recalled:

> The bell used to ring in the morning at, it was quarter to eight because the men used to be at the "pick up" at eight o'clock, see what they call the "pick-up" to get their different jobs. It used to ring at twelve for lunch time and again at one o'clock to start work. Then it used to ring for knock-off at five o'clock. It would also ring on Sundays for the church services and for Sunday school. All our lives were regulated by that bell. (Wanganeen 1987, 32)[4]

Doris Graham (née Edwards), born 1912, also a Point Pearce/Burgiyana resident stated:

> The men used to gather at the tank for work when they rang an old bell, up by the Superintendent's office at eight o'clock in the morning. They used to ring that bell at twelve o'clock too for dinner and at five o'clock to knock off

work ... Before my time, with the old people, they used to get up at six o'clock in the morning when the bell rang, and have breakfast at half past six in the morning. At nine o'clock there'd be school until lunch time. Everything had to be done like that. They were really rostered. Had to be on time even to the ringing of the bell—a bell to go to school, a bell to knock off for lunch and a bell to knock off work ... You'd be docked half a day's pay if you missed the bell ... On Sunday it would ring at eleven o'clock for Sunday service, two o'clock for Sunday school, and seven o'clock for service at night, and for service again on Monday night. (Graham and Graham 1987, 16, 35–36)

An additional recollection comes from the short story told by Phoebe Wanganeen (née Stuart, born 1925 [Kartinyeri 2002, 184]) of her lived experience at Point Pearce/Burgiyana as recorded by Gwen Pitcher in Edwards, Wanganeen, and Agius (1987, 11): "Everything at Point Pearce seemed to be ruled by the bell that the white superintendent rang. It rang to tell the men to start work. It rang for the start of school. It rang to tell the people to collect their milk, to collect their letters, to go to church, and even to go to bed."

Point Pearce/Burgiyana families in this period would often leave their houses on the mission station and spend time in shacks on the coast during allowed breaks. Pitcher (in Edwards et al. 1987, 11) poignantly writes: "Auntie Phoebe and family loved being there [at their Galadri shack]. They were free to run around and do what they pleased. The sandy beach was close by and the children swam and ran through the sand all day long. They could hear the bell, but it was far away."

Lewis O'Brien (born 1930 [O'Brien 2007, 84]) also recalled the evening regime, "Yeah, work's finished, and then it used to ring from nine o'clock at night to lights out" (Wood and Westell 1998, 12). Irene Agius (née Sansbury, born 1931 [Kartinyeri 2002, 277]) told Wood and Westell (1998, 12), "[w]e lived by the bell ... Bell rang at eight o'clock when the men would go to work ... Rang for after recess time, rang for dinner. Rang for afternoon, rang for morning and afternoon tea for the men ... And after school." Analyzing these oral histories (in combination with historical sources) reveals that the Point Pearce/Burgiyana bell/s rang at the times illustrated in Table 1.1.

Taken together it is hard not to view this institutionalization of time and labor through a Foucauldian lens (see also Attwood 2000, 53; Lydon 2009, 105). Indeed, the oral histories above leave one in no doubt that the imposition of the timetable through the ringing of the bell was a destructive force increasingly experienced as a form of systemic control. In this regard Foucault (1977) writes: "The principle that underlay the time-table in its traditional form was essentially negative; it was the principle of non-idleness: it was forbidden to waste time, which was counted by

God and paid for by men; the time-table was to eliminate the danger of wasting it—a moral offence and economic dishonesty." While we do not seek to provide a detailed Foucauldian exegesis of the bells of Point Pearce/Burgiyana it is pertinent to consider further some of his central tenets, also from *Discipline and Punish*, which focus on the production of "docile bodies" through the "psychological monitoring and control of individuals" (Kelly 2017).

Gramsci's (1971) key ideas of "hegemony" (false consciousness) and the manufacturing of "consent" via ideology, also inform us of how the bell (an icon of Empire) and its controllers sought to alter and eradicate Narungga collective memory and replace it with dominant collective memory. For Gramsci (1971), "false consciousness," by concealing

Table 1.1. Bell schedule using oral history and historical archive sources.

Time	Activity (approximate year)
0600	Get up or rise (1870, 1893, pre-1912)
0645	Rise (summer) (1915)
0630	Breakfast (1870, pre-1912)
0700	Rise (1900)
0715	Rise (winter) (1915)
0745	Men go to "pick up" (post-1897)
0800	Men gather for work to begin (1893, 1915, post-1912, post-1931)
0900	Morning service (1870), school (pre-1912)
0930	School (1900)
1100	Sunday service (pre-1912, 1915)
1200	Lunch time or dinner (post-1897, post 1912)
1230	Break school for dinner (1870)
1300	Start work after lunch (post-1897), finish work (Saturday) (1915)
1400	Sunday school (pre-1912)
1430	Sunday school (1915)
1700	Knock off (post-1897, post-1912), knock off work (winter) (1915)
1800	Tea (1870), finish work (summer) (1915)
1900	Evening service and prayers (1870, 1900), Sunday service (pre-1912, 1915)
2100	Retire to bed and lights out (1870, 1900, post-1930)

Sources: Oral history (Graham and Graham 1987; Wanganeen 1987; Wood and Westell 1998; Fowler 2015); historical archive sources (McArthur 1876; Higgins 1893; Octopus 1900; Archibald 1915).

contradictions and the authoritarian routine using bells, would keep the "other" from recognizing and rejecting their oppression. Drawing upon the works of Gramsci (1971) we define "bell hegemony" as the encounter using its power to manufacture mission ideology as "official knowledge" and the creator of hegemonic welfare.

Taken to this endpoint then, the story of Point Pearce/Burgiyana's bells becomes a trajectory within a singular understanding of the "notion of missions as paradigmatic sites of dominant colonial power" (Lydon and Ash 2010, 2). This conclusion, and its foregrounding, is most vital—the destructive nature of colonization should never be underplayed. However, a deeper analysis of the material culture and oral histories of the mission bells also allows for the telling of other important stories about the lives of people at Point Pearce/Burgiyana including the role of the material world in culture contact, maritime cultural landscapes, and agency and resistance (through spatial and sonic means). These themes are further interrogated below.

Tangible Bell Connections

Ships' Bells: Connections and Maritime Cultural Landscapes

In the period of transition from mission to station, following State control, we know more about the origins of Point Pearce/Burgiyana bells. A close analysis of the oral histories of this period, combined with a study of the material remains, reveal maritime connections. Situated near Point Pearce/Burgiyana is Port Victoria/Dharldiwarldu, once a busy international port which, after 1939, became the only port in the Spencer Gulf where sailing ships continued to call (Moody 2012, 48).[5] There are at least two ships whose stories most closely relate to the bells at Point Pearce/Burgiyana: *Songvaar* (1912) and *Notre Dame D'Arvor* (1920).

The wreck of *Songvaar* is well-known to the Point Pearce/Burgiyana community, including its origin, wrecking event, location, and continued use as a night fishing drop, specifically for "tommies" (tommy ruff, *Arripis georgianus*) (Fowler 2015, 291; Fowler and Rigney 2017, 63). *Songvaar*, formerly *Barcore*, was a three-masted iron ship built in 1884 in Stockton, England, and employed on the Australian grain run by a Norwegian company at the time of loss ("The Wrecked Songvaar: Washed by the Waves." *The Advertiser* 18 April 1912, 9). It was traveling from Port Victoria/Dharldiwarldu when it wrecked in the channel between Wardang Island/Waraldi and Point Pearce Peninsula /Burgiyana on 14 April 1912. A non-Indigenous man, Leo Simms, was assisting with the salvage of *Songvaar* in February 1915 when the boat in which he was traveling sank due to rough weather off Point Pearce Peninsula/ Burgiyana. Moody (2012, 81, 261) recorded the actions of two fourteen-year-old Aboriginal residents from Point Pearce/Burgiyana in the rescue of Simms and his crew: "Stanley Smith and Clifford Edwards, saw the boat go down and put to sea in a small dinghy from the Point Pearce jetty and rescued the two men."

Salvage operations to refloat the vessel, by means of recovering the wheat cargo and pumping the hold, occurred continuously for about twelve months after the wrecking event (1912–13), with subsequent unsuccessful attempts in August and September 1914 and February 1917. After this time, the wreck was finally capsized and broken during a gale and the entirety of the vessel became submerged (Edwards 1934, 50; Seamew 1946, 4). Thus, for over five years *Songvaar* was "gradually being despoiled of all movable fittings" ("Turn of the Tide: Romance of Wheat Cargo." *The Register* 24 April 1915, 8).

The *Songvaar's* bell became, for a time, the one that tolled at Point Pearce/Burgiyana. Doris Graham confirmed this, stating that the bell she remembered was one that "[w]e saw ... when we were in Port Victoria. It's in the Museum there" (Graham and Graham 1987, 16; see also Perry 2013). This bell remains on display at the Port Victoria Maritime Museum—it was originally donated by Point Pearce Primary School in 1972 (see Figure 1.3). However, how the bell came to be in Point Pearce/ Burgiyana's possession is not known. Was it salvaged by Point Pearce/ Burgiyana residents soon after *Songvaar* wrecked? Did Superintendent Bray recover the bell at the same time he recovered *Songvaar's* binnacle (which is also on display at the Port Victoria Maritime Museum with the exhibition label stating: "Donated by Max Bray in memory of his father A. H. Bray, the former Superintendent of Point Pearce Aboriginal Reserve, who found the binnacle on the Point Pearce Beach close to where the *Songvaar* sank")? Regardless, a deeper consideration of this artifact reveals a more complex interplay between the maritime industry in the vicinity of Point Pearce/Burgiyana, the actions and agency of Aboriginal residents, and the deployment of objects in colonizing acts.

Another ships' bell is also attributed to Point Pearce/Burgiyana. Olga Fudge recalled the following:

> The mission bell, I think, I'm not quite sure, I don't know whether it's that one or the one before that, was supposed to come off that ship that got wrecked over at Wardang Island [Waraldi], at Hungry Bay.[6] It was the ship *Notre Dame D'Arvor* (Wanganeen 1987, 32).

Figure 1.3. The *Songvaar,* formerly *Barcore,* bell. (Image courtesy of the Port Victoria Maritime Museum. Photograph by Wendy Brusnahan, 17 September 2017.)

The three-masted barque *Notre Dame D'Arvor*, built in Nantes, France in 1902, was also engaged in the grain trade. Approaching Wardang Island/ Waraldi to anchor before loading wheat at Port Victoria/Dharldiwarldu in 1920, the vessel grounded on the rocks. About two months after grounding, it was accidently burnt ("Fire Completes Wreck: French Ship Burnt Out." *The Register* 3 May 1920, 7). The location of the *Notre Dame D'Arvor* bell is not currently known.

Given the above information it is clear that Point Pearce/Burgiyana had a series of bells, at least two of which originated from local shipwrecks. Fowler and Rigney (2017, 62–63) revealed numerous shipwreck and rescue events and shipping mishaps involving Point Pearce/Burgiyana, its boats and the Aboriginal people living there, particularly in the waters around Wardang Island/Waraldi. Oral histories did not mention salvage activities by Point Pearce/Burgiyana residents at these vessels for reuse, yet it is likely to have happened. It appears that the systematic salvage of locally owned stranded or sunken vessels for reuse in boatbuilding occurred at a later period (Rait 2002, 12).

Fowler and Rigney (2017, 70–71) have argued that Aboriginal connections are poorly recognized when celebrating anniversaries of such wrecking events or other notable maritime occurrences (see also Rigney 2002, xii–xiii). Indeed, at Point Pearce/Burgiyana, Aboriginal people interacted daily with non-Indigenous fishermen and sailors (see Roberts, Fowler, and Sansbury 2014, 28–29). Approaching the bells from a maritime perspective also allows an exploration of Aboriginal agency in this colonial sphere, rather than the sole focus of the "impact of colonialism" on Indigenous peoples being a "unilateral perspective of terminal narratives" (Buscaglia 2017, 642).

It is not uncommon that ship's bells are among the first objects salvaged or souvenired from a shipwreck and, given the fifteen shipwrecks in the very nearby vicinity to Point Pearce/Burgiyana (Department of the Environment and Energy 2017), any number of these may have made their way to the mission. Although, with the earliest reference to a bell at the mission being in 1870 by Kühn, just two years after the establishment of the mission, it is difficult to ascertain its origin. The earliest local wreck is *Agnes* (1876); although, given that Kühn traveled widely during his early years of establishing the mission (Krichauff 2013, 63), he may have sourced the bell from elsewhere on Yorke Peninsula/Guuranda. For example, the three-masted iron barque *San Miguel* (1865) wrecked at Tiparra Reef, Moonta/Munda Bay, while the single-masted wooden cutter *Blanche* (1865), the cutter *Ben Morowie* (1870), and *Juno* (1870) wrecked at Wallaroo/Wadla waru (Department of the Environment and Energy 2017). The first bell may also not have been a ship's bell. English founders supplied the great majority of bells in Australia (Keating 1979, 103), and it is possible that the Moravian mission in Europe supplied this bell. Alternatively, foundries in Australia were producing bells by around the mid-nineteenth century (Keating 1979, 110).

Exploring tangible objects, such as bells, characterizes the wider acoustic ecology of the mission, revealing connections to the maritime industry in the area, and in particular a continuing association with sites long after the event (Till 2014; Fowler and Rigney 2017, 63). Long-term engagements are more readily understood through such curated objects than through historical records, which primarily focus on major moments and events (Fowler and Rigney 2017, 63), although, as illustrated below, "sound ... belongs to the realm of 'activity' rather than 'artefact'" (Watson 2001, 180).

Spatial and Sonic Agency and Resistance

Western constructs of nature/culture perceived that areas were open to control or colonization by others (Helmreich 2011, 132). Missionaries aimed to create boundaries where they did not exist in nature through the spatial layout of mission settlements, by imposing new forms of settlement organization and space and time routines (Griffin 2000, 22; Lydon and Ash 2010, 2; Keating 2012). The geometric or cadastral grid of "white" fences and legal boundaries forced the settlement and movement patterns of Indigenous peoples to occur within, around, and between these spaces (Di Fazio 2000; Smith and Beck 2003, 66; Byrne 2008). Local histories, however, often separate Indigenous and non-Indigenous geographic spaces, with the mission featured as the only space Indigenous peoples inhabited after missionization, creating the illusion that Indigenous peoples seemingly vacated other parts of the landscape (see commentary in Nash 1984; Howitt 2001; Byrne and Nugent 2004, 11; Roberts et al. 2014, 29). However, "it is not uncommon for multiple cultural landscapes to exist in the same physical space" (Westerdahl 2011, 333).

Due to the coastal location of Point Pearce/Burgiyana and its proximity to the sea (a "natural" feature), the spatial boundaries put in place by missionaries could at times be countered by Point Pearce/Burgiyana residents—total control in this regard was not consistently achieved (see Smith and Beck 2003). The accessibility of the ocean to Aboriginal peoples at Point Pearce/Burgiyana provided a source of subsistence during the mission period (Narungga people continue to be known as great fishers, as already noted) (Bennett 2007, 90); and indeed missionaries often encouraged (or allowed) the supplementation of resources through traditional foraging practices in order to achieve self-sufficiency (Attwood 1989, 65). Thus, missionary attempts to fully enclose and domesticate landscapes were often unsuccessful (Attwood 1989, 65). The aforementioned use of Wardang Island/Waraldi by Point Pearce/Burgiyana for grazing further facilitated access to spaces outside the spatial and sonic remit of the bell. Indeed, the success of Point Pearce/Burgiyana in the late nineteenth and into the twentieth century depended on utilizing every available piece of land, including Wardang Island/Waraldi (Wanganeen 1987, 55; Moody 2012, 113). The transport of sheep progressed from using launches to a purpose-built, large two-masted ketch, *Narrunga* (Roberts et al. 2013, 80–86; Fowler et al. 2014, 14–15). About seven Aboriginal families stayed on the island to run the sheep, and Point Pearce/Burgiyana people continue to be highly active in the waters off the Peninsula and around Wardang Island/Waraldi as well as other nearby islands (Wood and Westell 1998, 18).

The sonic authority of the mission faded when Aboriginal peoples left Point Pearce/Burgiyana and crossed the sea to Wardang Island/Waraldi and other nearby islands. There are spaces where the sound of the bell did not reach, either physically or cognitively. While Phoebe Wanganeen, for example, could hear the bell from the beach at Galadri, a distance of just over 5 km from Point Pearce/Burgiyana (Edwards et al. 1987, 11; Wood and Westell 1998, 12) (see Figure 1.4),[7] there is no record of a bell being present on Wardang Island/Waraldi, either in oral histories or historical archives (Fowler et al. 2014). It is important to note that there is also no record of a church or religious services on the island, therefore, those people living there were not subjected to the same religious regimes as those at Point Pearce/Burgiyana. A lack of interest given to the living situation on Wardang Island/Waraldi by the superintendent in the mission documents indicates an "out of sight, out of mind" mentality towards the Point Pearce/Burgiyana community living and working there (Fowler 2015, 315). Furthermore, permission to travel around Wardang Island/Waraldi was not required, unlike on the mainland. Oral histories also describe Wardang Island/Waraldi as allowing a level of freedom from mission life, as portrayed by Fred Graham (born 1932 [Kartineryi 2002, 119]): "Well, you can wander around the island with no one to stop you … you can go fishing, do what you like, no one there to tell you what to do. On the mission? Obey the law. That was the difference, you had freedom over there [Wardang Island/Waraldi], no freedom up here [Point Pearce/Burgiyana]" (Fowler et al. 2014, 20).

Living away from the confines of the settlement and its rules, known as "living away from the bell," occurred not only at Wardang Island/Waraldi, but also at fringe camps such as Wadjadin and Hollywood (Wood and Westell 1998, 11–12). Hollywood, for example, was a place where many Narungga people lived when they were not allowed on Point Pearce/Burgiyana due to the permit/exemption system (see

Mattingley and Hampton 1988, 46; Roberts et al. 2013, 89, as well as n. 3, this chapter). At this place people built their own shacks/tents and dug for their own water. Thus, while sound may have controlled the daily activities of Aboriginal people at Point Pearce/Burgiyana, it did not cross the mission's borders.

Aboriginal agency reveals that "[the] 'tactile' relationships between people and their material worlds" during colonial encounters are complex (van Dommelen and Rowlands 2012, 22). Today, the Point Pearce/Burgiyana community perceive the bell differently again.

"Community Sounds": New Contexts and Complexities

Finally, there is heritage, the bells that survive and what they mean to contemporary society (after Schofield 2014, 289). In 1966, the Point Pearce/Burgiyana Aboriginal Reserve Land, including Wardang Island/Waraldi, became vested in the Aboriginal Lands Trust—ending official government control—and has since been self-managed (Kartinyeri 2002, 70). While the mission/station bells, therefore, are significant for historical reasons, many values are also attached to the bells by the present community.

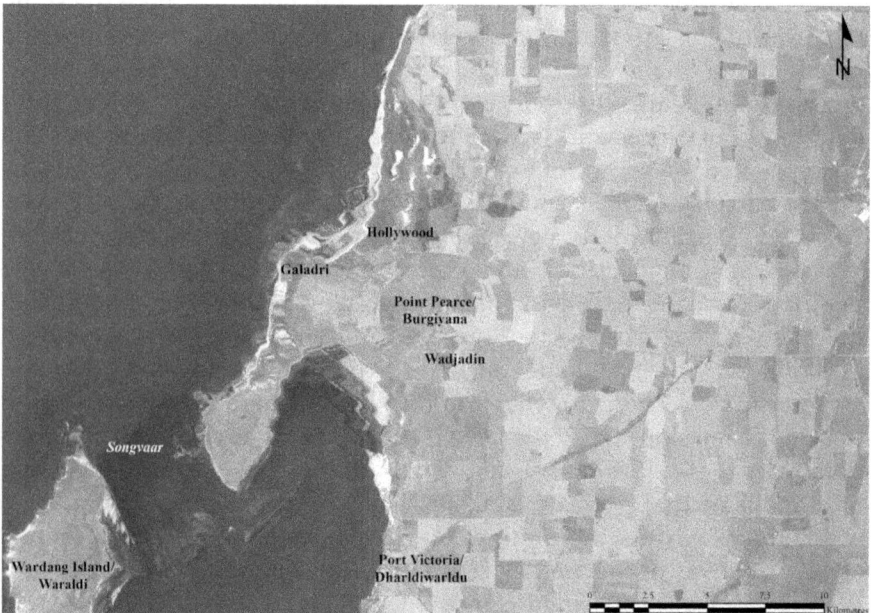

Figure 1.4. Soundscape: the sonic reach of Point Pearce/Burgiyana bells, given the known 5 km radius that the sound traveled. (Created by the authors, adapted from Schofield 2014, 290.)

Point Pearce/Burgiyana retains evidence of the influence of a mission-ary function, with a "regimented" street layout. The "new" church and hall, built in 1936, remain, and have indeed received continued renovation in recent decades (Wood and Westell 1998, 11, 27). At present, there is a bell located in front of the Point Pearce Hall, embossed with "John Danks & Son Pty Ltd Melbourne Sydney," denoting a company established in 1859 (see Figure 1.5). While bell-founding in Australia remained overall an ad hoc production, John Danks & Son were one of two exceptions and are the Australian firm most closely associated with bell-founding (Keating 1979, 111–2). John Danks & Son made their most identifiable Danks bells after the turn of the twentieth century and reached their peak in bell production in the 1920s (Keating 1979, 114).

Figure 1.5. John Danks & Son bell currently used at Point Pearce Hall. (Photograph by Julie Mushynsky, 25 November 2013.)

Anglican Bishop John Stead donated the current bell, a spare from a church in Gladstone (a South Australian town 170 km to the north), to Point Pearce/Burgiyana where Doug Milera (a former Point Pearce/ Burgiyana resident) undertook its installation (Perry 2013). According to Perry (2013), the removal of the previous bell from the same location about twenty years earlier (ca. 1993) occurred because the framework was starting to break. Some members of the community requested this new bell as many people missed hearing it, particularly during events that maintain community cohesion, such as funerals (Perry 2013). Given the colonizing effect of bells at Point Pearce/Burgiyana, however, for other community members this decision, and thus the continued tolling of the bell, remains fraught.

The continued sonic existence of a bell ringing at Point Pearce/ Burgiyana now represents at once a multitude of concepts and emotions. For some it speaks to the maintenance of identity and community—perhaps even a contestation of authority, as it is now no longer the colonizers controlling the aural space (see Rath 2003, 2008; Mills 2014, 283). Indeed, Rigney has observed that counter memories to "bell hegemony" have always existed and Narungga pass these on to celebrate Narungga resistance. For others, it is a reminder of the painful outcomes of invasion and European settlement and thus a troubled and contested soundscape. In this sense the bell, as a sound artifact, has been "adopted and set in new contexts" producing differing (even opposing) functions and meanings (Both 2009, 7). Despite this tension the sound of a bell ringing at Point Pearce/Burgiyana remains a "community sound" that unites community members through their collective lived and historical experiences (Mills 2014, 281).

Conclusion

We know the location of two Point Pearce/Burgiyana bells today; the present bell located at the hall and the *Songvaar* bell located at the Port Victoria Maritime Museum. Arguably, at least two additional bells may have served the community: the *Notre Dame D'Arvor* bell and the original bell which commenced ringing by at least 1870, just two years after the establishment of the mission.

In maritime spheres of the past, "the bell of a vessel symbolizes the essence of the ship" (Hruska 2016, 44), serving a number of roles such as the marking of time, changing of the watch, drawing attention to danger and signaling ceremonial duties such as burial at sea. The bells of Point Pearce/Burgiyana have had and continue to serve multiple functions, at once controlling the lives of Aboriginal peoples and in some instances revealing their involvement in a wider sphere of movement that extended into a maritime landscape (Cross and Watson 2006, 115). While the interpretation of material culture from contexts of cross-cultural engagement is challenging, oral histories have provided invaluable insights. In addition, the current bell at the hall is "an active object" and a "rope hangs from it seeking to be used" (Hruska 2016, 46)—as its sound still rings across the landscape it remains replete with meaning, able to instigate emotion and memory.

Acknowledgments

The authors especially thank all of the Narungga organizations that approved and supported this research. We also acknowledge Eileen Wanganeen for her assistance with this project and for allowing the reproduction of Figure 1.2. We thank the Port Victoria Maritime Museum, particularly Wendy Brusnahan, for assistance with collection images. The Flinders University Social and Behavioural Research Ethics Committee approved this research (Project 5806).

Dr. Madeline Fowler is a maritime archaeologist whose research has centered on Aboriginal maritime cultural landscapes in Australia's historical period. She is particularly interested in decolonizing Australian maritime archaeology through the representation of Aboriginal and Torres Strait Islander peoples in research. Currently at the University of Southampton, Dr. Fowler is exploring ethical practices for engaging Indigenous communities in the study of the submerged landscapes of Australia's deep past.

Associate Professor Amy Roberts is an archaeologist and anthropologist who primarily works with Indigenous communities in South Australia. In particular, she collaborates with the Narungga people of Yorke Peninsula and Aboriginal people from the Mid Murray and Riverland regions. Prior to her appointment as an academic at Flinders University, Amy worked as an "expert" for a number of native title cases—including for the First Peoples of the River Murray and Mallee Region, which achieved a successful determination.

One of Australia's most respected Aboriginal educationalists, **Professor Lester-Irabinna Rigney** is a descendant of the Narungga, Kaurna, and Ngarrindjeri peoples of South Australia. He is an expert on Aboriginal education and is best known for his theorization of Indigenist Research Epistemologies. He is a research fellow at Kings College, London, and Professor of Education at the Centre for Research in Education at University of South Australia. Professor Rigney has worked across the Pacific on Indigenous Education from New Zealand to Taiwan and Canada.

Notes

1. The reader should note the use of Narungga toponyms (e.g., Guuranda, Burgiyana, and Dharldiwarldu), where available, in conjunction with other place names is a requirement of the community and in accordance with the current orthography published by the Narungga Aboriginal Progress Association (2006). Indeed, it is important to remember that the naming of places is always power laden in character (Berg and Kearns 2009) and has played a key role in the "colonial silencing of [I]ndigenous cultures" (Vuolteenaho and Berg 2009, 1).
2. Kühn was superintendent of the mission from 1867 to 1880, C. R. Goode served from 1880 to 1882, T. M. Sutton served from 1882 to 1893, B. G. Edwards served from 1893 to 1894, B. Lathern served from 1894 to 1909, followed by F. Garnett (Archibald 1915, 5). During the period from 1867–1915, trustees ran Point Pearce/Burgiyana (Archibald 1915).
3. Mattingley and Hampton (1988, Chapter 6) detail later destructive legislative amendments such as exemption clauses. Roberts et al. (2013, 89) provide the following summary about exemption: "… a legislative provision under the *Aborigines Act Amendment Act 1939*. This provision was an 'invidious form of discrimination' which ultimately had the effect of declaring certain Aboriginal individuals and families as 'honorary whites' (Mattingley and Hampton 1988, 49). Such a declaration could be made by the Aborigines Protection Board even if the person concerned had not applied—and was sometimes employed as a punitive measure (Mattingley and Hampton 1988, 48)."
4. Although this quote is unascribed in Wanganeen (1987) the author of the compilation indicated that these were the words of Olga Fudge (Eileen Wanganeen, pers. comm. to Amy Roberts, 24 June 2014).
5. Exemplified by the fact that for the year ending June 1934, forty coastal steamships, 239 coastal sailing ships, ten interstate steamships, and twelve overseas sailing ships arrived there (Moody 2012, 38).
6. Note the only other shipwreck in the vicinity of Hungry Bay is *Investigator* (1918).
7. It is possible to hear bells from some distance when the wind is in the right direction (Keating 1979, 127).

References

Archibald, T. S. 1915. *Yorke's Peninsula Aboriginal Mission Incorporated: A Brief Record of its History and Operations*. Adelaide: Hussey & Gillingham.

Attwood, Bain M. 1989. *The Making of the Aborigines*. Sydney: Allen & Unwin.

_____. 2000. "Space and Time at Ramahyuck, Victoria, 1863–85." In *Settlement: A History of Australian Indigenous Housing*, ed. Peter Read, 41–54. Canberra: Aboriginal Studies Press.

Ball, Megan. 1992. "The Lesser of Two Evils: A Comparison of Government and Mission Policy at Raukkan and Point Pearce, 1890–1940." *Cabbages and Kings: Selected Essays in History and Australian Studies* 20: 36–45.

Bennett, Michael. 2007. "The Economics of Fishing: Sustainable Living in Colonial New South Wales." *Aboriginal History* 31: 85–102.

Berg, Lawrence D., and Robin A. Kearns. 2009. "Naming as Norming: 'Race,' Gender and the Identity Politics of Naming Places in Aotearoa/New Zealand." In *Critical Toponymies: The Contested Politics of Place Naming*, ed. Lawrence D. Berg and Jani Vuolteenaho, 19–52. London: Ashgate.

Both, Arnd Adje. 2009. "Music Archaeology: Some Methodological and Theoretical Considerations." *Yearbook of Traditional Music* 41: 1–11.

Buscaglia, Silvana. 2017. "Materiality and Indigenous Agency: Limits to the Colonial Order (Argentinean Patagonia, Eighteenth–Nineteenth Centuries)." *International Journal of Historical Archaeology* 21: 641–73.

Byrne, Denis. 2008. "Counter-Mapping in the Archaeological Landscape." In *Handbook of Landscape Archaeology*, ed. Bruno David and Julian Thomas, 609–16. Walnut Creek: Left Coast Press.

Byrne, Denis, and Maria Nugent. 2004. *Mapping Attachment: A Spatial Approach to Aboriginal Post-Contact Heritage*. Hurstville: Department of Environment and Conservation (NSW).

Comaroff, Jean, and John Comaroff. 1986. "Christianity and Colonialism in South Africa." *American Ethnologist* 13(10): 1–22.

_____. 1991. *Of Revelation and Revolution: Christianity, Colonialism, and Consciousness in South Africa*, Vol. 1. Chicago: University Chicago Press.

Cross, Ian, and Aaron Watson. 2006. "Acoustics and the Human Experience of Socially Organised Sound." In *Archaeoacoustics*, ed. Christopher Scarre and Graeme Lawson, 107–16. Cambridge: MacDonald Institute Monographs.

Department of the Environment and Energy. 2017. "Australian National Shipwreck Database." Retrieved 15 November 2017 from http://www.environment.gov.au/heritage/historic-shipwrecks/australian-national-shipwreck-database.

Di Fazio, Bianca C. 2000. *Living on the Edge: An Exploration of Fringe Camp Occupation in Beltana, Flinders Ranges*. Unpublished Honours thesis, Flinders University.

Edwards, A. D. 1934. "Wrecks at Wardang Is. and Port Victoria: Disastrous Chapters in S.A.'s Maritime History." *The Adelaide Chronicle*, 8 November, 50.

Edwards, Clifford, Phoebe Wanganeen, and Josie Agius. 1987. *Bookayana Stories: Childhood Memories of Bookayana (Pt. Pearce)*. Adelaide: Education Department of South Australia.

Foucault, Michel. 1977. *Discipline and Punish: The Birth of the Prison*. London: Penguin Books.

Fowler, Madeline. 2015. *"Now, are you going to believe this or not?"* Addressing *Neglected Narratives through the Maritime Cultural Landscape of Point Pearce Aboriginal Mission/Burgiyana, South Australia.* PhD diss., Flinders University.

Fowler, Madeline, and Lester-Irabinna Rigney. 2017. "Collaboration, Collision, and (Re)Conciliation: Indigenous Participation in Australia's Maritime Industry—A Case Study from Point Pearce/Burgiyana, South Australia." In *Formation Processes of Maritime Archaeological Landscapes*, ed. Alicia Caporaso, 53–78. New York: Springer.

Fowler, Madeline, Amy L. Roberts, Jennifer F. McKinnon, Clem O'Loughlin, and Fred Graham. 2014. "'They Camped here Always': Archaeologies of Attachment to Seascapes via a Case Study at Wardang Island (Waraldi/Wara-dharldhi), South Australia." *Australasian Historical Archaeology* 32: 14–22.

Graham, Doris May, and Cecil Wallace Graham. 1987. *As We've Known It: 1911 to the Present.* Underdale: Aboriginal Studies and Teacher Education Centre.

Gramsci, Antonio. 1971. *Selections from the Prison Notebooks of Antonio Gramsci.* New York: International Publishers.

Griffin, Darren. 2000. *"A Christian Village of South Australian Natives": A Critical Analysis of the Use of Space at Poonindie Mission, South Australia.* Unpublished Honours thesis, Flinders University.

Helmreich, Stefan. 2011. "Nature/Culture/Seawater." *American Anthropologist* 113(1): 132–44.

Higgins, R. 1893. "Point Pearce Mission Station." *Adelaide Observer*, 2 December, 43.

Howitt, Richie. 2001. "Frontiers, Borders and Edges: Liminal Challenges to the Hegemony of Exclusion." *Australian Geographical Studies* 39: 233–45.

Hruska, Benjamin J. 2016. *Interpreting Naval History at Museums and Historic Sites.* Lanham: Rowman & Littlefield.

Kartinyeri, Doreen. 2002. *Narungga Nation.* Adelaide: Doreen Kartinyeri.

Keating, Claire. 2012. *"We Want Men Whose Hearts Are … Full of Zeal": An Investigation of Cross-Cultural Engagement within the Weipa Mission Station (1898–1932).* Unpublished Master's thesis, Flinders University.

Keating, John D. 1979. *Bells in Australia.* Carlton: Melbourne University Press.

Kelly, Mark. 2017. "Michel Foucault (1926–1984)." In *Internet Encyclopedia of Philosophy*, ed. James Fieser and Bradley Dowden. Retrieved 27 November 2017 from http://www.iep.utm.edu/foucault/.

Krichauff, Skye. 2008. *The Narungga and Europeans: Cross-Cultural Relations on Yorke Peninsula in the Nineteenth Century.* Unpublished Master's thesis, University of Adelaide.

_____. 2011. *Nharangga Wargunni Bugi-Buggillu: A Journey through Narungga History.* Adelaide: Wakefield Press.

_____. 2013. "Narungga, the Townspeople and Julius Kühn: The Establishment and Origins of the Point Pearce Mission, South Australia." *Journal of the Anthropological Society of South Australia* 37: 57–72.

Lydon, Jane. 2009. *Fantastic Dreaming: The Archaeology of an Aboriginal Mission.* Lanham: AltaMira Press.

Lydon, Jane, and Jeremy Ash. 2010. "The Archaeology of Missions in Australasia: Introduction." *International Journal of Historical Archaeology* 14: 1–14.

Mattingley, Christobel. 2017. "Fudge, Olga Dagmar (1896–1993)." *Australian Dictionary of Biography*, National Centre of Biography, Australian National University. Retrieved 26 September 2017 from http://ia.anu.edu.au/biography/fudge-olga-dagmar-17846/text29434.

Mattingley, Christobel, and Ken Hampton, eds. 1988. *Survival in Our Own Land: "Aboriginal" Experiences in "South Australia" since 1936: Told by Nungas and Others*. Rydalmere: Hodder & Stoughton.

McArthur, J. 1876. "A Week at the Point Pearce Aboriginal Mission Station." *Yorke's Peninsula Advertiser and Miners' and Farmers' Journal*, 10 November, 1.

Mills, Steve. 2014. *Auditory Archaeology: Understanding Sound and Hearing in the Past*. Walnut Creek: Left Coast Press.

Moody, Stuart M. 2012. *Port Victoria's Ships and Shipwrecks*. Maitland: S.M. Moody.

Narungga Aboriginal Progress Association. 2006. *Nharangga Warra: Narungga Dictionary*. Maitland: Wakefield Press.

Nash, David. 1984. "The Waramungu's Reserves 1892–1962: A Case Study in Dispossession." *Australian Aboriginal Studies* 1: 2–16.

O'Brien, Lewis. 2007. *And the Clock Struck Thirteen: The Life and Thoughts of Kaurna Elder Uncle Lewis Yerloburka O'Brien*. Kent Town, South Australia: Wakefield Press.

Octopus. 1900. "A Model Mission: Point Pearce Station." *The Advertiser*, 29 June, 6.

Perry, N. 2013. "New Bell Ringing at Point Pearce." *Yorke Peninsula Country Times*, 30 April.

Peters, Edward N. 2001. *1917 Pio-Benedictine Code of Canon Law*. San Francisco: Ignatius Press.

Rait, Fiona. 2002. "The Launching of the *Doris May*." *Yorke Peninsula Country Times*, 12 December.

Rath, Richard Cullen. 2003. *How Early America Sounded*. Ithaca: Cornell University Press.

———. 2008. "Hearing American History." *Journal of American History* 95(2): 417–31.

Rigney, Lester-Irabinna. 2002. "Foreword." In *Alas, for the Pelicans! Flinders, Baudin and Beyond*, ed. Anne Chittleborough, Gillian Dooley, Brenda Glover, and Rick Hosking, ix–xiv. Kent Town: Wakefield Press.

Roberts, Amy L., Madeline Fowler, and Tauto Sansbury. 2014. "A Report on the Exhibition Entitled 'Children, Boats and "Hidden Histories"': Crayon Drawings by Aboriginal Children at Point Pearce Mission (SA), 1939." *Bulletin of the Australasian Institute for Maritime Archaeology* 38: 24–30.

Roberts, Amy L., Jennifer F. McKinnon, Clem O'Loughlin, Klynton Wanganeen, Lester-Irabinna Rigney, and Madeline Fowler. 2013. "Combining Indigenous and Maritime Archaeological Approaches: Experiences and Insights from the '(Re)Locating *Narrunga* Project,' Yorke Peninsula, South Australia." *Journal of Maritime Archaeology* 8(1): 77–99.

Roberts, Amy L., Adrian Mollenmans, Quenten Agius, Fred Graham, Jeffrey Newchurch, Lester-Irabinna Rigney, Fred Sansbury, et al. 2016. "'They Planned their Calendar...they Set up Ready for what they Wanted to Feed the Tribe': A First Stage Analysis of Narungga Fish Traps on Yorke Peninsula, South Australia." *The Journal of Island and Coastal Archaeology* 11(1): 1–25.

Schofield, John. 2014. "The Archaeology of Sound and Music." *World Archaeology* 46(3): 289–91.

Seamew. 1946. "Graveyard of Ships May Become a Tourist Resort." *The Advertiser,* 18 May, 4.

Smith, Anita, and Wendy Beck. 2003. "The Archaeology of No Man's Land: Indigenous Camps at Corindi Beach, Mid-North Coast New South Wales." *Archaeology of Oceania* 38(1): 66–77.

Till, Rupert. 2014. "Sound Archaeology: Terminology, Palaeolithic Cave Art and the Soundscape." *World Archaeology* 46(3): 292–304.

van Dommelen, Peter, and Michael Rowlands. 2012. "Material Concerns and Colonial Encounters." In *Materiality and Social Practice: Transformative Capacities of Intercultural Encounters,* Joseph Maran and Philipp W. Stockhammer, 20–31. Oxford: Oxbow Books.

Vuolteenaho, Jani, and Lawrence D. Berg. 2009. "Towards Critical Toponymies." In *Critical Toponymies: The Contested Politics of Place Naming,* ed. Lawrence D. Berg and Jani Vuolteenaho, 1–18. London: Ashgate.

Wanganeen, Eileen, ed. 1987. *Point Pearce: Past and Present.* Underdale: Aboriginal Studies and Teacher Education Centre.

Watson, Aaron. 2001. "The Sounds of Transformation: Acoustics, Monuments and Ritual in the British Neolithic." In *The Archaeology of Shamanism,* ed. Neil S. Price, 178–92. London: Routledge.

Westerdahl, Christer. 2011. "Conclusion: The Maritime Cultural Landscape Revisited." In *The Archaeology of Maritime Landscapes,* ed. Ben Ford, 331–44. New York: Springer.

Wood, Vivienne, and Craig Westell. 1998. *Point Pearce Social History Project, Yorke Peninsula, South Australia.* Unpublished report. Parkside: Australian Heritage Commission.

Chapter 2

Colonization, Sámi Sacred Sites, and Religious Syncretism, ca. AD 500–1800

Inga-Maria Mulk and Tim Bayliss-Smith

Introduction

In this chapter, we discuss changes in the religious beliefs and practices of Sámi hunting society in northern Fennoscandia over the past two millennia, and we consider in what ways archaeological evidence might help us to interpret these changes. This long-term perspective is relevant because religious change in this region did not take the form of sudden "conversion," and initially it was not even associated with "colonialism" in the strict sense. Only after the nation states of Norway, Sweden, Finland, and Russia were fully established in the late Medieval period did a state-sponsored colonization process begin along the states' northern borders. As elsewhere in the world, the Christianity of the frontier colonists influenced the beliefs and practices of Indigenous peoples, but for the Sámi in northern Europe the effects were variable in time and space. The impulse towards Christian conversion became overwhelming only in the seventeenth century with the activities of militant Lutheran missionaries, whereas the archaeological evidence suggests that "conversion" was actually the culmination of a long and slow process of religious change.

In this chapter, we use the term "religion" to mean the *lived religion* of people, in other words, the beliefs and practices that are both inside and outside religious institutions (Nordberg 2018, 140). A lived religion encompasses both lay people and religious experts, occupies both the private and the public spheres, and includes aspects of people's everyday lives as well as formal festivals and special events. Following Nordberg (2018), we make no sharp distinction between, say, Old Norse *seiðr*, Sámi shamanism, and Lutheran Christianity, seeing all three as the lived religions of people in northern Fennoscandia, past and present.

We discuss in this chapter evidence for interactions between Sámi and their neighbors from the Metal Age (1800 BC) up until Viking times (AD 800–1050). These pre-Christian interactions include those with Germanic (Norse) Pagans to the south and with other Finno-Ugrian language-speakers to the east. Using Insoll's (2004) model of religious conversion involving stages of "inclusion," "syncretism," and "displacement," we conclude that there were marked variations in the rate at which different Sámi societies progressed through these stages, before reaching the Christian "orthodoxy" that characterizes Sámi society today. The Mountain Sámi, for example, resisted assimilation into the ethnicity and religion of colonizing Swedish farmers, fishers, and traders, and despite some signs of "syncretism" their Christian conversion did not take place until after the Early Modern period. One reason for the delay was the spiritual connections between Sámi hunters, fishers, and herders and the wider landscape, making the church-based rituals of Christianity unattractive. We conclude that the "conversion" of the Sámi is by no means a simple story of colonialism, and that the archaeological evidence helps to map a more complex history and varied geography of various forms of religious "syncretism."

Sámi Ethnicity

The Sámi are an Indigenous people who speak different dialects of Finno-Ugrian Sámi languages and inhabit large tracts of Arctic and sub-Arctic Norway, Sweden, Finland, and the Kola peninsula and Karelia in northwest Russia. Much of the evidence that we review comes from burials, rock art, and sacrificial sites in northern Sweden, which is the area historically called Norrland. This region is sub-divided into Northern Norrland and Southern Norrland. Northern Norrland covers the historical provinces of Norrbotten, Västerbotten, and Lappland, while Southern Norrland covers the remainder of the region: Gästrikland, Medelpad, Ångermanland, Jämtland, and Härjedalen.

Using Northern Norrland evidence from Sámi sacrificial sites we can reconstruct a changing pattern of votive practices involving metal artifacts, such as arrowheads and pendants, beads, silver coins, antlers, and animal bones. We suggest that these practices need to be interpreted in the context of colonial contacts that led to new religious ideas and rituals. The evidence from rock art and burial practices also suggest that Sámi concepts of the sacred were not fixed and "traditional" but instead were dynamic and syncretic. Until their full conversion to Lutheran Christianity about 200–300 years ago, the Mountain and Forest Sámi maintained animistic and shamanistic ideas about the cosmos, and they inhabited a cultural landscape in which secular and sacred were interwoven. However, the actual practices of Sámi religion were always accommodating new ideas derived in part from their changing external connections.

It has been suggested that these external linkages provide the rationale for the initial formation of Sámi ethnic identity. Ethnicity emerges in the context of transactions across social boundaries, particularly social interactions, trade, and exchange (Barth 1969). Hansen and Olsen (2004, 31) consider that what later consolidated as Sámi ethnicity originated towards the end of the last millennium BC, when the northern hunter-gatherers experienced cultural dissimilarity from the agricultural groups of the south. The impacts of intergroup transactions on spiritual beliefs and ritual practices ("religion") were neither geographically uniform nor historically unchanging, and therefore any surviving archaeological evidence for Sámi religion will reflect an ongoing process of interaction with neighboring groups. We conclude that pre-Christian religious ideas are unlikely to have been monolithic, static or uniform across the wide terrain of the Sámi area.

The Sámi worldview, in its overall structure, was the westernmost extension of a widespread North Eurasian belief system (Anisimov 1963; Hultkrantz 1994). Throughout this vast area there was an animistic-shamanistic way of seeing the world. The Sámi variant of this worldview emerged during the post-glacial period, after people had moved into ice-free tracts of Fennoscandia and northwest Russia. These societies were not isolated, maintaining contact with neighboring groups (Bäckman and Hultkrantz 1985; Odner 1985; Ahlbäck 1987; Hansen and Olsen 2004; Forsberg 2010). Archaeological and linguistic evidence suggests that in prehistory their main contacts were with farmers and pastoralists in central and southeast Europe, while to the east there were strong interactions with other Finno-Ugrian language speakers with links extending as far as the Ural Mountains and western Siberia (Zachrisson 1997; Carpelan, Parpola, and Koskikallio 2001; Hansen and Olsen 2014).

With the onset of the Roman Empire and the spread of agriculture, Nordic-Germanic groups to the south were also extending their contacts. The southern influence increased during the first millennium AD when livestock husbandry, production of dried fish and seal oil, and small-scale farming were adopted along northern Atlantic and Bothnian coasts, along with trading. As a result there was some assimilation to Nordic or North Germanic languages and ethnicity among Sámi populations, for example in the fjords of northern Norway and in southern parts of the Gulf of Bothnia (Ramqvist 1983; Hansen 1990; Lindqvist 1994; Welinder 2003; Broadbent 2010). The northernmost Sámi area in Fennoscandia was not annexed by Sweden until after AD 1300 (Wallerström 1995a). A more formal process of colonization sponsored by the Lutheran church and Swedish state began after 1600 (Loeffler 2005).

All connections to the outside world intensified with the fur trade of the Viking Age and Medieval period, between the ninth century AD and about 1600 (Wallerström 1995a; Mulk 1996). The fur trade represented the frontier of colonialism in northern Europe, and the furs from northern Fennoscandia were important in supply chains. For example, many of the furs that were traded through Novgorod originated in northern Sweden. There was a particular demand for the winter furs derived from six animal species (marten, squirrel, ermine, fox, lynx, and beaver) as well as furs and leather products from reindeer (Ahnlund 1946; Zachrisson 1984, 1989; Mulk 1994a, 1996). Wealth objects derived from the fur trade provided an important index of cultural interchange, as seen for example in archaeological finds from Sámi sacrificial sites.

Religious Conversion

As already indicated, the beliefs and practices described in historical sources from the seventeenth to the nineteenth centuries reflect an already altered form of Sámi religion. Using the concept of religious "syncretism" we suggest that the *lived religion* of the Sámi was the outcome of a long process of blending and fusing of different religious traditions, following cultural interchange with Finnish, Karelian, Russian, and Scandinavian neighbors, both Pagan and Christian. Scholars in other regions of the world have argued that religious "conversion" does not generally involve "a sudden and total transformation in which a prior religious identity is wholly rejected and replaced by a new one" (Eaton 1996, 269; Insoll 2003, 2004), as can happen under colonialism with intense missionary activity. Instead, change usually takes place slowly, and with different stages and effects in different societies.

Stage 1 represents the prior stage of *tradition* in which local beliefs are not subject to major challenge from contacts with outsiders. Societies in this "traditional" state will still absorb new beliefs and may undergo many changes in religious practice, but probably the pace of change will be slow. In stage 2 (*inclusion*) the supernatural agencies of the new religion become accepted in local cosmologies alongside local divinities, but without any fundamental change in the pre-existing cosmology.

In stage 3 we see the emergence of *syncretism*, where local practices are adapted rather than being totally abandoned. The new concepts are merged with the local ones, and the names of deities are used interchangeably. Insoll (2004, 132–34) sees religious syncretism as the likely outcome in cases where the old and the new concepts of time and/or place are markedly incompatible.

Stage 4, if it happens, occurs after *displacement* of the old religion has taken place. Traditional ideas and practices become completely subordinate to the new religion, and they become relegated to the status of lingering folk beliefs that have limited credibility. We finally reach stage 5 (*orthodoxy*), which may happen only in cases where conversion to a world religion such as Islam or Christianity takes place. It occurs when an increasing integration leads to the local religion conforming more and more to orthodox global norms. In this chapter, we examine how well this model matches the archaeological record for the Mountain Sámi in northern Sweden, reviewing briefly the evidence from rock art, sacrificial sites, and graves.

Approaches to Sámi Religion

The emphasis in research on Sámi religion has been on artifacts and sites of religious significance, such as rock art, sacrificial sites, graves, and drums. Scholars like Qvigstad (1926) in Norway, Manker (1957) in Sweden, and Itkonen (1946) in Finland have documented sacred sites and objects across the whole of northern Fennoscandia. Earlier generations documented aspects of religious belief, and this body of sources has been reinterpreted by more recent scholars (e.g., Bäckman 1975, 2005; Bäckman and Hultkrantz 1978, 1985; Ahlbäck 1987; Rydving 1993, 2010; Äikäs 2011).

There is a risk, however, that by isolating "religion" as an analytical category we may lose sight of the holistic nature of Sámi cosmology. The Sámi inhabited a sacred landscape in which beliefs and rituals found a particular focus on certain mountains, cliffs, caves, waterfalls, and springs, some of which were visited for sacrificial offerings (Mulk and Bayliss-Smith 2007; Mulk 2014, 2017). The "cultural landscape" approach recognizes that landscapes exist in people's minds as well as "out there" in nature. Even today in northern Fennoscandia, landscapes that appear to some observers as untouched wilderness are likely to be perceived by the

Sámi as reflecting past and present livelihoods, communal social values, myths, memories, and spiritual meanings (Mulk and Bayliss-Smith 1998, 2007). From our reconstruction of the cosmology of Sámi hunting society before the onset of reindeer pastoralism around AD 1600, we argue that the entire landscape would have been imbued with religious meanings, and ritual practices would have involved everyone within the society on an almost daily basis (Mulk and Bayliss-Smith 2006, 114–15).

It is now generally agreed that Sámi ethnic identity was not forged in isolation but emerged in the context of interaction with neighboring populations (Barth 1969; Odner 1983; Olsen 1986). Several of the groups with which the Sámi interacted provided them with new ideas about what was "sacred" and how this alternative world of the spirits and deities should be acknowledged (Rydving 1993; Mebius 2003; Äikäs and Salmi 2013).

More recent scholars have emphasized instead the role of internal change within northern hunting societies, leading to the adoption of new ethnic (including religious) identities. Ethnicity is therefore seen as a social process among actors whose identity is in a permanent state of renegotiation. The archaeological signal of this process may be unclear or ambiguous, but sometimes the interactions between contrasted societies can quickly lead to the adoption of new symbols of ethnic identity that will be displayed in material culture (Barth 1969; Hodder 1979; Odner 1983; Olsen 1985). Colonial contacts will lead to an intensification of social interactions, and religion is part of the new identities that people form through this process.

Christian Conversion on the Bothnian Coast

At the same time as Sámi in southern areas were forming new identities (so-called assimilation), further north on the Bothnian coasts of northern Norrland there were still Indigenous communities with an economy based on hunting, fishing, and trading. We can call these people Bothnian Sámi, and we can also assume that they traded with the Forest and Mountain Sámi who lived inland, acting as brokers in the acquisition of furs and the supply of prestige goods of southern or eastern origin.

On the Bothnian coast the presence of this Sámi seal-hunting and fishing community is shown by the numerous circular huts of Sámi type, including iron-working sites. These sites are associated with seal hunting and oil production in the period AD 200–1200, with the largest proportion of charcoal samples dating to the Viking Age ca. 800–1000 (Broadbent 2006; Broadbent 2010, 142–43). At Stora Fjäderägg island several stone rings are interpreted as Sámi sacrificial sites, while at Grundskatan there is a Sámi bear burial dated to the eleventh century (Edvinger and Broadbent 2006; Broadbent 2010, 77–82).

On the south Bothnian coast at Hornslandsudde in Rogsta parish, Hälsingland, Broadbent (2010, 131–39) identified similar circular sites that are dated to the period ca. AD 300–950. Here the evidence indicated that up until ca. AD 600 there were Sámi seal-hunters living alongside other people of the Early Nordic Iron Age, suggesting "the co-existence of two groups in the region, one a hunter-gatherer/herding/trading group of Saami and the other an agrarian-based/trading Germanic community" (Broadbent 2010, 139).

By AD 1279 all sealing sites on the Bothnian coast had been abandoned, at a time of both climatic and political change. Broadbent (2010, 221) suggested that abandonment was primarily caused by Swedish colonization, the expansion of Christianity and the "assimilation" of coastal Sámi hunters and herders, or perhaps their displacement inland. In the 1300s, the Roman Catholic Church was well established among the farming settlements. It was probably soon after this period of church building that most of the Bothnian Sámi adopted both Catholicism and Swedish ethnicity, moving swiftly from Christian "inclusion" towards "displacement."

As well as Germanic settlers, Finnish groups also colonized parts of the northern Bothnian coast and Torne river, beginning in the Viking Age or early Medieval period (Fjellström 1987; Wallerström 1995a, 2000). It was probably the descendants of these farmers who became known as *birkarlar*, brokers who monopolized trade between the inland Sámi and the Swedish crown during the period ca. AD 1300–1600. Another group active in this trade was known as *hälsingarna*.

In the first millennium AD we can therefore distinguish three main groups living in northern Fennoscandia: (1) farming communities with Germanic ethnic identity living along the coastlines of north Norway and the Gulf of Bothnia; (2) groups of coastal Sámi living more sedentary lives as seal hunters, fishers, and farmers alongside the Germanic or Finnish communities, and gradually adopting their ethnicity; and (3) the inland Sámi who resisted adoption of foreign identities and maintained an economy of hunting, gathering and fishing, fur trading, and later reindeer herding (Figure 2.1).

We can hypothesize that all three groups exchanged religious ideas in the Bronze Age and Iron Age, which was a period of relatively balanced economic and political relations. As late as the Viking period the Sámi and Nordic peoples maintained close relationships based on trade and marriage (Storli 1991; Hansen and Olsen 2004). For example, some

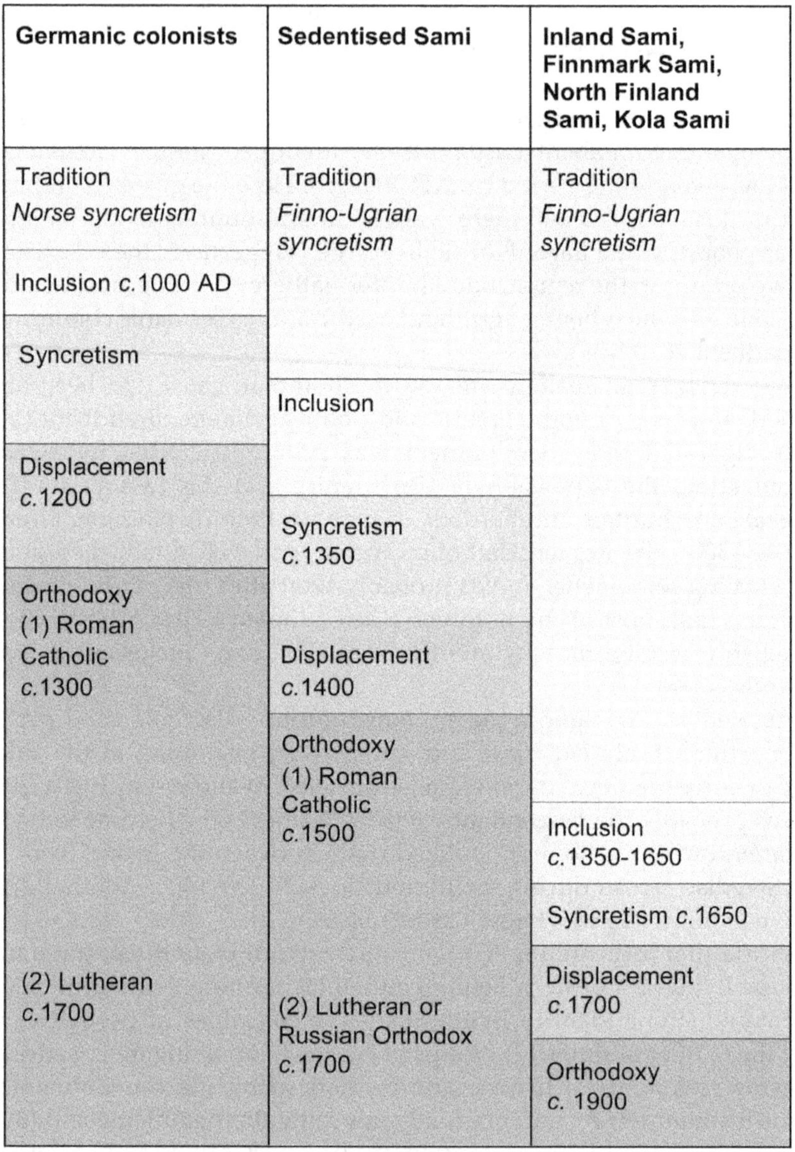

Germanic colonists	Sedentised Sami	Inland Sami, Finnmark Sami, North Finland Sami, Kola Sami
Tradition *Norse syncretism*	Tradition *Finno-Ugrian syncretism*	Tradition *Finno-Ugrian syncretism*
Inclusion c.1000 AD		
Syncretism		
	Inclusion	
Displacement c.1200		
	Syncretism c.1350	
Orthodoxy (1) Roman Catholic c.1300	Displacement c.1400	
	Orthodoxy (1) Roman Catholic c.1500	
		Inclusion c.1350–1650
		Syncretism c.1650
(2) Lutheran c.1700	(2) Lutheran or Russian Orthodox c.1700	Displacement c.1700
		Orthodoxy c. 1900

Figure 2.1. Tentative model of the conversion to Christianity of the three main ethnic groups living in northern Scandinavia: (a) Germanic colonists on the Atlantic coasts of north Norway and the Gulf of Bothnia; (b) sedentized Sámi farmers-fishers in the same two areas; and (c) the reindeer hunting/herding Sámi of inland regions. In the period of so-called "tradition," before ca. AD 1000, all three groups were engaged in religious interchanges involving Old Norse, Finnish, and Sámi religious beliefs and practices. Thereafter the dominant process was one of conversion to Christianity, but with much local variation. (Created by the authors.)

Sámi concepts of sorcery were absorbed into Old Norse religion (*seiðr*), while Sámi shamans were much respected in the Viking Age for their special powers (Price 2002; Äikäs and Salmi 2013). However, after the adoption of Christianity in south Scandinavia about AD 1000–1100 the balance of power began to shift, and Germanic colonists in the north saw advantages in early conversion to the new religion. To serve this population, churches were established in Norway after AD 1200 at some coastal sites, and in Sweden in the fourteenth century. The sedentized Sámi populations living as farmers and fishermen in coastal regions also began to convert at this time, as they switched to Norwegian, Swedish, or Finnish ethnicity.

Christian Conversion in Jämtland

Welinder (2003), in his study of Christian conversion in Jämtland, saw economic interests as providing the key to the religious choices made by different groups. Prior to the eleventh century the Jämtlandic elite with their warriors and retainers, and the Sámi who lived in the forest periphery, maintained different burial practices, but the two were linked by their close connection to Nordic rituals organized by the elite, land-owning chieftains.

Around AD 1000 there is evidence from Jämtland of an expansion of population and increasing surplus, both from new farms and from the forest periphery (iron ingots, elk hides). This surplus was organized by the elite and traded through their external alliances, which increasingly meant negotiations with Christian chieftains and kings. To maintain its exchange networks the farming elite accepted Christianity, but some Sámi retainers in Jämtland made a different choice and reaffirmed their Sámi ethnicity. Welinder (2003, 527) suggests that the Sámi elite saw an advantage in becoming independent of Germanic society by directly trading their surplus from hunting, fishing, and iron smelting to gain possession of display-objects and hoarded silver. In addition, we suggest that for Sámi hunters their spiritual links to hunting and fishing sites, settlements, and sacred sites in the wider landscape could have provided another reason for their rejection of the church-based rituals of Christianity, as reported much later by Högström ([1747] 1980, 210) in Gällivare.

Further north the Sámi also resisted the adoption of Germanic identity, despite some signs of "inclusion" and even perhaps "syncretism" (*sensu* Insoll 2003, 2004) in the later Medieval period. Phebe Fjellström (1962) suggested that Sámi cultures in northern Sweden and north Norway began to include ideas and symbols derived from the Catholic Church.

However, the stage of full "displacement" by the Christian religion was delayed until the period of intensive Lutheran missionary activity in the seventeenth and eighteenth centuries (Rydving 1993).

Why did the Sámi in the northern Sámi area move so slowly from the pre-existing Finno-Ugrian tradition towards Christian "inclusion," "syncretism," and finally "displacement"? Probably, the reasons for religious incompatibility between the nomadic Sámi and the church were conceptual as well as logistic. Sámi ritual practices were at sacred sites located within their *sijdda* territories in the natural landscape. Therefore their semi-mobile life style, settlement pattern and close connection to hunting and fishing sites meant that Sámi rituals of sacrifice and worship made little sense if they were focused on churches (Rheen [1671] 1897, 27; Högström [1747] 1980, 210; Mulk 1994a, 254; Kleppe and Mulk 2006).

Evidence from Sámi Graves

Burial customs provide us with further insights into changing religious beliefs. Only in recent decades has a more holistic picture of Sámi funerary practices emerged (Zachrisson 1997; Schanche 2000). From this overview, two main categories of graves have been distinguished: scree graves (Sw. *urgravar*) and forest burials (Sw. *skogsgravar* or *insjögravar*). Forest burials are found in the south Sámi area of southern Norrland whereas the scree graves have a more northerly distribution, being found over a long period and across the whole of northern Norway and Sweden. More than two hundred scree graves have been investigated in Mortensnes in Varanger fjord. Assessments of their age are based on about thirty radiocarbon dates and they include the oldest yet found, dating from the first millennium BC (Kleppe 1974, 1977; Schanche 2000, 166). Audhild Schanche regards scree graves and associated rituals and beliefs as becoming established at that time in the Varanger region. They then spread westward along the coast of north Norway and also inland, reaching the central and south Sámi area in the medieval period (Schanche 2000, 190).

Forest burials from the south Sámi area have been excavated at Krankmårtenhögen (Ambrosiani, Iregren, and Lahtiperä 1984) and Vivallen in Härjedalen (Hallström 1944; Zachrisson 1989), although the Sámi ethnic identity of these southern sites has not always been acknowledged. There is also probably a third category of Sámi graves, cremation graves (Sw. *brandgravar*) with stone settings and cairns, which are found in the central Sámi area of north Norrland, i.e., Norrbotten and Västerbotten. The oldest date from the beginning of the first millennium

AD and they continue until about AD 1200 (Manker 1961; Rahtje 2001; Hedman 2003; Liedgren and Johansson 2005, 284).

It is their morphology that distinguishes the scree graves from forest burials. In both types the bodies were laid onto birch bark or wrapped within it. In some cases, the bark was shaped and sewn with roots to fit the body, and sometimes it was decorated with geometrical designs. Occasionally the dead person was buried in a sledge or a coffin (Manker 1961; Storå 1971; Kleppe 1974, 1977; Schanche 2000). The scree grave is a type particularly associated with Mortensnes cemetery in Varanger, but today we can also recognize this type elsewhere in graves that are under cliffs, in caves, or constructed from stone slabs.

After AD 1300, however, an increasing proportion of graves shows evidence that Sámi in the south had chosen new burial practices (Zachrisson 1997) and perhaps a new ethnicity (Welinder 2003). The switch took place in Varanger fjord in the seventeenth century (Odner 1992, 18) but happened much earlier in areas suitable for farming, as in Jämtland (Welinder 2003). When living in close proximity to Norwegian, Finnish, or Swedish communities, and especially if pressurized by missionary activity, most sedentized Sámi moved quickly through the Christian conversion stages of "inclusion," "syncretism," and "displacement." It was the Sámi living inland in mobile groups of hunters and fishers, and later reindeer herders, who resisted this process.

Schanche (2000) sees the spread of scree graves as reflecting a process of growing social integration in Sámi society. This more integrated Sámi society shared religious ideas, including those that determined the rituals and practices of burial. From around AD 800 up to the time of Christian conversion, we see the formation of a more widespread Sámi ethnicity with much stronger connections to Finno-Ugrian groups than to Nordic (Germanic) ones.

The forest burials are a type with a more southerly distribution, and, like the scree graves, they reflect Sámi funeral practices over a long period. The oldest come from Krankmårtenhögen in Härjedalen and date from 300 BC, while the last ones are from around AD 1300. It would appear that the forest burial tradition first appeared in the southern parts of the south Sámi area and was already widespread there at the end of the first millennium BC. These dates are derived from graves in Dalarna, Härjedalen, Jämtland, Gästrikland, Medelpad, and Ångermanland. What all these graves have in common is their position in the landscape—either along lake shores, on peninsulas, or on headlands.

Like the scree graves the forest type of burial also changes through time, with three periods identifiable according to Fossum (2006). The large cemetery at Krankmårtenhögen belongs to the first period, and it has a definite link to Sámi hunting society (Zachrisson 1997). After AD 1200 forest burials are restricted to southern Norrland and probably are connected to the important iron industry of the area, with local Sámi workers employed by Nordic chiefs from the coastal region (Welinder 2003).

Forest burials after AD 800 seem to have a strong connection to the spread of agriculture in southern Norrland and the beginnings of a division in ethnic identities between Sámi and Germanic groups. After 1200, when these forest graves disappear, we can infer that the sedentized Sámi had themselves become part of the Nordic agrarian society, with "displacement" of their old beliefs and practices quickly followed by "syncretism" and Catholic orthodoxy.

Rock Art as a Reflection of Religious Belief

At the beginning of the first millennium AD hardly any rock art was still being produced in northern Fennoscandia, but the scratched images that have survived at the Badjelánnda site in Laponia, northern Sweden, are an exception. At this site the production of images continued until Early Modern times, so Badjelánnda can provide us with evidence for the changing religious beliefs of those who visited the site (Mulk and Bayliss-Smith 2006; Mulk 2009, 2014).

Three different phases of rock art are represented (Figure 2.2). The earliest images (Phase 1) appear to be contemporary with the quarrying of asbestos at the site. They are rather uniform anthropomorphic figures that date perhaps to the Metal Age (ca. 1800–500 BC) or early Iron Age (500 BC–AD 800). Phase 2, which consists of varied images of boats, reindeer and humans, can be dated to the Viking Age (AD 800–1050) and/ or the early Medieval period (AD 1050–1350). In the zone of most recent soapstone quarrying there are also a few graffiti, including the date 1673, carved to commemorate visits to the site in the Early Modern period and more recent times (Phase 3).

We have proposed that the Phase 1 images at Badjelánnda are standardized symbols of the supernatural, with anthropomorphic figures representing deities, possibly the prime female deity *Máttaráhkká* (Mulk and Bayliss-Smith 2001, 2006; Mulk 2004, 2014, 2017). These symbols reflect an unmodified "cosmic" worldview, with parallels to the rock art of Alta and other sites in northern Fennoscandia (Mulk 2014). Evidence of asbestos quarrying at the site suggests a connection to the period of Asbestos Ceramic ware, ca.1800 BC–AD 400 (Carpelan 1979). It has been argued that asbestos ware was used for rituals including food offerings, as in the Seitaure sacrificial site (Serning 1956, 135; Mulk 1996, 55).

Figure 2.2. Superimposed images from part of the Badjelánnda site. The sailing boat is from Badjelánnda Phase 2, with details of rigging, steering oar, furled sail, and anchor that were characteristic of the Nordic *knarr* type of boat, dating from ca. AD 800–1350. The boat is superimposed on a large Phase 1 anthropomorph that can tentatively be identified as a "cosmic" symbolic representation of *Máttaráhkká*. In these images, we see a new "historical" worldview emerging in the Viking Age. At this time, Sámi hunting society was assimilating new images from Sámi-Norse interaction, but within the context of traditional meanings provided by Sámi cosmology. (Created by the authors, adapted from Mulk and Bayliss-Smith 2006, 8.)

This pottery has also been found at Valkeisaari in Eastern Finland at an archaeological site that is adjacent to rock paintings. In front of the painted images at Valkeisaari is a fireplace and fragments of textile/ asbestos ware, some flints, an anthropomorphic stone, bones, and plant remains including *Chenopodium album* (fat-hen), an edible plant whose seeds were eaten as porridge. The Valkeisaari site is dated to the Metal Age or possibly later and is interpreted as a ritual deposit associated with the preparation, consumption, and sharing of food (Lahelma 2006, 3–21). We suggest that the quarrying of asbestos from the cliff face at Badjelánnda also had religious meanings, requiring the production of images in the context of rituals and offerings.

The more varied images of Badjelánnda Phase 2, while still permeated by the symbolic meanings of Sámi cosmology, also begin to reflect Sámi-Nordic interaction in the Viking or early Roman Catholic period. We see at this time a more "historical" style of depiction, as shown in the detailed pictures of sailing boats and reindeer. Iconic details of boats, such as steering oars, anchor, sails and rigging, derive from maritime technologies of the period ca. AD 800–1350. The sacrificial sites and graves have demonstrated how the Viking Age and early Medieval period was a time of intense fur-trading activity, particularly with eastern areas. As a result, some "inclusion" of ideas from outside is likely, with some elements of "syncretism" in the pre-Christian Sámi religion. The objects imported show that Sámi traditions potentially were open to eastern (Finnish, Karelian, and Russian), western (Scandinavian), and southern (Germanic) influences. For the inland Sámi of northern Norrland the main period of "inclusion" of Christian (i.e., Roman Catholic) ideas probably began in the mid-fourteenth century, in other words, after Phase 2 of the rock art at the Badjelánnda. However, the images from Phase 2 show that already in the Viking Age and early Medieval times new ideas were infiltrating the world of Mountain Sámi reindeer hunters.

Phase 3 is dated by the graffiti "1673.VI" carved in the main zone of soapstone quarrying, when the sacred character of the Badjelánnda site was in dispute. In late Medieval or Early Modern times the Mountain Sámi became reindeer-herding nomads and the Lutheran Protestant church entered its most militant phase. The result was Sámi-Christian "syncretism," followed by the "displacement" of Sámi religious beliefs. These were consequences of the intense confrontations with the Lutheran mission and the Swedish state, both of which challenged the validity of Sámi beliefs and persecuted the shamans (*noajdde*) (Rydving 1993). Increasingly, Badjelánnda was becoming merely a place of resource procurement, with a few graffiti to commemorate visits to the site.

Sacred Places and Sacrificial Sites

When we compare Badjelánnda to other sacred sites, we find that such places were usually located at outstanding natural formations in the landscape, such as mountains and lakes, islets, rapids, caves, and unusual rocks and stones (Qvigstad 1926; Itkonen 1946; Manker 1957). In Sámi cosmology these landforms were viewed as signifying a topographic anomaly, which in turn suggested liminality in relation to other worlds. Places that had significance for the Sámi in "economic" terms, because of their importance for fishing or hunting, inevitably also had a strong spiritual significance. Some cliffs or boulders were marked with *siejdde*-stones or wooden idols, *värromuorra* (e.g., Rheen [1671] 1897, 37–45). Other sacrificial sites were constructed as circular stone structures or ring-shaped enclosures of reindeer antlers, or were made out of wood as altar-like platforms, *luovve* (Hallström 1932; Manker 1957; Vorren 1985; Vorren and Eriksen 1993; Mulk 1994b; Edvinger and Broadbent 2006).

Through his fieldwork and interviews with Sámi informants, Manker (1957, 299) identified over five hundred sacrificial sites and sacred places in northern Sweden. We can divide them into two groups: those associated with mountains, cliffs and caves; and those connected to water. Analyzing over one hundred Sámi sacred sites in northern Finland, Äikäs (2011) found a similar range of sites again divisible into mountain/rock/cave sites and sites in close proximity to water. In Sweden, archaeological investigation by Hallström (1924, 1932) yielded finds from eleven of the major sacrificial sites: Bolnnuvuoddu (Pålnovuoddo), Viddjavárri in Rávttasjávri (Rautasjaure), Sáivva (Saivo), Unna Sáivva, Átjekoaivve (Átjekåive), Skerffe (Skerfe), Vidjáguojkka (Vidjakuojka), Siejddejávrre (Seitaure), Gråträsk, Vindelgransele, and Bäsksjö (Figure 2.3). This material provided the basis for later work by Inga Serning (1956). More recently, Zachrisson investigated Mörtträsket in Västerbotten which Wallerström identified as another sacrificial site (Zachrisson 1984; Wallerström 1995b).

The sacrificial finds from these twelve sites in northern Sweden are a major source of material for studies of Sámi society and its role in the trade of northern Europe. The sites contain bone and antlers (mainly of reindeer), arrowheads, and votive objects, including in some cases artifacts from Novgorod, Perm, and other places in eastern Europe and silver coins minted in western Europe. Serning (1956, 162) distinguished six different areas of origin: Scandinavia, Finland, Russia, northwestern Europe, the eastern Baltic area, and objects manufactured locally by the Sámi themselves. Until recently all finds have only been dated by their association with certain artifacts, which, when they are dateable, mostly

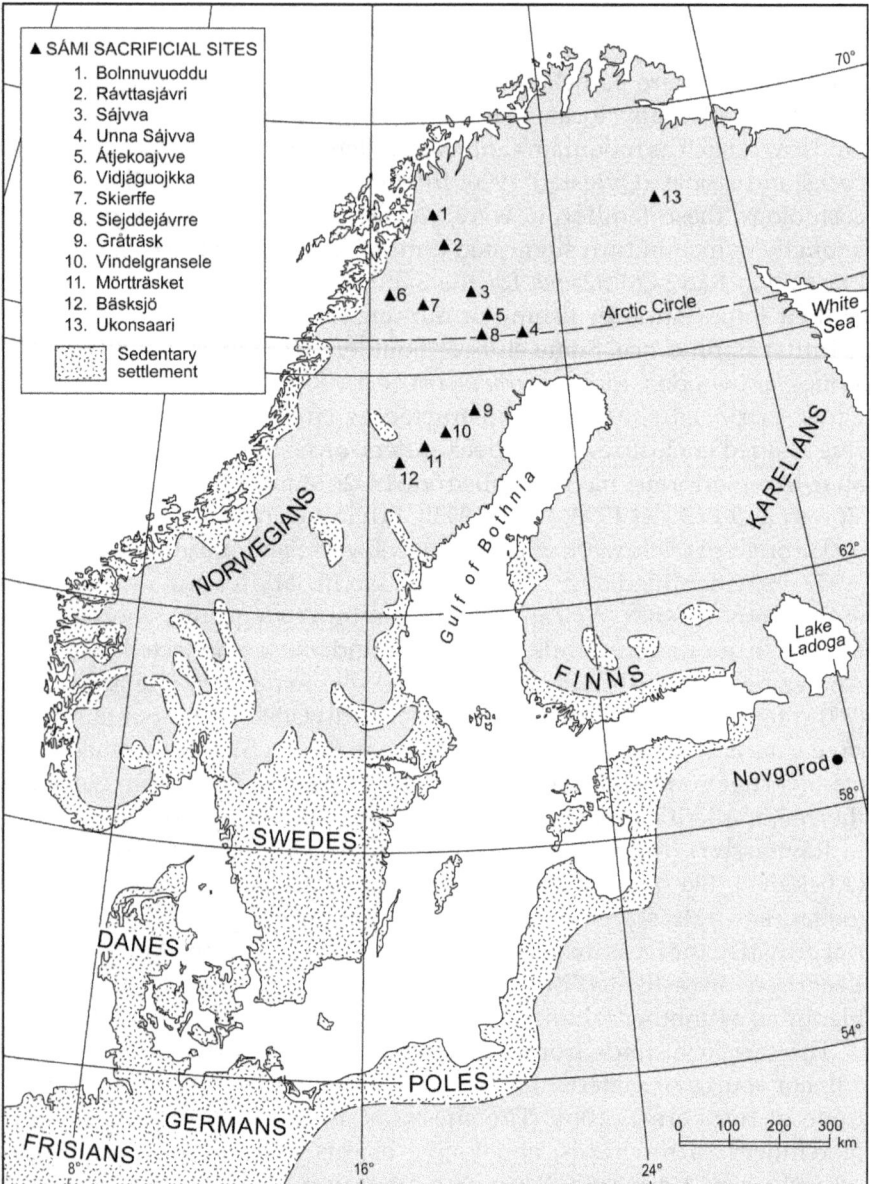

Figure 2.3. Fenno-Scandinavia at ca. AD 1000, showing (a) the Sámi sacrificial sites (triangles) (adapted from Mulk 1994a, 170); (b) the approximate boundary of sedentary Scandinavian settlement (adapted from Clarke 1994, 49); and (c) some of the neighboring peoples who were connected to the Sámi in northern Sweden through the fur trade. (Created by the authors.)

come from the eleventh to fourteenth centuries AD, although there are isolated objects that are either older or younger.

When we compare the twelve investigated sites in northern Norrland with sites elsewhere, we find major similarities in the finds reported from north Finland, the Kola peninsula, and the Pechora region in northwest Russia (Ovsyannikov and Terebikhin 1994; Äikäs and Salmi 2013). For example, the Ukonsaari sacrificial site in Lake Inari in northern Finland was inside a cave within an enclosure of reindeer antlers. It contained bones of reindeer and other animals, and an earring with filigree decoration of eastern type from the Perm region of Russia dated to the twelfth century (Bradley 2000, 3–5; Ucko 2001; Okkonen 2007).

The Sámi continued to visit and use their sacrificial sites right into Early Modern times. In the year 1747, for example, Sáivva still exerted a sufficiently powerful influence on local Sámi for it to be desecrated by a Swedish missionary (Högström [1747] 1980). After about AD 1300, however, first coins and then other metal objects become less and less frequent as votive offerings (Mulk 2009; Salmi et al. 2015).

Sacrificial Offerings and Religious Meanings

The pendants in the sacrificial sites belong to a Finno-Ugric world of symbols. Some are in the form of animals (horse, reindeer) or birds (mainly ducks, loons, and other waterfowl). An amulet of bronze from Viddjavárri in Rávttasjávri shows a reindeer calf, and it may represent the myth of Máttaráhkká and her son Mjandasj (Mulk 2005, 2009, 2014, 2017).

At a later period the pendants (trapezoid, cruciform, and circular) were locally produced in pewter or bronze. Many are shaped like the webbed foot of a waterfowl (or perhaps an axe), or they are cruciform. The motifs appear to be copied after prototypes from the east (Serning 1956, 167), and some are similar to pendants manufactured during the thirteenth century in Novgorod and Polotsk (Zachrisson 1984, 197). In Sámi traditions of the eighteenth century, bird-shaped amulets symbolized the bird from the holy mountain, Saiovolodde or Passelodde, and they served as the shaman's guardian and helping spirit (Rydving 2010).

The cruciform pewter pendants from Mörtträsket, again probably from the fourteenth century, appear to be imitations of Russian Byzantine crosses (Zachrisson 1984). Many of the circular pendants have motifs that resemble the crosses on certain Viking Age coins and bracteates (Figure 2.4). There is a particular resemblance to crosses on English coins minted by Ethelred II between ca. 997–1003 (Long Cross type), which

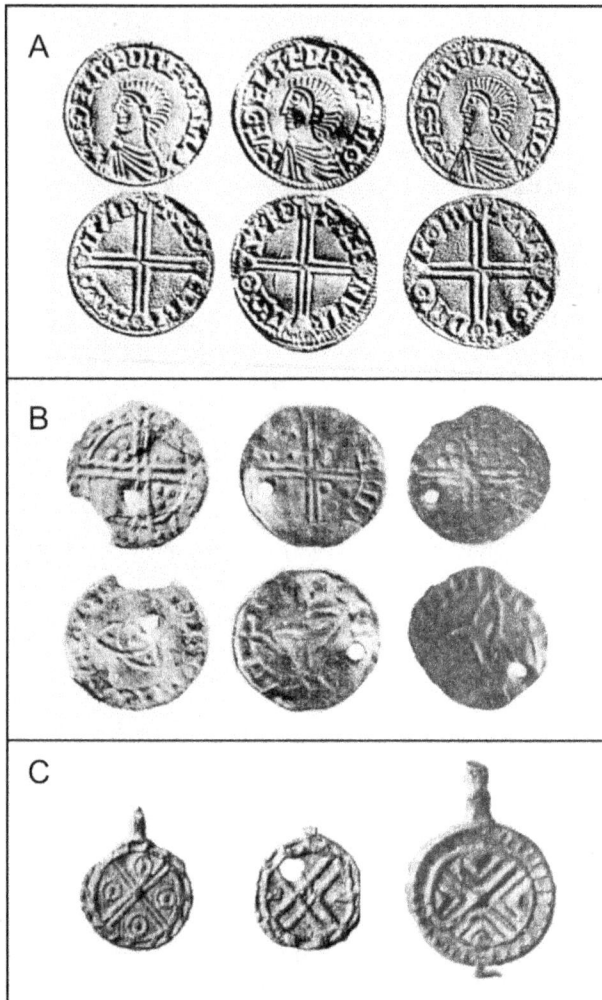

Figure 2.4. (A) Three coins of the Long Cross type minted in England in the reign of Aethelred II (978–1016). (B) The Long Cross motif copied onto Norwegian coins of the Triquetra type dating from the reign of Harald Hardråde (1047–66). These coins were perforated by the Sámi and deposited at the sacrificial sites at Rávttasjávri (left and middle) and Unna Sáivva (right); the positions of the perforations show that the motif was intended by the Sámi to be displayed as a diagonal cross. (C) The Long Cross motif transferred as a diagonal cross onto Sámi pewter pendants of probable fourteenth century and deposited at Mörtträsket sacrificial site. (Sources: (a) adapted from North 1994, plate 13, reproduced with permission of Spink and Son Ltd; (b) adapted from Skaare 1976, 264, 267, 268, reproduced with permission of Kulturhistoriskmuseum, Oslo; (c) adapted from Zachrisson 1984, 45, reproduced with permission of Inger Zachrisson.)

themselves were prototypes for some of the twelfth century coins from Sweden (Sigtuna type) and Norway (Zachrisson 1984, 45).

The cross that we see on pendants of Sámi manufacture is not the Christian cross, but instead is a diagonal cross resembling those seen by Samuel Rheen ([1671] 1897) at sacrificial sites in the Lule Sámi area. Rheen described a platform (*luovve*) on which "they erected Thor's idols smeared with blood, and with several crosses on their breasts," diagonal crosses which Rheen also depicted (Manker 1957, 26, 301). Similar crosses were also engraved on wooden poles (*värromuorra*), for example the one shown to Manker (1957, Figure 249) at a sacrificial site in Västerbotten. Diagonal crosses appear to have been a "key symbol" for the Sámi, like certain animals (reindeer, elk, bear) and waterfowl. The webbed feet of waterfowl shown on brooches and pendants convey certain religious ideas. All these symbols had shamanistic meanings when used in votive contexts (Mulk 2009, 2014).

Tallgren (1934, 153, 180f) suggested that much of the north European fur trade involved an exchange of objects that were known to have religious significance to Finno-Ugric peoples. He drew parallels between the fur trade in northern Fennoscandia and the situation in Pechora in northern Russia. The Pechora shamans collected together furs that were passed on to traders from the Kama area, and later from Novgorod, and they received in return objects with shamanistic significance.

Votive Offerings and Religious Syncretism

When did votive offerings at Sámi sacrificial sites begin? The earliest C14 date is from a bear mandible from Unna Sáivva that was deposited in the period AD 540–770 (Salmi et al. 2015, 12). Much earlier use is suggested for Seitaure, where a small bowl made of asbestos ceramic ware was excavated suggesting continuity of sacrificial offerings since the first millennium BC (Serning 1956, 135; Mulk 1996, 55). However, the majority of finds from sacrificial sites are later. Chronologically the finds can be divided into four groups: before AD 800, 800–1350, 1350–1650, and after 1650, with the period 800–1350 seeing the greatest activity (Serning 1956).

The dateable objects such as traded imports of jewelry and coins might suggest that far fewer objects were being deposited by the Sámi between ca. AD 1350 and the seventeenth century, but many non-dateable artifacts may have been deposited after this date. For example arrowheads of iron and pewter pendants are of local manufacture and they continued to be produced long after AD 1300 (Wallerström 1995b, 186). We see similar pendants hanging on drums collected in the period AD 1650–1750 (Manker 1938).

New evidence from Viddjavárri showed that at this site there were actually more sacrifices of meat and antlers in the period ca. AD 1450–1650 than during earlier times, which Mulk (2005, 2009) interpreted as meaning that votive activity by the Sámi continued but with a transition "from metal to meat." More than half of the osteological material collected by Hallström from Viddjavárri, amounting to 34 kg, consisted of reindeer antlers. The reindeer bones are from animals more than two years old and derive from the less meaty parts of the animal. C14 analysis was carried out on a random sample of this material. Ten of the twelve dates were in the range AD 1450–1650, which means they are younger than the dateable artifacts and silver coins (Mulk 2005, 2009).

At Unna Sáivva radiocarbon dates were analyzed for eight of the animal bones originally collected by Hallström. The youngest was a reindeer mandible dated to the period 1440–1640, while another three dates on reindeer bone were from the fifteenth century (Salmi et al. 2015, 12). As at Viddjavárri, a continuing ritual use of Unna Sáivva is indicated from ca. AD 1300 until the seventeenth century (Mulk 2009).

It seems that reindeer offerings peaked in the period just before the sacrificial sites were abandoned, which was in the seventeenth and eighteenth centuries AD according to documentary sources. Increasingly the metal offerings were replaced by reindeer antlers, especially antlers from large male animals, and bones from younger reindeer (Salmi et al. 2015, 15). From other evidence we know that wild reindeer hunting was still important in the seventeenth century (Mulk 2009, 127–29), but at Unna Sáivva the sacrificed animals could have been domesticated reindeer (Salmi et al. 2015, 16). Whether wild or domesticated, the rising importance of reindeer to the Sámi necessitated gifts to spirits in the other world.

Even after Christian conversion it is clear that the sites were still being visited (Manker 1957). After the Mountain Sámi experienced Christian "inclusion" and the shaman's rituals had ceased, rather than being displaced by Christianity most people's beliefs were syncretic for several generations, as testified by Lutheran priests (Rydving 1993). Even today, a respect for sacrificial sites continues among some Sámi (Mulk 1994b, 130).

Silver Coins: Origins and Fluctuations

Silver coins have so far been found and recorded in five of the ten sacrificial sites that have been excavated in northern Sweden. The site at Rávttasjávri is located under a south-facing cliff, while the other sites are next to rich fishing lakes in the forest areas. Rávttasjávri yielded 424 coins, Gråträsk 166 (but some may have been dispersed before the archaeological inventory), and Unna Sáivva 36. Two other sites that were rich in other metal objects had very few coins—only three were found at Bäsksjö, and one at Mörtträsket.

The provenance of these coins was first established by Jammer and others (Jammer et al. 1956, 184–218; Malmer 1961, 226–376; Skaare 1976, 179; Zachrisson 1984). The total coin assemblage derives from a wide range of ultimate sources, which reflects the widespread nature of fur trading contacts at this period. The mints with known sources are

Table 2.1. Location of the mints for 630 silver coins found in five Sámi sacrificial sites.

Location of mints	Rávttasjávri	Unna Sáivva	Gråträsk	Bäsksjö	Mörtträsket	Total
Coins from identifiable mints	1	0	4	0	0	5
Caliphate						
Poland	0	1	0	0	0	1
Germany: Frisia	38	13	13	0	1	65
Germany: North (a)	28	7	2	1	0	38
Germany: South (b)	23	5	6	0	0	34
Germany: unknown	12	0	2	0	0	14
Denmark	5	1	4	1	0	11
England	26	4	6	0	0	36
Norway	274	1	116	0	0	391
Sweden	0	0	0	1	0	1
Coins from unknown or uncertain mints	17	4	13	0	0	34
Totals	424	36	166	3	1	630

Sources of data: Jammer et al. 1956; Malmer 1961, 244; and Zachrisson 1984, 42.

Notes: (a) Lower Lorraine, Rhineland, Lower Saxony, Westphalia; (b) Upper Lorraine, Thuringia, Hesse, Franconia, Swabia, Bavaria.

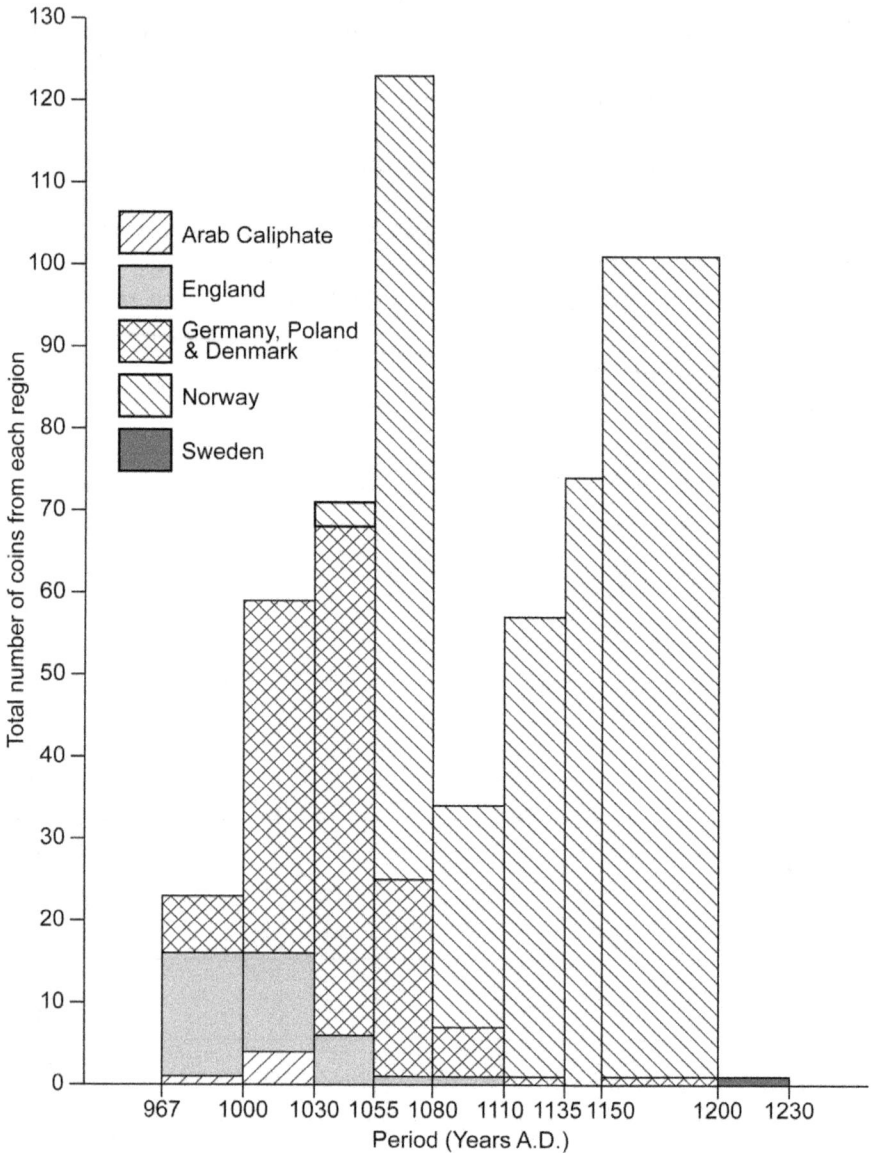

Figure 2.5. The total number of coins minted in various regions and deposited in five Sámi sacrificial sites, according to the approximate period when they were minted. The data represent the 545 coins that are identifiable to both place and period, from Rávttasjávri (350), Unna Sáivva (30), Gråträsk (162), Bäsksjö (2), and Mörtträsket (1). There are in addition a further 34 coins from unidentifiable mints, and 51 coins from identifiable mints but where the period of minting cannot be established. (Created by the authors, based on data in Table 2.1).

located in the Caliphate, Poland, Germany, Frisia, England, Denmark, and Norway (Table 2.1 and Figure 2.5). The English and Danish coins are mostly well preserved, but the condition of the others is generally bad. The Arabic coins are only fragmentary, as are nearly half of the German and Norwegian coins. With one exception, each of the complete coins has been pierced, often quite crudely by a blow from a metal knife or spike. In many cases there were still traces of knotted strands of wool threaded through these holes (Serning 1956; Malmer 1961, 314–16), suggesting that when used as votive objects they were hung as pendants.

We can also analyze the total assemblage according to the dates when the coins were minted. The oldest coin is an Arabic dirhem from AD 967, and the absence of the much more prolific, earlier tenth-century dirhems is notable. The German and Friesland coins mostly date from the end of the tenth to the beginning of the twelfth century AD, the majority being minted in the first half of the eleventh century (Figure 2.6). The English coins are somewhat earlier and mostly come from the reigns of Ethelred II (979–1016) and Cnut (1016–1035). There are a few Danish coins from the mid-eleventh century, and they disappear at the time when Norwegian coins first appear. The relative proportions from different periods within the English and German coin assemblage suggest that most of the coins were acquired by the Sámi in the mid-twelfth century.

Coins minted in Norway (both Helgeland and Gresli types) dominate the assemblage that is dated to the second half of the twelfth century. There appears to be two peaks in the coin distribution, in the mid-eleventh century (mainly German, English, and Norwegian coins) and in the mid to late twelfth century (almost entirely Norwegian coins). Malmer (1961, 364–66) and Skaare (1976, 31, 72) have argued that for the Norwegian coins this broadly reflects variations in the rate at which the Sámi were importing coins to northern Sweden, and that that was in turn influenced by the availability of coinage. In the late eleventh and early twelfth centuries Norwegian coinage was being minted on a much smaller scale.

It is difficult to know if the patterns shown in Figures 2.5 and 2.6 reflect real variations in ritual activity and/or opportunities for trade with different places, or whether they merely reflect fluctuations in the quantity of coins as opposed to other objects entering the region from the various sources. In the twelfth century AD practically all the coins originated ultimately in Norway. The end of the deposition of these coins around 1200 may signal an important shift in trading patterns, because in the following two centuries we see an increased influx into northern Sweden of metal objects from Finland.

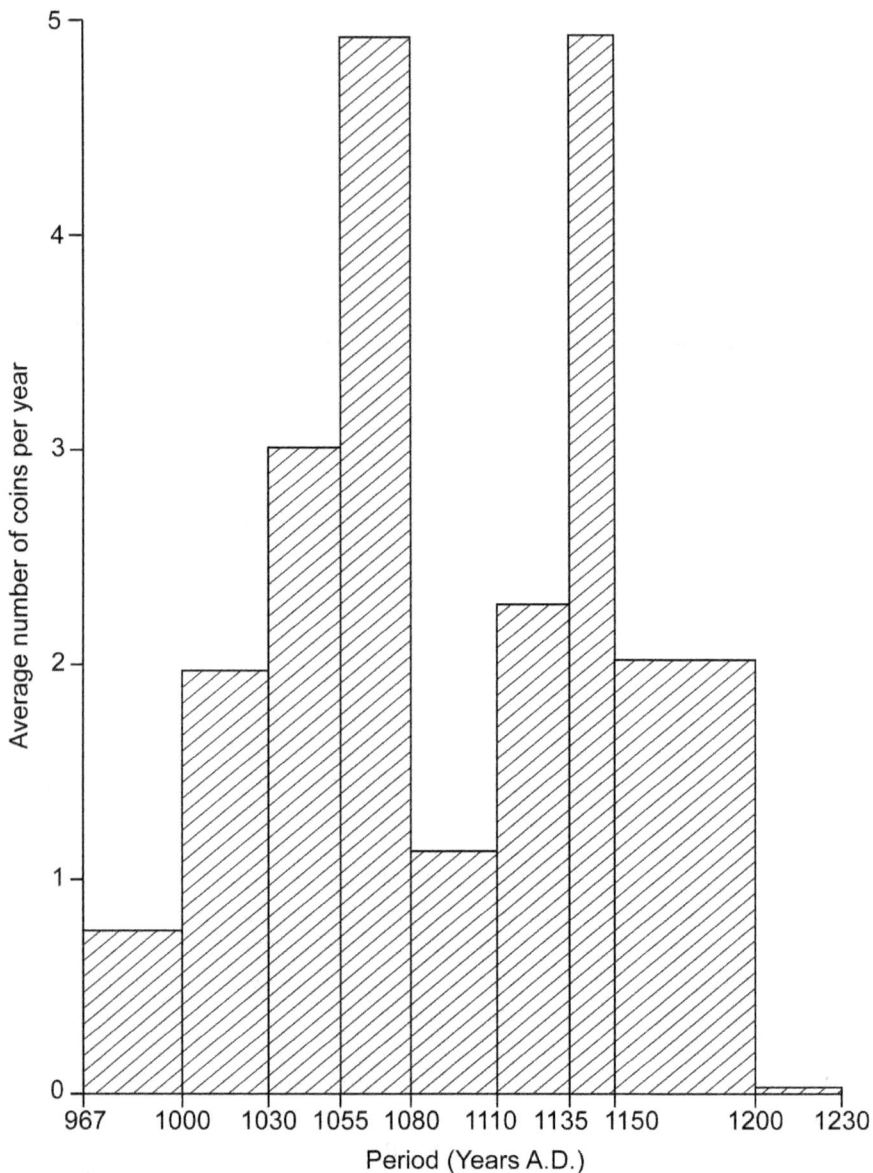

Figure 2.6. Chronological distribution of coins (per year based on date of minting) at five Sámi sacrificial sites. The average annual rate of deposition has been calculated based on the period when the coins were minted. (Created by the authors, based on data in Table 2.1).

There are certainly some indications that the Sámi who were trading to the north began to be taxed at this time (*Finnskatt*) through bailiffs appointed by the Norwegian crown. Tax was calculated in money even if it was paid in kind, and this replaced the earlier system of barter between the Sámi and surrounding ethnic groups. The thirteenth century also saw the beginning of colonization in Tornedalen and along the coasts of the Gulf of Bothnia, initially by settlers from Finland, while the Catholic Church and the Swedish state also began to extend their influence (Vahtola 1980; Wallerström 1995a). This period seems to mark a new stage in the incorporation of the Sámi of northern Sweden into the European economy, even though the interior was not subject to formal colonization for another four hundred years.

Conclusion

The evidence of coins and other metal artifacts suggests that the use by the Sámi of places for sacrificial offerings probably peaked in the period ca. AD 800–1350, but use of these places certainly continued for at least another three hundred years, continuing even after the period of enforced Lutheran conversion in the seventeenth century. For example, when passing by, the Sámi sometimes left small offerings of tobacco or alcohol (Manker 1957, 75). Although offerings of antlers or meat may have ended, the Christian Sámi continued to respect these sites and to some extent they still do. We must conclude that even beyond the period of "syncretism" after ca. 1650, and well into the time of religious "displacement," the Sámi continued to treat the sacred places of their ancestors with ritual and respect.

From our summary of the evidence from Sámi graves we concluded that three types can be distinguished, characteristic of north, central, and southern areas of Sámi territory, with the northern scree type spreading southwards to cover a large area in the medieval period. It is tempting to see this spread in mortuary practices as reflecting the emergence of a more homogeneous form of Sámi ethnicity during the period ca. AD 800–1300. This was the period that also saw a peak in activity at sacrificial sites (ca. 1000–1200) involving coins, jewelry, and other metal deposits, and also Phase 2 of soapstone quarrying and rock art at the Badjelánnda site. In graves and sacrifices this new regional identity seems to have been symbolized by objects that indicate foreign connections, especially connections to the Finno-Ugrian cultures to the east that were accessed via trading links to Finland, Karelia, and Russia.

At the same time an alternative response to external contact is shown by the abandonment of forest burial practices by Sámi living in the south of Norrland, and by the rise of agrarian cultures in that region that seem to signal assimilation by the Sámi into Nordic ethnicity. After AD 1300 rapid conversion of these groups to Christianity can be inferred. Further north, however, the inland populations of Sámi hunters and fishers continued with their syncretic Finno-Ugrian religion, and the new cremation graves that we see in central Norrland may be evidence of strong eastern influences which arrived with an intensification of the fur trade.

For a long time during the medieval period the Sámi in northern Sweden seem to have acknowledged only in minor ways the inclusion of new Christian deities and beliefs. A full engagement with Christianity was delayed until the Lutheran Church arrived after 1600, resulting in a brief period of syncretism followed by enforced displacement of the Sámi religion by Christianity by about 1800. For most Sámi, the stage of Lutheran orthodoxy had arrived by the twentieth century, although it is worth noting that a distinctive Laestadian Christian revival began after 1850 especially among the North and Lule Sámi, representing perhaps a new variant of Christian beliefs in which some older Sámi elements have re-emerged.

Acknowledgments

The research which forms the basis for this chapter took place while Inga-Maria Mulk was head of the Sámi division and later Director of Ájtte Swedish Mountain and Sámi Museum, Jokkmokk, Sweden. Tim Bayliss-Smith was a lecturer in the Department of Geography, Cambridge University, and is a Fellow of St. John's College, Cambridge. Their joint fieldwork at the Badjelánnda rock art site in the Laponia World Heritage Area was funded by the above institutions, and it took place with the support of Sirkas Sameby which uses this area as pasture for summer reindeer herding. We also thank Tiina Äikäs and the late Mark Blackburn (Fitzwilliam Museum, Cambridge) for their suggestions, and Philip Stickler, cartographer at the Cambridge Geography Department, for his excellent work on the figures.

Inga-Maria Mulk is the former director of Ájtte, the Swedish and Sámi Museum. After reading archaeology at Uppsala university she did her doctoral research at Umeå University, where her dissertation was published in 1994. She has done field excavation in North Norway and Sweden, especially in the Lule valley. The initial focus of her research was on settlement sites, hunting pits, and seasonal mobility during the Sámi Iron Age and medieval times. More recently, she has also written about Sámi sacrificial sites, cultural landscape, and rock art. She served for many years on the Council of the World Archaeological Congress, and she has also been active in documenting the Sámi cultural heritage in the Laponia World Heritage Area.

Tim Bayliss-Smith was a geography lecturer and professor in Cambridge from 1973 to 2015. His current research in the Solomon Islands focuses on agricultural intensification, population change, and colonialism.

References

Ahlbäck, Tore, ed. 1987. *Saami Religion. Scripta Instituti Donneriani Aboensis* XII. Stockholm: Almqvist & Wiksell.

Ahnlund, Nils. 1946. "Nordländska skinnskatter." *Saga och sed* 4: 32–55.

Äikäs, Tiina. 2011. "From Fell Tops to Standing Stones: Sacred Landscapes in Northern Finland." *Archaeologia Baltica* 15: 16–21.

Äikäs, Tiina, and Anna-Kaisa Salmi. 2013 "'The Sieidi is a Better altar/ the Noaidi's Drum a Purer Church Bell': Long Term Changes and Syncretism at Sámi Offering Sites." *World Archaeology* 45(1): 64–82.

Ambrosiani, Björn, Elisabeth Iregren, and Pirjo Lahtiperä. 1984. *Gravfält i fångstmarken. Undersökningarna av gravfälten på Smalnäset och Krankmårtenhögen, Härjedalen.* Rikatikvarieämbetet och Statens Historiska Museer Rapport, vol. 6. Stockholm: Riksantikvarieämbetet.

Anisimov, Arkadii F. 1963. "Cosmological Concepts of the Peoples of the North." In *Studies in Siberian Shamanism,* ed. Henry N. Michael, 157–229. Toronto: University of Toronto Press.

Bäckman, Louise. 1975. *Sáiva: Föreställningar om hjälp och skyddsväsen i heliga fjäll bland samerna. Acta Universitatis Stockholmiensis.* Stockholm Studies in Comparative Religion vol. 13. Stockholm: Almqvist & Wiksell.

———. 2005. "The Noaidi and His Worldview: A Study of Saami Shamanism from an Historical Point of View. *Shaman* 13(1–2): 29–40.

Bäckman, Louise, and Åke Hultkrantz, eds. 1978. *Studies in Lapp Shamanism. Acta Universitatis Stockholmiensis.* Stockholm Studies in Comparative Religion 16. Stockholm: Almqvist & Wiksell.

———, eds. 1985. *Saami Pre-Christian Religion: Studies on the Oldest Traces of Religion among the Saami. Acta Universitatis Stockholmensis 5.* Studies in Comparative Religion 25. Stockholm: Almkvist & Wiksell.

Barth, Fredrik. 1969. "Introduction." In *Ethnic Groups and Boundaries,* ed. Fredrik Barth, 9–38. Oslo: Universitesforlaget.

Bradley, Richard. 2000. *An Archaeology of Natural Places.* London: Routledge.

Broadbent, Noel. 2006. "The Search for a Past: The Prehistory of the Indigenous Sámi in Northern Coastal Sweden." In *People, Material Culture and Environment in the North*, Proceedings of the 22nd Nordic Archaeological Conference, ed. Vesa-Pekka Herva, 13–25. Studia humaniora ouluensia 1. Oulu: University of Oulu.

———. 2010. *Lapps and Labyrinths: Saami Prehistory, Colonization and Cultural Resilience.* Washington, DC: Arctic Studies Center and Smithsonian Institution Scholarly Press.

Carpelan, Christian. 1979. "Om asbestkeramikens historia i Fennoskandien." *Finskt Museum* 85(1978): 5–25.

Carpelan, Christian, Asko Parpola, and Petteri Koskikallio, eds. 2001. *Early Contacts between Uralic and Indo-European: Linguistic and Archaeological Considerations.* Memoires de la Société Finno-Ougrienne 242. Helsinki: Suomalais-Ugrilainen Seura.

Clarke, Helen. 1994. "Society, Kingship and Warfare." In *Cultural Atlas of the Viking World*, ed. James Graham-Campbell, 38–57. London: BCA.

Eaton, Richard M. 1996. *The Rise of Islam and the Bengal Frontier, 1204–1760.* Berkeley: University of California Press.

Edvinger, Britta Wennstedt, and Noel Broadbent. 2006. "Sámi Circular Sacrificial Sites in Northern Coastal Sweden." *Acta Borealia* 23(1): 24–55.

Fjellström, Phebe. 1962. *Lapskt silver.* Skrifter upgivna geneom landsmåls- och folkminnesarkivet i Uppsala, Ser. C1:3. Uppsala: Landsmåls- och folkminnesarkivet i Uppsala.

———. 1987. "Älvdalskultur kring Bottenvikens nordliga spets ur etnologiskt perspectiv." In *Nordkalotten in en skiftande värld—kulturer utan granser ock stater över gränser*, ed. Kyösti Julku. *Studia Historica Septentrionalia* 14, vol. 2: 36–58. Rovaniemi: Societas Historica Finlandiae.

Forsberg, Lars L. 2010. "The Spread of New Technologies in Early Fennoscandia: A View without Boundaries." In *Transference: Interdisciplinary Communications 2008/2009*, ed. Willy Østreng. Oslo: CAS. Retrieved 30 March 2019 from https://cas.oslo.no/about-cas/booklets/seminar-booklets/.

Fossum, Birgitta. 2006. *Förfädernas land: En arkeologisk studie av rituella lämningar i Sápmi, 300 f.Kr—1600 e. Kr.* Studia Archaeologica Universitatis Umensis 22. Umeå: Umeå University.

Hallström, Gustaf. 1924. "Fornminnen. Sverige." In *Geografisk, topografisk, statistisk beskrifning*, ed. Otto Sjögren, 919–22 (Jokkmokk), 928–31 (Gällivare). Stockholm: Wahlström & Widstrand.

———. 1932. "Lappska offerplatser." In *Arkeologiska studier tillägnade H.K.H. Kronprins Gustaf Adolf*, 111–13. Stockholm: Svenska Fornminnersföreningen.

———. 1944. "Gravfältet i Vivallen i Funäsdalen." *Heimbygdas tidskrift* 1(Fornvårdaren 8): 305–44.

Hansen, Lars-Iver. 1990. *Samisk fångstsamfunn og norsk høvdingeøkonomi.* Oslo: Novus Forlag.

Hansen, Lars-Iver, and Björnar Olsen. 2004. *Samernas historie fram til 1750.* Oslo: Cappelen akademisk forlag.

———. 2014. *Hunters in Transition: An Outline of Early Sámi History.* Leiden: Brill.

Hedman, Sven-Donald. 2003. *Boplatser och offerplatser.* Studie Archaeological Universitatis Umensis 17. Umeå: Umeå University.

Hodder, Ian. 1979. "Social and Economic Stress and Material Culture Patterning." *American Antiquity* 44: 446–54.

Högström, Pehr. [1747] 1980. *Beskrifning öfwer de til Sweriges Krona lydande Lapmarker.* Stockholm: Lars Salvius.

Hultkrantz, Åke. 1994. "Religion and Environment among the Saami." In *Circumpolar Religion and Ecology: An Anthropology of the North*, ed. Takashi Irimoto and Takato Yamada, 347–74. Tokyo: University of Tokyo Press.

Insoll, Timothy. 2003. *The Archaeology of Islam in Sub-Saharan Africa.* Cambridge: Cambridge University Press.

———. 2004. *Archaeology, Ritual, Religion.* London: Routledge.

Itkonen, Toivo I. 1946. *Heidnische Religion und späterer Aberglaube bei den finnischen Lappen.* Memoires de la Société Finno-Ugrienne 87. Helsinki: Suomalais-Ugrilainen Seura.

Jammer, Vera, U. S. Linder Welin, Mats P. Malmer, and Nils L. Rasmusson. 1956. In *Mynten i de Lapska offerplatsfynden. Lapska offerplatsfynd från järnålder och medeltid i de svenska lappmarkerna*, ed. Inger Serning, 183–218. Acta Lapponica 11. Stockholm: Nordiska museet.

Kleppe, Else J. 1974. *Samiske jernalderstudier ved Varangerfjorden.* Magistergradsavhandling, University of Bergen.

———. 1977. "Archaeological Material and Ethnic Identification: A Study of Lappish Material from Varanger." *Norwegian Archaeological Review* 10: 32–46.

Kleppe, Else J., and Inga-Maria Mulk. 2006. "Religion Embedded in the Landscape: Sámi Studies and the Recognition of Otherness." In *Samfunn, symboler og identitet: Festskrift til Gro Mandt på 70-årsdagen*, ed. Randi Barndon, Sonja M. Innselet, Kari K. Kristoffersen, and Trond K. Lødøen, 363–376. Nordisk 3, Universitetet i Bergen Arkeologiske Skrifter. Bergen: University of Bergen.

Lahelma, Antti. 2006. "Excavating Art: a 'Ritual Deposit' Associated with the Rock Painting of Valkeisaari, Eastern Finland." *Fennoscandia Archaeologica* 23: 2–23.

Liedgren, Lars, and Mikael Johansson. 2005. "An Early Norrland Age Stone-Setting from Lake Uddjaur in Arjeplog." In *En lång historia... festskrift till Evert Baudou på 80-årsdagen*, ed. Roger Engelmark, Thomas B. Larsson, and Lillian Rathje, 275–95. Archaeology and Environment 19. Umeå: Institutionen för Arkeologi och Samiska Studier, Umeå universitet.

Lindqvist, Anna-Karin. 1994. "Förromersk och romersk järnålder i Ångermanlands kustland. En mångkulturell variation inom en region." In *Järnålder i Mittnorden*, ed. Kurt Gullberg, 83–100. Studier i Österbottens förhistoria 3. Vasa: Acta Antiqua Ostrobothniensia.

Loeffler, David. 2005. *Contested Landscapes/Contested Heritage: History and Heritage in Sweden and Archaeological Implications Concerning the Interpretation of the Norrlandian Past.* Archaeology and Environment 18. Umeå: Department of Archaeology and Sámi Studies, Umeå University.

Malmer, Brita. 1961. "A Contribution to the Numismatic History of Norway during the Eleventh Century." In *Commentationes de nummis saeculorum IX–XI in Suecia repertis*, ed. Nils L. Rasmussen and Lars O. Lagerkvist, 226–376. KVHAA Handl. Antikv. 9. Stockholm: Almkvist & Wiksell.

Manker, Ernst. 1938. *Die Läppische Zaubertrommel.* Acta Lapponica 1. Stockholm: Nordiska museet.

_____. 1957. *Lapparnas heliga ställen: Kultplatser och offerkult i belysing av Nordiska museets och lantantikvariernas fältundersökningar.* Acta Lapponica 13. Stockholm: Nordiska museet.

_____. 1961. *Lappmarksgravar: Dödsföreställningar och gravskick i lappmarken.* Acta Lapponica 17. Stockholm: Nordiska museet.

Mebius, Hans. 2003. *Bissie: studier i samiskt religionshistoria.* Östersund: Jengel.

Mulk, Inga-Maria. 1994a. *Sirkas: ett Sámiskt fångstsamhälle i förändring Kr.f.–1600 e. Kr.* Studia Archaeologica Universitatis Umensis 6. Umeå: University of Umeå.

_____. 1994b. "Sacrificial Places and their Meaning in Saami Society." In *Sacred Sites, Sacred Places,* ed. David Carmichael, Jane Hubert, Brian Reeves, and Audhild Schanche, 121–31. London: Routledge.

_____. 1996. "The Role of the Sámi in Fur Trading during the Late Iron Age and Nordic Medieval Period in the Light of the Sámi Sacrificial Sites in Lapland, Northern Sweden." *Acta Borealia* 13: 47–80.

_____. 2004. "Hällristningar i Padjelanta och myten om Mandasj." In *Samisk forhistorie: Rapport fra konferense i Lakselv 5–6 september 2002,* ed. Mia Krogh and Kerstin Schanche, 81–102. Varanger: Várjjat Sámi Musea Câllosat/Varanger Samiske Museums Skrifter.

_____. 2005. "Viddjavárri: en samisk offerplats vid Rávttasjávri i ett samhällsperspektiv." In *En lång historia … Festskrift till Evert Baudou på 80-årsdagen,* ed. Roger Engelmark, Thomas B. Larsson, and Lillian Rathje, 331–48. Archaeology and Environment 19. Umeå: Umeå University.

_____. 2009. "From Metal to Meat: Continuity and Change in Ritual Practices at a Saami Sacrificial Site, Viddjavárri, Lapland, Northern Sweden." In *Máttut-Máddagat. The Roots of Saami Ethnicities, Societies and Spaces/Places,* ed. Tiina Äikäs, 116–33. Oulu: Giellgas Institute.

_____. 2014. "Depictions in Sámi Rock Art of the Mother Earth Figure." In *Art and Shamanhood,* ed. Elvira E. Djaltchinova-Malec, 47–69. Budapest, Warsaw, and Torun: Akademiai Kiado, Polish Institute of World Art Studies, and Tako Publishing House.

_____. 2017. "Máttaráhkka: Conceptions and Representations of Mother Earth in Sámi Myths, Rituals, Rock Art and Material Culture." In *Shamanhood and Mythology: Archaic Techniques of Ecstasy and Current Techniques of Research,* ed. Attila Mátéffy and György Svabados, 349–69. Budapest: Akadémiai Kiadó.

Mulk, Inga-Maria, and Tim Bayliss-Smith. 1998. "The Representation of Sámi Cultural Identity in the Cultural Landscapes of Northern Sweden: The Use and Misuse of Archaeological Evidence." In *The Archaeology and Anthropology of Landscape,* ed. Peter J. Ucko and Robert Layton, 358–96. London: Routledge.

_____. 2001. "Anthropomorphic Images at the Padjelanta Site, Northern Sweden." *Current Swedish Archaeology* 9: 133–62.

_____. 2006. *Rock Art and Sámi Sacred Geography in Badjelánnda, Laponia, Sweden: Sailing Boats, Anthropomorphs and Reindeer.* Archaeology and Environment 22. Umeå: Umeå University.

_____. 2007. "Liminality, Rock Art and the Sámi Sacred Landscape." *Journal of Northern Studies* 1–2: 95–122.

Nordberg, Andreas. 2018. "Old Customs: The Vernacular Word *Seiðr* and Its Cognates in the Study of (Lived) Religion in Viking and Medieval Scandinavia." *Temenos* 54: 125–47.

North, Jeffrey J. 1994. *English Hammered Coinage, Vol. 1 Early Anglo-Saxon to Henry III c. 600–1272*. London: Spink & Son.

Odner, Knut. 1983. *Finner og terfinner*. Occasional Papers in Social Anthropology 9. Oslo: Oslo University.

———. 1985. "Saamis (Lapps), Finns and Scandinavians in History and Prehistory: Ethnic Origins and Ethnic Processes in Fenno-Scandinavia." *Norwegian Archaeological Review* 18(1–2): 1–35.

———. 1992. *The Varanger Saami. Habitation and Economy AD 1200–1900*. Oslo: Scandinavian University Press.

Olsen, Bjørnar. 1985. "Arkeologi og etnicitet; et teoretisk og empirisk bidrag." In *Arkeologi og etnicitet*, ed. Jenny-Rita Naess, 23–32. Ams-Varia 15. Stavanger: Arkeologisk Museum i Stavanger.

———. 1986. "Norwegian Archaeology and the People without (Pre-) History: Or How to Create a Myth of a Uniform Past." *Archaeological Review from Cambridge* 5(1): 25–42.

Okkonen, Jari. 2007. "Archaeological Investigations at the Sámi Sacrificial Site of Ukonsaari in Lake Inari." *Fennoscandia Archaeologica* 24: 29–38.

Ovsyannikov, Oleg V., and Nicolay M. Terebikhin. 1994. "Sacred Space in the Culture of the Arctic Regions." In *Sacred Sites, Sacred Places*, ed. David Carmichael, Jane Hubert, Brian Reeves, and Audhild Schanche, 44–81. London: Routledge.

Price, Neil S. 2002. *The Viking Way: Religion and War in Late Iron Age Society*. Uppsala: Uppsala University Press.

Qvigstad, Just K. 1926. *Lappische Opfersteine und heilige Berge in Norwegen*. Oslo EtnografiskaMuseums Skrifter 1(5). Oslo: A.W. Broggers.

Rahtje, Lillian. 2001. *Amasonen och jägaren: Kön/genderkonstruktioner i norr*. Studia Archaeologica Universitatis Umensis 14. Umeå: Institutionen för Arkeologi och Samiska Studier, Umeå Universitet.

Ramqvist, Per H. 1983. *Gene: On the Origin, Function and development of Sedentary Iron Age Settlement in Northern Sweden*. Archaeology and Environment 1. Umeå: University of Umeå.

Rheen, Samuel. [1676] 1897. *En kortt Relation om Lapparner Lefwarne och Sedher, wifd-skippellser sampt i många stycken Grofwe wild-farellsser*, ed. Karl B. Wiklund. Nyare bidrag till kännedom om de svenska landsmålen och svensk folklif 17.1. Uppsala: H. Wretman.

Rydving, Håkan. 1993. *The End of Drum-Time: Religious Change among the Lule Saami, 1670s–1740s*. Acta Universitatis Upsaliensis, Historia Religionum 12. Uppsala and Stockholm: Almqvist & Wiksell.

———. 2010. "The birds of the *noaidi*." In *Tracing Sámi Traditions: In Search of the Indigenous Religion among the Western Sámi during the 17th and 18th Centuries*, ed. Håkan Rydving, 125–34. Oslo: The Institute for Comparative Research in Human Culture, Novus Forlag.

Salmi, Anna-Kaisa, Tiina Äikäs, Markus Fjellström, and Marte Spangen. 2015. "Animal Offerings at the Sámi Offering Site of Unna Saiva: Changing Religious Practices and Human–Animal Relationships." *Journal of Anthropological Archaeology* 40: 10–22.

Schanche, Audhild. 2000. *Graver i ur och berg: Samisk gravskikk og religion fra förhistorisk til nyere tid*. Karasjok: Davvi Girji.

Serning, Inger. 1956. *Lapska offerplatsfynd från järnålder och medeltid i de svenska lappmarkerna*. Acta Lapponica 11. Stockholm: Nordiska museet.

Skaare, K. 1976. *Coins and Coinage in Viking Age Norway: The Establishment of a National Coinage in Norway in the XI century, with a Survey of the Preceding Currency History*. Oslo: Universitetsforlaget.

Storå, Nils. 1971. *Burial Customs of the Skolt Lapps*. FF Communications 210. Helsinki: Academia Scientiarum.

Storli, Inger. 1991. "De østlige smykkene fra vikingtid og tidlig middelalder. Norsk Arkeologisk Selskap." *Viking* 1991: 89–104.

Tallgren, Ane M. 1934. "Die 'altpermische': Pelzwarenperiode an der Pecora. Excavationes et Studia." *Finska Fornminnesföreningens Tidskrift* 40: 152–81.

Ucko, Peter J. 2001. "'Heritage' and 'Indigenous Peoples' in the 21st Century." *Public Archaeology* 1(4): 227–38.

Vahtola, Jouko. 1980. *Torniojoki- ja Kemijokilaakson asutuksen synty. Nimistötieteellinen ja historiallinen tutkimus. The origins of settlement in the Tornio and Kemi river valleys*. Studia historica septentrionalia 3. Rovaniemi: Societas Historica Finlandiae.

Vorren, Ørnulf. 1985. "Circular Sacrificial Sites and Their Function." In *Saami Pre-Christian Religion: Studies on the Oldest Traces of Religion among the Saamis*, ed. Louise Bäckman, and Åke Hultkrantz, 69–82. Stockholm Studies in Comparative Religion 25. Stockholm: Almqvist & Wiksell.

Vorren, Ørnulf, and Hans Kristian Eriksen. 1993. *Samiske offerplatser i Varanger*. Tromsø Museums Skrifter 24. Tromsø: Nordkalottförlaget.

Wallerström, Thomas. 1995a. *Norrbotten, Sverige och Medeltiden: Problem kring makt och bosättning i en europeisk periferi*, vol. 1. Lund Studies in Medieval Archaeology 15(1). Stockholm: Almqvist & Wiksell.

———. 1995b. "A Merchant's Depot and a Hiding Place for Stolen Goods: Or Saami Sacrificial Sites? A Source-Critical Look at Gråträsk and Mörtträsket Finds." In *Thirteen Essays on Medieval Artefacts*, ed. Lars Ersgård, 167–87. Meddelanden från Lunds universities historiska museum 1993–1994, NS 10. Stockholm: Almqvist & Wiksell International.

———. 2000. "The Saami between East and West in the Middle Ages: An Archaeological Contribution to the History of Reindeer Breeding." *Acta Borealia* 17(1): 3–39.

Welinder, Stig. 2003. "Christianity, Politics and Ethnicity in Early Medieval Jämtland, Mid Sweden." In *The Cross goes North: Processes of Conversion in Northern Europe, AD 300–1300*, ed. Martin Carver, 509–30. York: York Medieval Press, University of York.

Zachrisson, Inger. 1984. *De samiska metalldepåerna 1000–1350 i ljuset av fyndet från Mörtträsket, Lappland*. Archaeology and Environment 3. Umeå: Umeå University.

———. 1989. "The So-called Scandinavian Cultural Boundary in Northern Sweden in Viking Times: Ethnic or Socio-economic?" *Acta Borealia* 1988(1/2): 70–97.

———. 1997. *Möten i gränsland: Samer och germaner i Mellanskandinavien*. Statens historiska museum, Monographs 4. Stockholm: Statens historiska museum.

Chapter 3

Seeking the Indigenous Perspective

Colonial Interactions at Fort Saint Pierre, French
Colonial Louisiane, AD 1719–1729

LisaMarie Malischke

Introduction

The remains of Fort Saint Pierre are located on the Yazoo Bluffs
northeast of present-day Vicksburg, Mississippi, USA. The site was
archaeologically excavated between 1974 and 1977 (Brown 1975, 1979),
with a reexamination of the artifacts, excavation notes, and primary and
secondary documents relating to the fort performed in 2015 (Malischke
2015). The fort was built near the confluence of the Yazoo and Mississippi
rivers by French colonial soldiers in AD 1719 and occupied for ten years
(Figures 3.1 and 3.2). There were no recorded incidents of trouble between
the fort's soldiers and the neighboring Yazoo, Koroa, and Ofo Native
people during this time, and select excavated objects demonstrate daily
exchange and interaction. Other Native groups brought violence to the
fort, indicating a wider regional unrest. The end of the Yazoo Bluffs settlement was violent and eventually led to mutual death, destruction, and
ultimately, abandonment. The reasons for this remain a mystery, but the
event itself highlights the complex two-way nature of colonial encounters
discussed throughout this volume.

In this chapter, I attempt to understand the Indigenous viewpoint
by applying a postcolonial ethnohistorical approach to the written and
material record. Though the artifacts in this case study come from several
iterations of a French colonial military and commercial fort, I use the
assemblage to examine the cultures of the neighboring Native groups

"from the symbolic products of their actions, including material arti-facts" (Axtell 1979, 2). Though many ethnohistorians work directly with extant Indigenous groups, here is a case where no living members of the Yazoo Bluffs Native peoples are known. Yet, the methods of ethnohistory can still be applied to the data, especially when reading the primary documents with a postcolonial eye. Also, though the pinnacle of the colonial history of this region is one synchronic event—the massacre of nearly everyone living in the region—I provide a diachronic narrative and description to understand the provincial sociopolitical situation in the region (Axtell 1979, 6). Lastly, per Michael E. Harkin (2010, 125), I use the available documentary sources to "understand the dialogic dimen-sions of culture encounter and exchange" between the French garrison members and local Native peoples. I try to do this in a "politically com-mitted" way (Harkin 2010, 123), that gives voice and strength to these silenced voices, including making this publication available to the public during 300th anniversary celebrations as a chance to commemorate and honor a difficult history.

In order to analyze what unfolded between French colonists and the Native peoples of the Yazoo Bluffs, I provincialized local history by plac-ing it within the context of early eighteenth-century Native and European relations in the Lower Mississippi Valley. This mixed-methods approach

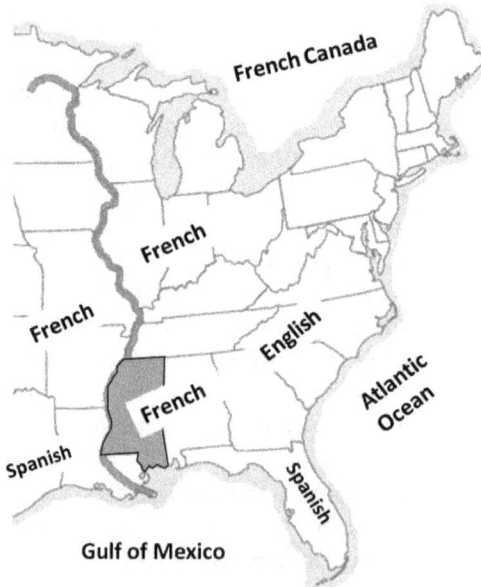

Figure 3.1. Regions of eastern North America claimed by European colonial powers in the first decades of the eight-eenth century. Native peoples inhabited all of the lands shown on map. The state of Mississippi is shaded. (Map created by LisaMarie Malischke.)

Figure 3.2. Map of Fort Saint Pierre produced by Officer Dumont de Montigny. Map reproduction courtesy of the Norman B. Leventhal Map & Education Center at the Boston Public Library. Licensed for use under a Creative Commons Attribution Non-Commercial Share Alike License (CC BY-NC-SA).

can be applied to historical situations where collaborative research with modern Native peoples is not possible. In the absence of nearby archaeological settlement remains ascribed to specific Native groups, Fort Saint Pierre offers a case of Indigenous archaeology being applied to a European colonial site in order to "see" the Native neighbors amongst the soldiers as well as to inform the interpretations of activities within the fort. I reanalyzed the assemblage to tease out manifestations of material needs, wants, and exchange products present at Fort Saint Pierre which, in turn, represent French and Native interactions, discourse, agreements, disagreements, and Native agency. The end goal of this research is to provide a voice for the "voiceless" Native groups of the Yazoo Bluffs. It is no small story to tell, as it was their collective power that changed the course of colonial imperialism in the region, limiting European development for the next century through small group resistance, but paying a high cost that decimated member populations.

Historical Background

The archaeological site called Haynes Bluff, located in Warren County, Mississippi, on the bluffs of the Yazoo River, has been interpreted as the joint village of the Yazoo, Koroa, and Ofo peoples. When recorded in 1853, the site had seven earthen mounds and a large plaza (Brain 1988, 196). Excavations at the site revealed historical artifacts dating to 1700 (Brain 1988, 211–12). By 1955, the site was reduced to three small mounds and one large mound, all of which were disturbed in some fashion (Phillips 1970, 430–33). Further destruction of the site took place in 1967, but limited excavations were allowed in 1974 (Brain 1988, 200–4). The archaeological remains indicated a historical occupation of the site, along with mound-building activities, structural remains, historical burials, and evidence of middens (Brain 1988, 209–47). No further work has been done on the site, or with the artifacts collected over time from Haynes Bluff, since the excavations and examinations performed in 1974.

The Yazoo, Koroa, and Ofo people were rarely mentioned in French documents of the time. The Jesuit priest Charlevoix, who travelled to Fort Saint Pierre, stated that the Yazoo, Koroa, and Ofo all resided in one village (de Charlevoix 1977, 91, 132). The editor of that volume noted that the Koroa were allied to the Natchez, with customs similar to those of the Natchez (O'Neill n. 6 cited in de Charlevoix 1977, 132). A segment of the Koroa may have even resided alongside the Natchez in a neighboring village (Lieb 2008, 3). Charlevoix himself recorded that in 1722, the

French feared the formation of a political group involving the Yazoo with the populous Choctaw, Chickasaw, and Natchez (de Charlevoix 1977, 229). At this time, the Chickasaw predominantly were spread throughout northern Mississippi, while the Choctaw were in the southeastern portion of Mississippi and in parts of Alabama (Swanton 1971, 177, 180).

Researchers disagree regarding how these ethnic groups related to one another. The Koroa were likely Tunican speakers (Swanton 1952, 187; Brain 1988, 285); the Yazoo were either Tunican (Kunkel 1951, 176; Swanton 1952, 194) or Muskhogean (Brain 1988, 284); and the Ofo were likely Siouan speakers, possibly originating in Ohio (Swanton 1971, 231; Brain 1988, 283). The Tunica people were living in the Yazoo Bluffs when the French first encountered them in the 1680s, but later moved south of Natchez, where the Mississippi River met the Red River (Swanton 1971, 193). This is where the Tunica resided during the occupation of Fort Saint Pierre.

In the most intensive study of any of these Native peoples, Ian W. Brown (1979, 64–69, 101, 105, 122, 431, 539, 542–68) determined that the French considered the Yazoo a polytheistic people who built small, round houses organized in hamlets around the principal village containing an earthen mound topped by a wooden temple. As access to European goods increased, the Yazoo employed metal kettles for rendering bear oil and procuring salt. Kettles thereafter replaced ceramic vessels as burial accompaniments. French pottery forms served as models for Native ceramics, and glass bottle fragments were used to create projectile points and hide-scrapers. Iron knives were used for daily work, and gunpowder and vermilion supplemented charcoal and red ochre in the creation of tattoos. As consumers with discerning tastes, these Native groups requested red and blue Limbourg cloth, woolen blankets, and white and blue beads. Between 1702 and 1719, these economic activities, as well as political concerns, turned French government attention to the Yazoo Bluffs and provided the impetus for construction of a fort at this locale.

During this time span (1702–19), before the building of the fort, the Yazoo, Koroa, and Ofo people became increasingly influenced by English imperial activities. By 1716, they were acting as conduits and brokers between English traders in slaves and deerskins, and larger regional Native groups such as the Chickasaw and Chakchiuma (Barnett 2012, 104–5). The Chickasaw, a populous and powerful group, were strongly allied with the English. Early French colonists visiting the region encountered Englishmen, Yazoo, and Chickasaw attempting to convince the Natchez people to "declare war on other nations, so as to bring in captives" (de Charlevoix 1900, 24). The French realized that a Yazoo-English-Chickasaw alliance posed a threat to their traffic on the Mississippi River and to their larger French imperial aspirations. To remedy this situation the French began construction of Fort Saint Pierre in 1719.

Fort Saint Pierre was envisioned as the nucleus of a commercial settlement for the production of tobacco (Dumont de Montigny 2012, 164). After a seemingly auspicious start with six hundred inhabitants and three hundred soldiers, illness, high mortality rates and drought soon contributed to the failure of the majority of surrounding *concessions* (plantations). Between 1722 and 1723, most of the post's French population moved 100 miles (161 km) south to the vicinity of Fort Rosalie among the Natchez Native people (now modern-day Natchez, Mississippi). This exodus from the Fort Saint Pierre area left only twenty or so civilians, and a much reduced military force. Fort Saint Pierre became an isolated outpost surrounded by Indigenous groups who far outnumbered the small French settlement.

Jean-François-Benjamin Dumont de Montigny was a literate officer assigned to the fort for several years, before, during, and after the exodus. In his memoir, he explained that the Yazoo, whom Dumont called friends of the French, ceded their lands for the fort, the associated commercial concessions, and the civilian and military homesteads (Dumont de Montigny 2012, 165). He described his role in laying out the design of the fort complex:

> And it was me whom he [de Graves] ordered … to lay out the fort in which we, our troops, our belongings, and those of the concession, would all be protected from attack by enemy Indians. I obeyed his orders. I outlined a fort with four bastions. … In each of the bastions, there were two gunports where cannons would be set up on their carriages. … On the inner side of the fort, there was a parapet four feet wide and two and a half feet high, so that one might fire over the top of the palisade if necessary. We also built a guardhouse next to the main entry, barracks, quarters for the officers, and a residence for the captain commandant, as well as four large storehouses and a room for the warehouse keeper (Dumont de Montigny 2012, 154–55).

Once construction of Fort Saint Pierre was completed, Dumont recorded that routine tasks dulled the soldiers and consumed their daily lives (Dumont de Montigny 2012, 189). Exchange and interaction with neighboring Native individuals evidently also became routine by design, as the French military and the Company of the Indies chose to pay the garrison with trade goods from the fort's warehouse. According to Dumont (2012, 165), "[T]he soldiers and workers, rather than being credited in money, were paid with merchandise that the men then traded to the Indians for food, such as corn, oil, beans, meat, etc." The material remains recovered archaeologically at the fort site are manifestations of exchange and interpersonal relations, exemplified below, that occurred at the Yazoo settlement between French colonists and the area's Native peoples.

Material Culture of Exchange

Written accounts document the range of merchandise available for exchange. This included fabrics that often do not survive archaeologically, metal items and containers, utensils, and small, everyday items. Merchandise may have included red and white wines and brandy, all provided in glass bottles. Offering a variety of items as payment to the troops may have been necessary, considering that the Superior Council repeatedly lamented in letters to the Company Directors how candle wax and olive oil frequently reached the fort in a rotten state, while cloth, blankets, shoes, straight pins, nails, and gunpowder were scarce at the best of times (Rowland and Sanders 1929, 259, 271, 314, 337, 460, 553, 559; and 1932).

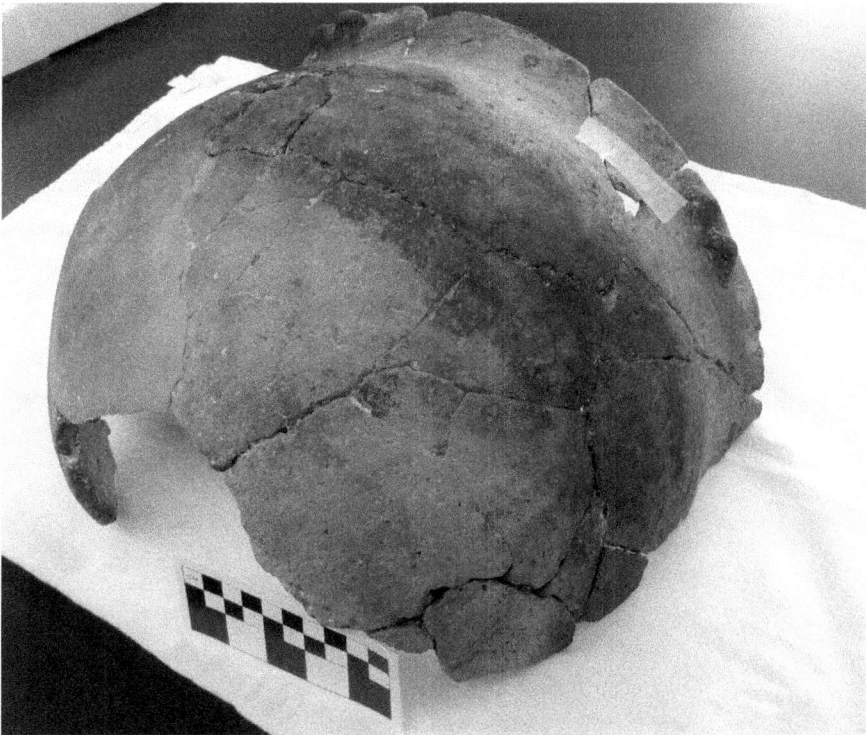

Figure 3.3. Mended Native cooking pot recovered from Fort Saint Pierre. (Photograph by LisaMarie Malischke.)

In exchange for these imported items, the Fort Saint Pierre French garrison likely received from Native neighbors processed leather hides, moccasins as replacement footwear, and foodstuffs such as corn, bear grease, sagamity, and game meat. Some of the food items must have been delivered in baskets or in Native-made ceramic vessels. Various foods were likely processed in Native ceramic cooking pots (Figure 3.3). Indeed, Native ceramics contemporaneous with the fort's occupation were the most numerous artifacts recovered from excavations within the fort perimeter (Malischke 2015, 147–48). Traditionally across southeastern North America, ceramic vessels were made by Native women, and food preparation was largely a female task. Women trapped small animals, processed hides, tended to agricultural fields, and gathered a wide assortment of wild plants and animal foodstuffs, while Native men primarily hunted large game (Swanton 1952, 1971). Therefore, the recovery inside the fort of abundant fragments of large Native-made cooking pots represents the work of local women and the foods provided by local women and men. The artifact assemblage contains many other items exchanged with Native peoples.

Glass beads (N = 237), manufactured in Europe and shipped to North America by the millions (Karklins 1985; Karklins, Dussubieux, and Hancock 2015), were recovered from all portions of the fort. The garrison soldiers likely obtained glass beads in payment from the warehouse and

Figure 3.4. Projectile point made from glass shard, recovered from Fort Saint Pierre. (Photograph by LisaMarie Malischke.)

then used the beads in strands or sewed them onto cloth or leather, for gifts or for trading purposes (Malischke 2015, 326).

To supplement conventional trade items, hungry or ill-clothed soldiers evidently turned to unconventional objects such as discarded glass and metal scraps. Unneeded glass from discarded containers was readily available to enlisted soldiers, whether curated whole or scavenged as fragments from waste piles. Seven modified glass hide-scrapers were recovered at Fort Saint Pierre, along with a single glass projectile point (Figure 3.4). As these artifacts attest, glass was occasionally modified by Native hands, likely as an end product of trade with the fort inhabitants.

Scrap metal scavenged from discarded French items, such as kettles and pans, was used by the Native neighbors in multiple ways. Twenty-two fragments of scrap sheet metal and thirteen tinkling cones were recovered from locations scattered across the most heavily trafficked areas of the fort. All are copper alloy, although their exact material remains to be determined. The variety of shapes and sizes of the recovered tinkling cones indicates that production of these decorative cones was a cottage industry (Figure 3.5). Several of the cones have rivets and rivet holes, attesting to their origin as portions of patched (and well worn) kettles.

Figure 3.5. Tinkling cones recovered from Fort Saint Pierre. (Photograph by LisaMarie Malischke.)

It is quite likely that the Yazoo, Koroa, and Ofo produced tinkling cones themselves, but the recovery of these thirteen cones at the fort indicates their probable manufacture by French soldiers. Three of the tinkling cones and some scrap sheet metal were recovered in the fort's parade ground, possibly indicating that this was a trading space. An eyewitness to the 1729 attack on the fort recounted how Yazoo and Koroa warriors had no problem getting inside the fort that day, perhaps because the parade ground routinely served as a trading and meeting place.

The presence of tinkling cones within the fort is particularly interesting because these are true cross-cultural objects. They were created by imitating a Native style of deer-hoof janglers, but made from imported metals, resulting in a tinkling sound when strung together. Throughout the extensive Native lands claimed by the French, these items were worn by Native men and women of all ages in their hair, on their persons dangling from ear and nose piercings, and on clothing and other items such as pouches and bags. French inhabitants of Canada and the western Great Lakes also adopted the wearing of tinkling cones along with their adoption of Native garments. However, such an adoption of Native clothing was not recorded for the troops stationed at Fort Saint Pierre, all of whom were born in France.

The use of standardized trade goods for exchange with neighboring Native groups was recorded by Dumont and evidenced by the recovery of glass beads. Expedient use of discarded items to supplement trade goods is evidenced by the glass retouched hide-scrapers, a glass projectile point, tinkling cones, and the snipped scrap metal fragments. The high volume of Native ceramics recovered from the fort indicates what the French were receiving from these exchange events: foodstuffs in ceramic storage vessels and utilitarian cooking and serving ceramics. From the perspective of the colonial French, these apparently peaceful interpersonal exchanges belied increasing tensions among the Yazoo, Koroa, and Ofo people who had to contend with shifts in the region's political landscape.

Alliances, Violence, and the Political Landscape

Intergroup Native politics were complicated before the arrival of a substantial French presence in 1719 and became more so afterwards. In 1702, in response to previous provocations, the Koroa murdered three Frenchmen and barely escaped French retribution for this action. By 1706, French colonists noted a newly established sociopolitical relationship between the Yazoo and Chickasaw, and a burgeoning economic relationship between them and English traders, which grew unabated for the next ten years. To rectify this situation, in 1716, French colonial officials asked for an alliance with the Yazoo and made plans to build Fort Saint Pierre. Construction of the fort was delayed as funds were funneled to the Natchez area in response to violence in 1715–16, at the Grand Village of the Natchez, in what is called the First Natchez War (Swanton 1911, 196, 199; Barnett 2007, 61; Milne 2015, 59–62, 64–68). As an outcome of that war, Fort Rosalie was constructed atop a nearby bluff on the Mississippi River (Swanton 1911, 203). Despite their alliance with the leader, the Great Sun of the Natchez, the French now realized that not all Natchez villages wanted them as allies and, in fact, they were actively interacting with English merchants (Swanton 1911, 202; Milne 2015, 60–78).

Once construction of Fort Saint Pierre finally occurred in 1719, the French used their new post to attempt to attach the Yazoo and Koroa more firmly to their geopolitical interests. French envoy De Pailloux arrived in summer 1720 to persuade the Natchez and Yazoo, apparently unsuccessfully, to declare war on the Chickasaw. In the fall of 1721 the first vanguard of civilian colonists arrived at the Yazoo Bluffs, but disease killed more than half the group. Dumont and a second wave of settlers arrived late in 1721, prompting reconstruction and reconfiguration of Fort Saint Pierre in early 1722 (Wright field notes, 1977, Unit W824; Brown 1979; Dumont de Montigny 2012, 144, 154–55, 160; Malischke 2015, 350, 352–53).

The mission of the French envoy and the reconfiguration of a larger Fort Saint Pierre led the Chickasaw to attack the nearby Yazoo village around 25 May 1722. The fort's commander, M. de Grave, sent Governor Bienville in New Orleans a letter which explained that, "the Chickasaws had come to the Yazoo village and had carried off the few supplies which were there" (de La Harpe 1971, 209).

Soon after the Chickasaw raid on the Yazoo, the household of a sergeant of the garrison was attacked, with only his young son surviving. The responding soldiers saw, "blazes engraved on trees and learned from these that it was the Chickasaws who were making war on us. ... Our detachment brought back some loot, such as a kettle, pillows, brass plates, etc., that the Indians had dropped as they ran" (Dumont de Montigny 2012, 163).

This was not the end of the Chickasaw threat. A second letter from Commandant M. de Grave explained that:

> on June 5 two [Native] Cahoumas had arrived. They had been sent by their chief to warn that five parties of Chickasaws were coming to wage war on the Yazoos, Courois [Koroa] and Ofogoula [Ofo], and that because of this information these nations had sent their women and children into the fort. The Chickasaws, however, sent word that they did not intend to wage war, but

were coming to justify themselves for the murder of [the] Frenchmen for which they were not responsible. M. de Grave permitted the warrior Thioncouata and four of his men to come to the fort to present their explanation. (de La Harpe 1971, 209–10)

Thioncouata and his companions apparently came bearing animal pelts as gifts, but the explanation they provided regarding the attack was either not recorded or did not survive (Dumont de Montigny 2012, 163). It is still a mystery who, in the end, was blamed for the attack on the Yazoo settlement and sergeant's home and family.

The Jesuit Charlevoix offered some insight when he explained that the giving of the gifts and the smoking of the calumet pipe at the meeting described above was not simply restitution for the attack on the fort's sergeant, but instead was an overture on the part of the Chickasaw to make peace specifically with Governor Bienville and generally with the French (de Charlevoix 1900, 70). Despite this peace overture, Dumont (2012, 164) recorded that after this May 1722 event the inhabitants of Fort Saint Pierre, "were obliged to maintain a higher state of alert."

Months after the attack on the sergeant at Fort Saint Pierre other troubles led to the Second Natchez War (1722) involving inhabitants of Fort Rosalie. Small pox and long-simmering issues contributing to this conflict included French concession managers who ignored their Native neighbors and did not perform calumet pipe ceremonies, extensive French farming on contested lands, European livestock consuming Native cultivated plants, and European concepts of private property (Milne 2015, 88–91). In response, some Natchez damaged French crops, killed livestock, and attacked colonists and slaves (Milne 2015, 93–105).

French attitudes towards the Natchez, however, did not change. The Third Natchez War began a year later, in the fall of 1723, when small groups killed horses and cattle and attacked nearby concessions (Milne 2015, 106). The Natchez were divided by these conflicts and some sided with the French. Native people opposed to war wore armbands to signify their alliance with the French. Finally, after much inaction, Governor Bienville gathered troops, civilian militia, and Native allies and went on the attack (Milne 2015, 108–11). The French and their numerous Native allies began a scorched earth march, and along the way attacked several individual Natchez homesteads (Swanton 1911, 212–15).

Roughly six months after the end of the Third Natchez War, a second incident took place at Fort Saint Pierre. Despite a high state of alert in the spring of 1724, Dumont went alone to hunt in the woods surrounding the fort, where he was attacked and almost killed by a Chickasaw man. After a struggle, Dumont claimed he shot the Chickasaw man in the heart, scalped him, and then retreated to the safety of the fort (Dumont 2012, 189–90). The events that happened after this attack reveal much about the political position of the Yazoo caught between the French and the Chickasaw:

> After dinner, however, our commandant sent a man to fetch the chief of the Yazoo Indians, and having been shown the scalp, the chief told him that it was one of the Cris [short for Chickasaw], of a group of fifteen or so that had been scouting the area around our fort, and that I was very lucky to have been attacked by only one. The next day, the Yazoo Indians came to give me a calumet [pipe] congratulating me for my victory. My word — as long as I remained there, I no longer wanted to go hunting so early in the morning, and least of all alone. When we went hunting, there were seven or eight of us. (Dumont de Montigny 2012, 190)

The Yazoo people were aware of the presence of Chickasaw warriors in the vicinity of the fort, but they did not warn the garrison. Yet, the Yazoo either did not condone the attack on Dumont, or wanted to appear to condemn the attack, so they presented him a calumet peace pipe. High alert at Fort Saint Pierre was reinstated, and future hunting by the French was done in groups.

Nature intervened in 1724, with the French and Yazoo suffering equally from flooding and famine. Governor Bienville was recalled to France in 1725, leaving a void in French governance in the Louisiane colony. That same year the War Chief of the Natchez passed away leaving a similar void among the Natchez. By 1728, two more elderly pro-French Natchez leaders, the Natchez Great Sun and a Chief, had died. The new Great Sun was young and unprepared for leadership, and ultimately proved to be a weak ruler (de Charlevoix 1977, 117, 119).

The French-Native relationship in the Yazoo Bluffs region was affected by events elsewhere, particularly, contentious relations between French and Natchez at Fort Rosalie, and the struggle between the French and English for influence among the more populous Choctaw and Chickasaw. Perhaps it is unsurprising that both colonial and Native peoples of the Yazoo Bluffs region were caught up, in 1729, in the most violent of the French-Natchez wars, variously termed the Natchez Revolt, Natchez Uprising, or Natchez Massacre. The repercussions of this event ultimately destroyed the Fort Saint Pierre settlement, the French fort, and the majority of the neighboring Native groups (Brown 1979, 89–98; Malischke 2015, 337–49).

Despite extensive attention paid to the Natchez Uprising (Le Page du Pratz 1774; Swanton 1911; Cruzat 1925; Rowland and Sanders 1927; Le Petit 1950; Barnett 2007, 2012; Dumont de Montigny 2012; Milne 2015), historical documents and extant scholarship are mostly silent on its repercussions for the Yazoo and the Fort Saint Pierre settlement.

A Violent End

Even with warnings from the chronicler Dumont, Commandant Chepart of Fort Rosalie disregarded potential danger from the pro-English faction of the Natchez. On 28 November 1729, Natchez warriors surrounded French homesteads and entered Fort Rosalie under the guise of asking for hunting supplies. The French death toll came to 145 men, 36 women, and 56 children. Approximately 150 French women and children were taken captive, along with enslaved Africans who had remained neutral or who held military knowledge. One tailor and one carter were kept alive to transport looted items and to alter clothes (Dumont de Montigny 2012, 212–13, 236, 244; Milne 2015, 176–78).

Several Yazoo and Koroa warriors were visiting the Natchez settlement when the uprising took place, but they did not participate. Instead, they helped a French man escape to the Mississippi River (de Charlevoix 1977, 90; Dumont de Montigny 2012, 237, n. 14). A few days later, they offered the calumet pipe to the Natchez victors, and then departed for the Yazoo Bluffs.

Their trip upriver took almost two weeks. Upon arriving at the Yazoo Bluffs on the evening of 11 December 1729, these warriors killed the missionary stationed at Fort Saint Pierre, Father Souel; then chased his servant to the Jesuit's house, where he too was killed. A survivor of the attack on the fort, known only as "Aubry's wife," later explained that on the morning of 12 December 1729, the Yazoo and Koroa warriors came to the river where they first attacked her husband. He tried to shout a warning but was silenced by a tomahawk. The Yazoo and Koroa next went to the fort with a calumet pipe and, "entered without any difficulty with their tomahawks hidden under their robes." In her witness statement she explained that, "[T]hey had laid violent hands on all of the French who were fifteen in number, having spared only five women and four children. The fact that the Koroa women had lamented the death of the latter was what saved their lives" (Rowland and Sanders 1927, 99). During and after the attack, items looted from Fort Saint Pierre included guns, gun parts, gunpowder and lead shot, clothing, trade goods, and personal items. The warehouses of the king were picked clean (Malischke 2015, 148, 337–50).

Meanwhile, the Ofo were some distance away, possibly engaged in producing ceramic jars (Rowland and Sanders 1927, 100) or hunting (de Charlevoix 1977, 92). When the Ofo heard the news, Aubry's wife explained, they approved of what the Yazoo and Koroa had done and were sorry they had not participated. To make up for this, she reported, the Ofo later vigorously attacked three pirogues (a type of canoe) descending the Mississippi River from the Illinois Country.

Three weeks later, the Yazoo, with prisoners and looted items from the French fort and settlement, agreed to meet with the Chakchiuma who were acting as trading middlemen for the Chickasaw. To the Yazoo's surprise, the Chakchiuma and some Choctaw attacked them and "rescued" some of the women and children, and the looted possessions from the fort (Rowland and Sanders 1927, 100; de Charlevoix 1977, 96–97). Various Choctaw groups divided the prisoners and booty between them. French envoys had to pay high ransoms to retrieve the surviving captives and looted possessions from Fort Saint Pierre.

Discussion and Aftermath

Though motivations behind Yazoo, Koroa, and Ofo actions remain unclear at this historical remove, careful analysis of the written accounts, some of them by eyewitnesses, does offer clues to the viewpoints of these Native people. Dumont explained that Yazoo and Koroa warriors had traveled south to smoke the calumet with the Natchez yet were unaware of the plan to attack Fort Rosalie (Dumont de Montigny 2012, 237, n. 14). Their delay of several days before they offered the calumet pipe to the Natchez suggests they debated how to proceed in light of the new situation. Perhaps the Natchez destruction of the Fort Rosalie colonial settlement convinced the Yazoo and Koroa that the entire French colony could be destroyed.

By all accounts, the Yazoo and Koroa successfully replicated the Natchez attack on Fort Rosalie at Fort Saint Pierre. According to Aubry's wife, the warriors easily entered the fort under guise of presenting the soldiers with a calumet. They relied on familiarity and trust developed over years of daily interactions to gain access to the fort, invited inside by their trading partners, the French garrison.

Aubry's wife recounted how the Koroa women protested the imminent deaths of French women and children. This could be interpreted in two ways. Perhaps the Koroa women sought to save the French women with whom they shared some sense of sisterhood. More than likely, however, the Koroa women were thinking of capturing French women and children as potential adoptees, servants, slaves, and/or to bolster their bargaining position in future ransom negotiations.

From Aubry's wife, we know that the Ofo were not present during the attack on Fort Saint Pierre. This may have been a political strategy to remove themselves from the area during the attack. In the days following, Ofo warriors participated, along with Yazoo and Koroa warriors, in sporadic attacks on French people traveling down the Mississippi River. The eventual settling of the Ofo people outside of a rebuilt Fort Rosalie, to supply food to the garrison, seems to indicate that the Ofo policy of "waiting for the dust to settle" may have saved them from French retaliation, a fate that befell the Natchez, Yazoo, Koroa, and Chickasaw (Swanton 1971, 188, 195, 207, 232; de Charlevoix 1977, 120–24; Lieb 2008, 219–20).

After the destruction of both French forts, the Natchez, Yazoo, and Koroa were flush with colonial captives and goods, possibly destined for the English via the Choctaw and Chickasaw. But this did not occur. Instead, perhaps due to ill feelings at being left out of original plans, the Choctaw turned on the Yazoo and distributed the captured survivors and goods among several of their villages. Old, prewar enemies clashed, flipped sides, and created new alliances. French officials learned that the Natchez were actively recruiting allies from among the English trade network, most of whom were enemies to the French.

The aftermath of the Natchez Uprising was chaos for the participating Native groups. French officials enlisted a large army of colonists and slaves from New Orleans and marched against the Natchez, laying siege to the Grand Village. Possibly due to Choctaw and Chakchiuma attacks, the Yazoo and Koroa left the Yazoo Bluffs and scattered among the Natchez, the Chickasaw, and various other places (de Charlevoix 1977, 120–24). By 1734, the Yazoo and Koroa had disappeared from colonial written records. Swanton (1971, 188) recorded that the Koroa settled initially with the Chickasaw, but ultimately, with the Choctaw. He noted that Choctaw chief Allen Wright (1826–85) claimed Koroa descent (Swanton 1971, 188).

Less is known about the fate of the Yazoo. Acting in conjunction with the Koroa, they apparently moved to live with the Chickasaw and/or Choctaw. Evidence of the Yazoo ultimately residing with the Choctaw possibly could be seen in the two Choctaw towns named Yazoo, but this has yet to be confirmed (Swanton 1971, 195).

The Ofo settled for several decades, from about 1739 to 1758, outside of newly rebuilt Fort Rosalie, but later they joined the Tunica, and together moved to Marksville, Louisiana (Swanton 1971, 207, 232). It was noted in 1784 that the Ofo were living in a village eight miles above Pointe Coupée, Louisiana (Swanton 1971, 193, 232). Swanton, conducting field research in 1908, claimed to have met the sole survivor of the Ofo people. This survivor spoke the Ofo language and was at the time residing with the Tunica outside of Marksville (Swanton 1971, 232).

Fort Saint Pierre was never rebuilt, and French forces never visited the scene nor buried their dead. Judging from archaeological evidence, the fort was left to rot after an unsuccessful attempt to burn it following the attack (Malischke 2015). The Yazoo Bluffs were not resettled by French colonists or by Native groups and it remained essentially unoccupied until American settlement one hundered years later.

In the end, we can deduce the following: the Chickasaw, at the behest of the Yazoo, were in the Yazoo Bluffs region long before construction of Fort Saint Pierre. Because the Chickasaw attacked fort inhabitants on two separate occasions, they remained in the region throughout the French occupation of the fort. The populous Chickasaw and Natchez out-numbered the French settlement's occupants and local Native groups, although the latter were influenced by the power of these large groups.

After witnessing the destruction of Fort Rosalie, the Yazoo and Koroa allied with the Natchez and subsequently attacked Fort Saint Pierre. The Yazoo and Koroa were trying to maintain good relations with all Native peoples in the region during a precarious time. They probably also believed that an attack on Fort Saint Pierre would strengthen trade ties with the Chickasaw and the English, and confirm their alliance with the now powerful Natchez. The Ofo choose a different tactic, which enabled them to survive for a bit longer as a distinct group.

The history of Fort Saint Pierre demonstrates that with the fort's destruc-tion, the Yazoo, Koroa, and Ofo successfully resisted political and cultural domination by the colonial French. The French garrison became depend-ent upon a policy of paying enlisted soldiers with merchandise, which necessitated interpersonal trading with Native neighbors for foodstuffs and supplies. Despite a decade of peaceful exchanges in the Yazoo Bluffs region, troubled interactions between the French and Natchez villages to the south reverberated as far as Fort Saint Pierre. Internal power strug-gles between various Natchez factions condemned these distant unwit-ting victims. Powerful groups such as the Chickasaw and the Natchez made wide-ranging political decisions that finally culminated in actions to cleanse their lands of the French scourge.

Before the Uprising there were no recorded incidents of violence between the Fort Saint Pierre French and the Yazoo, Koroa, and Ofo. But long-standing intersocial goodwill was insufficient to prevent the destruction of a remote colonial outpost when faced with the larger politi-cal machinations that swept the region. By attempting to understand the Indigenous viewpoint, this chapter provides another strand to the mul-tivocal narrative of the Native experience in relation to French colonial Louisiane.

LisaMarie Malischke is an assistant professor of anthropology at Mercyhurst University and a historical archaeologist specializing in French and Native interaction and exchange, particularly French military forts and settlements stretching from the Great Lakes down the Mississippi River corridor to the Gulf of Mexico. Dr. Malischke has also worked in Cultural Resource Management (CRM) in the US on sites spanning the Mississippian to the archaeology of yesterday. She is a public archaeologist who has a passion for teaching and engaging with local communities through lectures, public exhibitions, site open houses, and historical reenactments.

References

Axtell, James. 1979. "Ethnohistory: An Historian's Viewpoint." _Ethnohistory_ 26(1): 1–13.

Barnett Jr., James F. 2007. _The Natchez Indians: A History to 1735._ Jackson: University Press of Mississippi.

_____. 2012. _Mississippi's American Indians._ Jackson: University Press of Mississippi.

Brain, Jeffrey P. 1988. _Tunica Archaeology._ Papers of the Peabody Museum of Archaeology and Ethnology 78. Cambridge: Peabody Museum Press.

Brown, Ian W. 1975. _Archaeological Investigations at the Historic Portland and St. Pierre Sites in the Lower Yazoo Basin, Mississippi 1974._ Master's thesis, Brown University.

_____. 1979. _Early 18th Century French-Indian Culture Contact in the Yazoo Bluffs Region of the Lower Mississippi Valley._ PhD diss., Brown University.

Cruzat, Heloise H., trans. 1925. "The Concession at Natchez. History of the Founding of the Colony and Its Destruction by the Natchez Indians." _Louisiana Historical Quarterly_ 8(3): 389–97.

de Charlevoix, Pierre-François-Xavier. 1900. _History and General Description of New France,_ vol. VI. Translated and edited, with notes, by John G. Shea. New York: Francis P. Harper Publisher.

_____. 1977. _Charlevoix's Louisiana, Selections from the History and the Journal._ Edited by Charles E. O'Neill. Baton Rouge: Louisiana State University Press.

de La Harpe, Jean-Baptiste B. 1971. _Historical Journal of the Settlement of the French in Louisiana,_ USL History Series 3. Virginia Koenig and Joan Cain (trans.), edited with annotations by Glenn R. Conrad. Lafayette: University of Southwestern Louisiana Press.

Dumont de Montigny, Jean-François-Benjamin. 2012. _The Memoir of Lieutenant Dumont, 1715–1747. A Sojourner in the French Atlantic._ Gordon M. Sayre (trans.), Gordon M. Sayre and Carla Zecher (eds.). Chapel Hill: University of North Carolina Press.

Harkin, Michael E. 2010. "Ethnohistory's Ethnohistory: Creating a Discipline from the Ground Up." _Social Science History_ 34(2): 113–28.

Karklins, Karlis. 1985. "Early Amsterdam Trade Beads." _Ornament_ 9(2): 36–41.

Karklins, Karlis, Laure Dussubieux, and Ron G. V. Hancock. 2015. " A 17th-Century Glass Bead Factory at Hammersmith Embankment, London, England." *BEADS: Journal of the Society of Bead Researchers* 27: 16–24.

Kunkel, Paul A. 1951. "The Indians of Louisiana, about 1700: Their Customs and Manner of Living." *Louisiana Historical Quarterly* XXXIV: 175–203.

La Page du Pratz, Antoine S. 1774. *The History of Louisiana, or of The Western Parts of Virginia and Carolina: Containing a Description of the Countries that lie on both Sides of the River Mississippi: With an Account of the Settlements, Inhabitants, Soil, Climate, and Products,* Translated from the French. New Orleans: Pelican Press, Inc.

Le Petit, Father Mathurin, S. J. 1950. *The Natchez Massacre.* Translated by Richard M. Hart. New Orleans: Poor Rich Press.

Lieb, Brad R. 2008. *The Natchez Indian Diaspora: Ethnohistoric Archaeology of the Eighteenth-Century Natchez Refuge among the Chickasaws.* PhD diss., University of Alabama.

Malischke, LisaMarie. 2015. *Heterogeneity of Early French and Native Forts, Settlements, and Villages: A Comparison to Fort St. Pierre (1719–1729) in French Colonial Louisiane.* PhD diss., University of Alabama.

Milne, George E. 2015. *Natchez Country. Indians, Colonists, and the Landscapes of Race in French Louisiana.* Athens: University of Georgia Press.

Phillips, Philip. 1970. *Archaeological Survey in the Lower Yazoo Basin, Mississippi, 1949–1955,* Papers of the Peabody Museum of Archaeology and Ethnology, Harvard University, 60. Cambridge: The Peabody Museum Press.

Rowland, Dunbar, and Albert G. Sanders, eds. and trans. 1927. *Mississippi Provincial Archives 1729–1740 French Dominion I. French-English-Indian Relations, Wars with the Natchez and Chickasaw Indians.* Jackson: Press of the Mississippi Department of Archives and History.

_____, eds. and trans. 1929. *Mississippi Provincial Archives 1701–1729 French Dominion II.* Jackson: Press of the Mississippi Department of Archives and History.

_____, eds. and trans. 1932. *Mississippi Provincial Archives 1704–1743 French Dominion III.* Jackson: Press of the Mississippi Department of Archives and History.

Swanton, John R. 1911. *Indian Tribes of the Lower Mississippi Valley and Adjacent Coast of the Gulf of Mexico,* Smithsonian Institution Bureau of American Ethnology Bulletin 43. Washington, DC: United States Printing Office.

_____. 1952. *The Indian Tribes of North America,* Smithsonian Institution Bureau of American Ethnology Bulletin 145. Washington, DC: Smithsonian Institution Press.

_____. 1971. *The Indian Tribes of North America,* Smithsonian Institution Bureau of American Ethnology Bulletin 145. Washington, DC: Smithsonian Institution Press.

Wright, William. 1977. Director's Field Notebooks for Fort Saint Pierre excavations. On file at the Mississippi Department of Archives and History, Jackson, Mississippi.

Chapter 4

A Clockwork Porridge

An Archaeological Analysis of Everyday Life in the
Early Mining Communities of Swedish Lapland in the
Seventeenth Century

Risto Nurmi

Introduction

The rise of mining enterprises in the northern part of Swedish Lapland
during the seventeenth century has been viewed as an iconic example
of Swedish colonial affairs in early modern Lapland (e.g., Nordin 2012,
2015; Naum 2017). The efforts and aims of the Swedish state—not to
mention the ways in which measures were executed—did indeed echo
colonial ideology and apparently also partly influenced the development
of a colonial atmosphere and a dichotomist view of the local, namely Sámi,
population in the north. However, the northern Sámi population played
a significant role in the emergence, development, and success of the early
mining affairs in the north, even though relations between the Sámi and
the mining companies have been considered problematic or even hostile
(e.g., Awebro 1983, 183–230; Lundmark 2008, 44–47; Ojala 2018, 214–16).

In this chapter, I aim to shed some light on the everyday life of the
early mining communities, with special reference to the role of the Sámi
population and the development of social relations between the people
and groups involved in the early mining communities. The approach is
based on an analysis of the archaeological material excavated at the first
two state-founded mining communities of Silbojokk and Kvikkjokk in
present-day western Norrbotten, Sweden. The excavated data from both
sites comprises an extensive and versatile collection of artifacts used in

everyday life and daily mining and refining works. For this discussion, I have chosen to concentrate on three different artifact groups in more detail: items related to food culture, items bearing ethnic markers, and items connected with industrialization. Through these case studies, I hope to be able to highlight the development of social relations between people in the context of everyday life in the mining community and to provide a more individual view than that offered by general narratives.

Early Mining in the North

Mining in Sweden has a long and successful history from the medieval period to the present. Sweden's plentiful mineral deposits and vast forest resources of fuel provided a beneficial environment for the development of the industry. The earliest historical documents that indicate systematic commercial mining activity in central Sweden date to the thirteenth century (Lindroth 1955, 24), and it is likely that these deposits of Stora Kopparberg were used already by the ninth century (Rydberg 1979, 28).

The medieval period was an era of growth, and by the seventeenth century, Sweden had become one of Europe's leading producers and exporters of iron and especially copper. The mines in Falun alone produced the majority of the copper on the European market at that time (Heckscher 1963, 84–88; Nordin 2015, 264). However, since the early sixteenth century, mercantile economic doctrines had developed within the state economy and eventually characterized the economic ideology of seventeenth-century Sweden (Heckscher 1963, 112–14). The seventeenth-century economic ideology and the political influence of Sweden in Europe raised the status of metals in the state economy and the social value of silver increased (Götlind 2005, 261–62; Nordin 2015, 252; cf. also Nordin 2012, 143–44, 159).

The expansion of the industry required both the development of production methods and an increasing amount of skilled labor. The flourishing mining industry had attracted a considerable number of immigrants to Sweden already since the medieval period. The fourteenth-century development of extraction methods took place largely thanks to German mining specialists who immigrated to Sweden. During the seventeenth century, the immigration of miners increased when Dutch investors became active on Swedish markets. Thanks to Dutch influence, many German, Dutch, French, and Wallonian miners moved to Sweden to work in the existing and newly founded mines and foundries, such as the new mining communities in Lapland (Lindroth 1955, 24, 26–28; Heckscher 1963, 101–9; Hildebrand 1992, 98–100; Boudin 2002; Nergård 2002; Nordin 2012, 159).

By the early seventeenth century, the State of Sweden began to place greater emphasis on investigating possibly exploitable resources in its northern realms. The surveying of mineral deposits was one important part of this process, and cartographers and officials were instructed to spread the word and persuade local people to inform them of the locations of potential mineral deposits (Awebro 1993, 361–63). This strategy eventually paid off in 1634, when the galena samples found on the slopes of Mount Nasafjäll (Figure 4.1) by Peder Olofsson, a Sámi

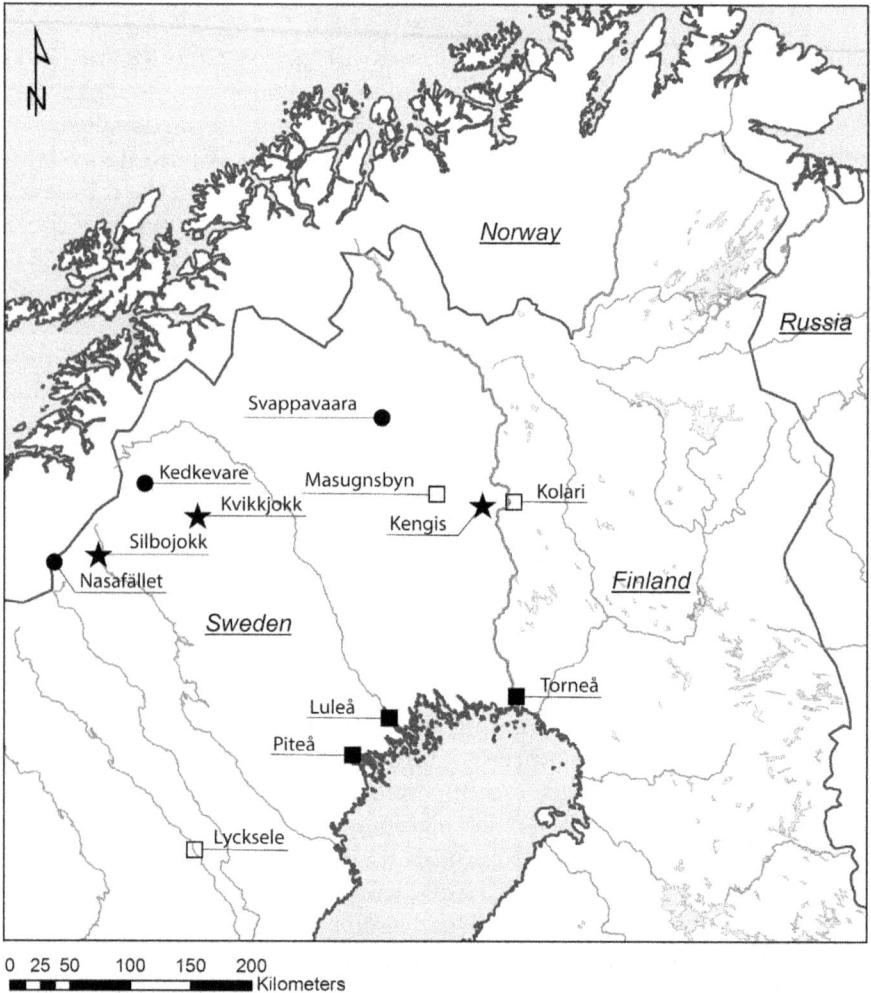

Figure 4.1. Locations of the sites mentioned in the text. (Drawing by Tiina Äikäs and Risto Nurmi.)

man, proved promisingly rich in silver (Bromé 1923, 62–63). Pressures to increase domestic silver production were high, as were expectations for the wealth that the endless northern domains could provide. The Crown therefore did not delay in launching mining enterprises concentrating on the newly found resources.

The first mining community in Swedish Lapland was founded in 1635 in Silbojokk on the western shore of Lake Sädvajaure (Figure 4.1) to refine the ore quarried from the slopes of Mount Nasafjäll (Bromé 1923, 61–64). The environmental conditions were harsh from the Swedish, or European, point of view. The Nasafjäll deposits were located at high altitudes near the peak of the mountain, above the tree line. Neither infrastructure nor permanent settlements were available within a radius of hundreds of kilometers, excluding the Norwegian coast on the other side of the mountains. Everything had to be imported and constructed. However, the region was not uninhabited. The nomadic mountain Sámi people had lived in the high inland regions since prehistory. The mountain Sámi were reindeer herders, hunters, and fishers, who were well adapted to life in the northern environment (e.g., Fjellström 1986; Kent 2014). For them, the conditions were normal, and their knowledge and "infrastructure" had an important role in the founding of the Silbojokk enterprise. Throughout the seventeenth century, the logistics of the mining enterprises in Lapland were highly dependent on Sámi reindeer (cf. Bromé 1923; Awebro 1983, 1989).

The foundry and mining community, including housing and storage facilities, as well as a church and churchyard, were built at the mouth of the small Silbojokk river forty kilometers away from the mines. Here, the rapids provided the water power needed in the refining process and Lake Sädvajaure connected the site with the logistically best available water route to the town of Piteå on the coast of the Bay of Bothnia, where the final refinery was located (Roslund 1992, 256).

The high expectations for the production figures of the Piteå silver works soon proved to be exaggerated. The original deposits were rich, but the size of the deposit turned out to be smaller than predicted, which meant that production rates soon decreased. The Crown's interest waned along with the declining production figures, and in 1649, the works were turned into private hands. A company consisting of Piteå merchants continued production until the works were destroyed by Danish-Norwegian troops in August 1659 (Bromé 1923, 243; Roslund 1989a, 72). The Piteå silver works (the name used for the ensemble of mine, foundry, and refinery) was founded to obtain silver, although the main product in terms of quantity proved to be lead (Roslund 1989a, 72). The overall production figures of the Silbojokk foundry ended up being approximately 880 kg of silver and 250 tons of lead as a side product. Not exactly "the West Indies of the Swedes" that councilor Carl Bonde envisioned in his rhetoric in 1635 (Bromé 1923, 64).

After losing Silbojokk and Nasafjäll, the Swedish Crown turned its attention toward the recently found new silver deposits in Kedkevare, upstream along the Lule river waterway some one hundred kilometers northeast of Silbojokk (Figure 4.1). The silver deposits were discovered in 1659, and the Crown's Board of Mines (*Bergskollegium*) granted a license to establish a mine and foundry in Kvikkjokk at the northernmost end of Lake Saggat, where the Kamajokk river enters the lake (Figure 4.1). The construction of the mining community began in March 1660 (Awebro 1983, 30–43). The Luleå silver works remained active until 1702, when it was closed for the first time. Mining and refining activities were continued sporadically in Kvikkjokk during the eighteenth and nineteenth centuries by private enterprises, but success remained modest (Awebro 1983, 156–82).

As state-organized mining enterprises were established on the headwaters of the Pite and Lule rivers, the privately funded mining enterprise of the Kengis works was launched in the northern reaches of the Torne river in the present-day region of Pajala (Figure 4.1). The enterprise was originally founded in 1644 by a group of Tornio merchants, and already in 1646, it was turned into the hands of the German entrepreneur Arend Grape. In 1652, he lost the company to his Dutch financiers Abraham and Jakob Momma, who were later ennobled with the name Renstierna (Awebro 1993, 365–371; Fagerwall, Salomonsson-Juuso, and Tervaniemi 2006, 18–23; cf. also Nordin and Ojala 2017). The Kengis works eventually became the most successful of the seventeenth-century mining enterprises in Swedish Lapland. Its main product was iron, but it also exploited the copper deposits of the Svappavaara mine. The Kengis works continued to function with varying success up to the early twentieth century, although its glory days remained in the late seventeenth century (Awebro 1993; Fagerwall et al. 2006).

Archaeologies of Early Northern Mining

The three early northern mining sites described here have been subject to increasing archaeological interest during the past few years. Since 2014, the history of northern mining has been studied by research groups at the University of Uppsala in Sweden (in the project "Mining Sápmi: Colonial Histories, Sámi Archaeology, and the Exploitation of Natural Resources in Northern Sweden," funded by Jernkontoret) and the University of

Oulu in Finland (in the project "Understanding the Cultural Impacts and Issues of Lapland Mining: A Long-Term Perspective on Sustainable Mining Policies in the North," funded by the Academy of Finland) (e.g., Ojala and Nordin 2015). These projects have produced quite a few research papers that have highlighted the cultural impact of the emerging mining industry on the sociocultural sphere of early modern Lapland (e.g., Naum 2016, 2017; Nordin 2015; Nordin and Ojala 2017; Ojala 2017, 2018; Ojala and Nordin 2015; Nurmi n.d.). Moreover, at least since the early 2000s, coastal erosion of the Sädvajaure reservoir has destroyed the remains of the Silbojokk foundry cemetery and unearthed the remains of the deceased. For this reason, Norrbottens Museum has conducted rescue excavations at the cemetery site during several field seasons from 2003 up to the present (cf. Lindgren 2015). In addition, Norrbottens Museum has also carried out small test and rescue excavations at several sites related to the Kengis works in the area of the Torne river (e.g., Lindgren 2014).

However, the archaeological history of the mining communities of Silbojokk and Kvikkjokk date farther back. The archaeological excavations in the residential area of the Kvikkjokk foundry were carried out in 1970 and 1971 as a part of the *Luleå Silverväg* project by the National Heritage Board. A total area of 750 square meters was excavated, consisting of several smaller squares and test trenches that concentrated on the residential area on the western bank of the Kamajokk river. The actual foundry site on the eastern bank of the rapids slightly upstream of the residential area was not studied. The excavation trenches were targeted on the locations of buildings that were marked on the detailed map of the foundry site from 1661 (Figure 4.2). The excavations proved the accuracy of the map. In addition, the excavations also revealed a burial ground on the southern side of the site (the cemetery had not been marked on the original map). The best-studied buildings were the foundry smithy (A1), a residential building (A3), another residential building (A5) with attached storage facilities (A6), and a storage building with a cellar (A4). These four buildings were quite comprehensively excavated, whereas others were only documented on the basis of the test trenches or pits. The stables and animal shelters on the riverbank were not excavated (Wallerström 1976).

The buildings and constructions on the site were arranged loosely in the form of a square. The stables and food storage buildings were located on the riverside to the east, and food preparation was concentrated in the southwestern corner of the complex. The two residential buildings were on the western side and the cellar and storage on the northern side. The distances between the buildings were long, up to several dozen meters. The buildings were constructed of logs on low stone footings without mortar. The fireplaces were built on slate foundations. The residential buildings were suitable for winter habitation. They had underfloor soil rafts and rather massive fireplaces. They had also been fitted with glass windows (Wallerström 1976).

The artifact assemblage from the Kvikkjokk excavations consisted of almost 2,500 finds (Table 4.1), excluding slag, bone fragments, and some window glass, which increase the quantity to three thousand finds or more. The finds date largely to the active period of the Kvikkjokk foundry, but as the site has been inhabited more or less intensively since the foundry was established, the assemblage also includes younger material. Most of the finds were concentrated in the remains of the largest building (A3). Over forty percent of the documented finds came from this building. The finds from the remains of the smithy (A1) form a significant share of the assemblage as well. The number of finds is actually equal to that from building A3, but ninety percent of the finds from the smithy are pieces of iron residue and iron artifacts.

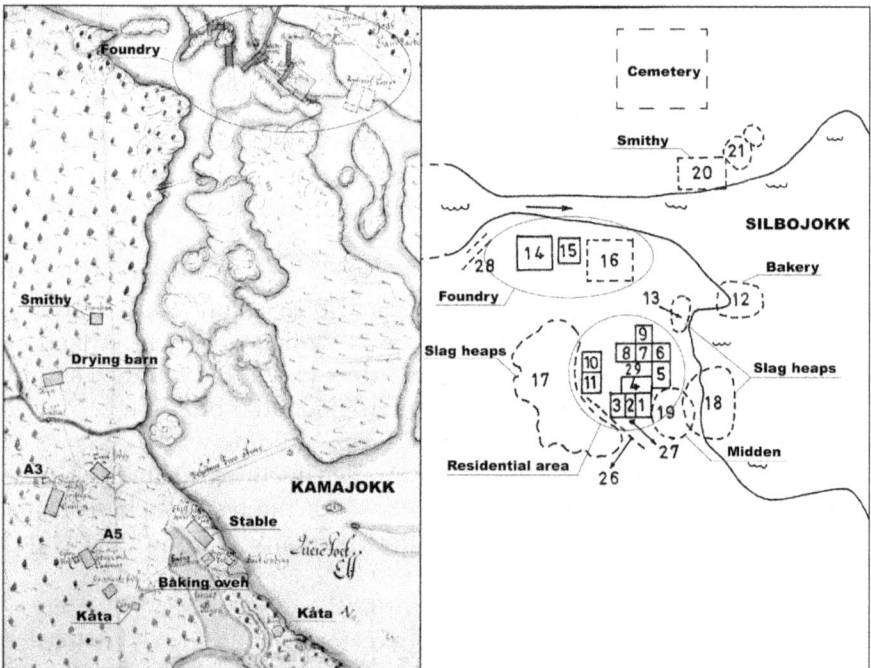

Figure 4.2. Left: a map of the Kvikkjokk foundry site from 1661. (Courtesy of Riksarkivet, Stockholm, Sweden.) Right: an outline map of the excavated remains at the Silbojokk foundry site. (Original drawing by Erik Nordberg, amendments by Risto Nurmi.)

Table 4.1. The list of archaeological finds from the Silbojokk and Kvikkjokk sites.*

Item type	Quantity of items/sherds	
	Silbojokk	Kvikkjokk
Ceramic Vessels		
red earthenware	529	401
faiences	83	8
stoneware	47	15
creamware/transfer printed wares	37	
Glass Vessels		
bottles	8	15
beakers	67	6
jar	8	
Clay Pipes	190	98
Household Items		
knife	37	14
fork	1	
antler spoon	14	1
brass spoon	1	1
brass dish	1	1
kettle	1	
cauldron	7	6
wooden vessel	1	
wooden lid	3	
barrel	6	
barrel tap	3	3
cloth seal	1	
scissors	5	1
knitting needle	1	
slikenstone	1	
millstone	2	
strike-a-lite flint	14	
strike-a-lite	2	1
Daily Economics		
horse shoe/shoe nails	6	2
lead pullet	2	1
gunflint	1	
key	7	2
fish hook	4	
scythe	1	1
clock index	2	
weight stone	5	
reindeer harness	4	
net needle	3	
net float	127	

Item type	Quantity of items/sherds	
	Silbojokk	Kvikkjokk
bone prick	1	
wood prick	5	
copper ring	3	
copper rivet	1	
wooden wheel	1	
rope	1	
chain	1	
Personal Items		
silver ring		1
brass ring	2	
copper pendant	2	
shoe	11	2
button	1	3
shirt clasp	1	4
belt buckle	2	
thimble	2	
brass chain		1
tin fitting		8
brass fitting	9	4
bone fitting	2	
glass pearl	1	2
Jew's harp		1
mirror		4
coin	9	7
rock crystal	12	9
purse frame	3	
drum hammer	1	
book clasp	1	
tweezers	1	
marble	1	
cloth	55	
string	8	
Tools		
anvil	4	1
hammer	11	11
sledge	1	3
axe	1	
adze	1	
shovel	5	1
hoe	3	
drill	1	1
wedge	5	
stamp	1	
scraper	2	

Item type	Quantity of items/sherds	
	Silbojokk	Kvikkjokk
grindstone	6	5
hammerstone	1	
pullet mold	1	
Structural Elements		
window glass	67	275*
window lead	2	
candlestick	5	1
stove tile	10	
door hook	11	6
lock	5	6
iron nail	332	293
clamp	8	6
brick	1	6
wall hook	8	
handle	3	
door knocker	1	
knob	1	
hinge	19	
Unidentified Artifacts		
wooden artifact	2	7
iron artifact	134	119
bone artifact	6	
lead artifact	2	
copper artifact	1	
stone artifact	2	
Raw Materials		
iron	8	969**
copper	9	1
brass	2	
lead	5	10
antler	1	
bone	13	
flint	11	
leather	7	
Total	2017	2428

Sources: The Silbojokk Data is collected from Swedish National Heritage Board database (RAÄ SMH 34358) and the Kvikkjokk data has been analyzed in Norrbotten's Museum archives by the author.

Notes

* This figure is not complete. The quantity of sherds was not available in all window glass units.

** Almost all pieces are from the remains of the smithy.

Rescue excavations were carried out at the Silbojokk foundry site in 1983, when plans to raise the water level of the reservoir exposed the Silbojokk foundry site to the danger of submersion. Eventually altogether four thousand square meters of the site were excavated during 1983 and 1984. The excavations concentrated on three separate research areas, of which Area I on the southern bank of the Silbojokk river included most of the building remains and was the main focus of research (Roslund 1989a). Area I included a tightly constructed building complex surrounded by slag heaps. The complex consisted of residential buildings, stables, storage facilities, and an older foundry, all set in the form of a tight rectangle and forming a closed courtyard inside. The preserved building remains on the site were quite comprehensively excavated (Roslund 1989a, 76–81). However, the assemblage lacks material from the higher social rank of the foundry. The house of the foundry master and other higher-ranking people at the site were submerged in the Sädvajaure reservoir already in 1953 when the lake level was elevated for the first time (Roslund 1992, 265). The newer foundry buildings (Area II) and bakery had been built farther away from the complex, the foundry on the riverbank over the rapids and the bakery closer to the lakeside (Figure 4.2). The smithy, church, and graveyard were located on the riverbank opposite the foundry buildings (Roslund 1989a, 76–81; Lindgren 2015).

The buildings were constructed of logs over low stone foundations. The building technique represents local traditions. The foundations were laid from local slate, which is naturally available at the site in plentiful quantities, and no mortar was used (Roslund 1989a). The building arrangement of the residential area formed a very tightly closed yard, almost like a fortress. Such an arrangement resembles the typical features of pioneering European colonial settlements, for example, in North America and South Africa (cf. Nurmi n.d.). The buildings were constructed of a series of rectangular dovetail-jointed log frames connected side by side, most likely under the same roof. The stables and storages were located on the southern side and the residential buildings on the eastern side. The northern side included the first foundry that had later been modified for residential use. On the western side, there was a cellar and a smokehouse. One residential building had been built inside the yard against the stables. The rest of the inner yard had been covered with slate. The fireplaces had been laid over a slate masonry base and built of slate and bricks. Buildings were fitted with glass windows, and some of the residential buildings had underfloor soil rafts insulating them for winter use. Floors were mostly wooden and, in some cases, laid with slate (Roslund 1989a).

The artifact assemblage from the Silbojokk excavations consisted of slightly more than two thousand finds (Table 4.1), excluding the slag, ore, and bone remains, which would increase the total quantity to over three thousand items. The quantity of items related to actual production was rather small, probably because all production facilities were transported to Kvikkjokk after production in Silbojokk ended. Overall, the assemblage resembles many find-compositions excavated at urban contexts of the same period. Most of the items are related to everyday household activities. Knives and spoons are common, as well as ceramics. Bullet molds and remains of fishing nets indicate that the community also hunted and fished for their food and was not dependent only on imported food items. Buttons, scissors, needles, and other small items, as well as evidence of handicrafts, indicate that people spent their spare time on the same activities as in towns and at rural estates (Roslund 1989a, 119–24).

Pots, Bowls, and Spoons—Notes on the Food Culture of the Foundry

Building and maintaining a successful mining community in a remote location far away from the existing logistics network and infrastructure required careful planning of the maintenance services for the site. The community needed sufficient amounts of daily foodstuffs, as well as facilities and staff to prepare daily meals. Both the Silbojokk and Kvikkjokk foundries were chiefly seasonally occupied sites, and most of the activity took place in the summer and autumn months. Only a small group of people lived on the sites year-round (Bromé 1923; Awebro 1983, 1986). Since these mining communities were seasonal work sites, their demographics differed from permanent residential contexts, such as towns and villages, of the same period. At Silbojokk and Kvikkjokk, workers did not move to the site with their families or build their own family homes in nearby areas. The Kengis works took a different approach. Kengis made long-term contracts with its workers, who often moved to the region with their families and occupied the site year-round (Lindmark 1963). This may have had an influence on the fact that many of the mining-related sites connected to the Kengis works (e.g., Kolari, Svappavaara, and Masungsbyn) have grown into active settlements and still exist today, even though the actual mining activity ceased centuries ago.

To provide meals for the workers, the works had their own hired cooks, and food supplies were acquired from multiple sources. Sabine Sten's (1989) osteological study of the Silbojokk data provides a good overview of the variety of meat supplies used in the early mining community. The majority (over eighty percent of the total quantity and seventy percent of the minimum number of individuals) of the domesticated species consisted of reindeer (*Rangifer tarandus*). In addition to this, the assemblage also included bovine (*Bos taurus*), sheep/goat (*Ovis aries/Capra hircus*), and pig (*Sus scrofa domesticus*) remains. According to Sten (1989, 172), the butchering technique used for the Silbojokk reindeer is exclusively Sámi. The traditional Sámi butchering technique involves only the use of a knife, and no bones are broken during the butchery, but joints are disarticulated (Itkonen 1948, 256; Sten 1989, 172). The hack marks caused by the use of axes or heavier blades are virtually absent in the Silbojokk bone assemblage (Sten 1989, 172). This means that not only was the reindeer meat obtained from the Sámi, but also that Sámi individuals were responsible for preparing the meat. In fact, both of the named cooks at the Silbojokk foundry were Sámi women. In an index of foundry workers from 1636, their names were marked with the modifier *lappkona* (Sámi woman) (Bromé 1923, 71). The ratio of excavated reindeer bone material (Sten 1989, 173) also strongly indicates that slaughtering was carried out on site. The other meat products were most likely imported to the site in a semi-finished or preserved state (cf. Sten 1989, 174). According to the information preserved, the foundry had no animal shelters except for the stables. Thus, very little animal husbandry probably took place on site (Sten 1989, 173).

Foodstuffs found at the Silbojokk foundry also consist of significant amounts of game animals, particularly birds, as well as fish. It is likely that part of this material was acquired by purchasing, as the fishbone assemblage includes cod, which is chiefly a North Sea species. The large quantity of willow grouse/willow ptarmigan (*Lagopus sp.*) indicates that these species were most likely systematically purchased from hunters in nearby areas. However, the archaeological assemblages at both sites clearly show that the communities were also highly self-sufficient in acquiring game and fish. Both assemblages include rifle bullets and fishing gear, such as parts of fishing nets, net needles, and hooks (Roslund 1989a, 121; Wallerström 1976; Table 4.1).

The built environment supports the idea that the communities were self-sufficient. The Silbojokk foundry site includes a cellar, smokehouse, and bakery/brewery. The Kvikkjokk complex includes a large stable and food storage building on the shore, as well as more storage facilities and an external baking oven closer to the residential buildings. In addition, the Kvikkjokk community had adopted cultivation. The building arrangement contains a drying barn (Figure 4.2), and the artifact assemblage includes pieces of a sickle or scythe and a millstone (Wallerström 1976; Table 4.1). The mining communities clearly aimed to create familiar surroundings for newcomers and provide them with daily necessities in the strange and remote environment. This may have been a part of the ideology aiming to modernize the wild, along with the construction of schools and churches (cf. the section "Elements of Industrial Society" in this chapter).

More accurate contextual data for the Silbojokk finds is unfortunately not available in the preserved records (Ling and Annuswer 1999). Thus, the contextual distribution of ceramic material from Silbojokk cannot be analyzed here. However, based on the Kvikkjokk data, the ceramic material appears to be highly concentrated in one particular building, which is named A3 in the excavation report (Figure 4.2). This is the largest building on the site, measuring 15 x 6.5 meters and consisting of two log frames and a corridor built between them (Wallerström 1976, 5). The remains of this building clearly yielded the highest concentration of finds on the site in general. The building has been interpreted as the most important building, or the administrative center of the site (Nordin 2012, 152), but based on the archaeological assemblage and particularly on the high concentration of ordinary dining vessels, I would lean toward interpreting it as the workers' quarters. At least this building appears to be the place in which most meals at the works seem to have been eaten.

The remains of commercially produced ceramic vessels form one of the major groups of archaeological finds at both sites. From this perspective, the assemblage follows the general pattern of archaeological assemblages at residential sites of the same period in Scandinavia (cf. Elfwendahl 1999; Rosén 2004; Rydström 2006; Nurmi 2011). Glazed red earthenware dominates the ceramic assemblage of both sites. Other ceramic materials are represented by only a modest amount of faience and stoneware at both sites. For example, all the stoneware pieces found at the Kvikkjokk site are from a single Bellarmine jug. The identified red earthenware vessel types in the assemblages consist mostly of dishes, bowls, and tripod pipkins. The presence of pipkins especially is very common in the Kvikkjokk assemblage. Roslund (1989b, 189) has also pointed out the significantly high frequency of pipkins at Silbojokk. This, together with the frequency of bowls, indicates the popularity of liquid-type meals, that is, soups and porridges. Soups and porridges were common meal types particularly among the poor and common people in western Fennoscandia (e.g., Talve 1990, 154; Sillanpää 2000, 25–26). However, the popularity of soups also fits well with the generally strong Sámi influence in the catering of the works. The cooks working at Silbojokk were Sámi, and meat and fish soups were the basis of traditional Sámi cuisine (Itkonen 1948, 253–95; Fjellström 1986, 261–89).

The popularity of pipkins is not the most conspicuous feature in the ceramic assemblages, however. The Kvikkjokk assemblage includes several vessels that could be described as "miniature vessels." These vessels, most of which are pipkins, are usually technically identical to normal-sized equivalents but strikingly small in size (Figure 4.3). For example, the rim diameter of a miniature pipkin could be less than ten centimeters. The most prominent example in the Kvikkjokk assemblage is a completely preserved tiny bowl or dish, which is only fifty-one millimeters in diameter and twenty-one millimeters high. Unlike the common bowls and dishes, this item has not been glazed, however. Miniature vessels are not totally unknown in northern ceramic assemblages, but they are generally rare. The only other assemblage from the Bothnian Bay region that also includes several examples of miniature vessels comes from the Pikisaari site in Oulu, Finland. This site dates to a slightly younger period from the mid-eighteenth century to the early nineteenth century (Herva 2006; Hyttinen et al. 2016; Huhtelin 2017).

Interpreting the function of these tiny little vessels is a much more complicated task than observing their presence in these contexts. The tiny size easily suggests children and their toys, but this interpretation has faced criticism (cf. Sipiläinen 2003, 296–97). The handicraft production and sale of toys had been common in Europe already since the medieval period, and ceramic workshops also made earthenware toys as a side

Figure 4.3. A small three-legged pipkin found at Kvikkjokk. (Photograph by Risto Nurmi.)

product (Sipiläinen 2003, 299). Handicraft toy manufacturing became more common by the eighteenth century, but, in practice, such toys remained the privilege of children of the higher social classes, and commercial toys began to spread to the wider social sphere in the north only in the 1920s (Lehto 1996, 15–24; 2004, 376). However, the contexts of the miniature vessels found at Pikisaari and Kvikkjokk cannot be considered as places where upper-class children would have lived. Although the Pikisaari community included families with children, almost all of them were poor working-class people (Hyttinen and Kallio-Seppä, in press), and there were no children at all at Kvikkjokk.

The function of these small vessels remains unclear. The medieval miniature vessels that have been found in Turku, for example, were extremely small, and out of the vessels found at Kvikkjokk, only the completely preserved bowl represents the same size category. The pipkins are slightly larger, up to ten centimeters in diameter, so they could have had some specific use other than as toys. In fact, even the abovementioned tiny bowl has a dark tint absorbed into the unglazed inner surface, indicating a particular kind of use. The question of why these small earthenware vessels appear to have been used particularly in the industrial communities still remains unanswered.

Another strong indication of the popularity of soups and porridges is the quantity of spoons in the archaeological assemblages of the sites. The Kvikkjokk finds include only two spoons—one made of brass and one of antler. The Silbojokk assemblage includes one brass spoon and fourteen antler spoons. The number of antler spoons is among the highest known at a single site in northern Scandinavia. Only a couple of sites in northern Norway have yielded a few more spoons per site (Skandfer 1996, 33–35). The antler spoon is strongly connected to Sámi material culture, but the item and its traditional decoration style originate from late Iron Age Scandinavian culture and only became popular among the Sámi people by the seventeenth century (cf. Nurmi 2009). Moreover, Roslund (1989a, 125–26) also notes that some of the spoons from Silbojokk feature a style and decoration that is not typical of traditional Sámi style.

Transcultural Community

The archaeological assemblages of Silbojokk and Kvikkjokk correspond quite well with urban archaeological assemblages of the same period, excluding the significant number of bone and antler artifacts found at Silbojokk (Roslund 1989a, 119, 127). Especially decorated bone and antler artifacts found in Lapland have been strongly connected with

Sámi material culture (e.g., Fjellström 1972; 1986, 449–75; Immonen 2006; Kent 2014, 164–65). According to historical documents, Sámi influence has been strong at both mining enterprises, and at Silbojokk there is clear evidence for the presence of Sámi people in the community, as discussed above. However, despite the obviously close everyday interaction, interpretations of the material culture at the sites tend to be much more segregating. The imported commercial items have been connected to Swedish and German occupants and the decorated antler artifacts and brass or copper pendants linked to the Sámi people (e.g., Nordin 2012, 152–56; Roslund 1992, 263–65).

Although the presence of Swedish and German as well as Sámi people at the foundry sites is indisputable, the Silbojokk region has not revealed any Sámi settlements of this period in spite of archaeological surveys conducted in the area (e.g., Awebro 1989, 39). The Kvikkjokk map (Figure 4.2) does include two buildings titled *kåta*. The word *kåta* refers to the traditional Sámi hut, but it also means a lightweight kitchen building in the Finnish rural building tradition (spelled *kota* in Finnish) (Vuorela 1975). Thus, the location of the other *kåta* right next to the large external baking oven could, in fact, indicate a kitchen building rather than a Sámi dwelling. On the other hand, the other *kåta* farther away from the residential area on the riverbank could be an actual Sámi dwelling (Figure 4.2). Here, the artifact and structural data between the sites are inconsistent with each other. The Silbojokk assemblage reveals a considerable amount of Sámi influence, but there is no evidence of Sámi dwellings nearby, whereas the Kvikkjokk assemblage lacks any sign of Sámi influence regardless of the presence of *kåta* buildings on the site.

Jonas M. Nordin (2012, 156) has noted that "Saami were working or staying there in the seventeenth century to a much greater extent than is suggested by the written record." Under closer scrutiny, on the basis of the archaeological assemblage and interpretations of historical documents related to Silbojokk (e.g., Bromé 1923; Awebro 1989), it appears that in the early phase of the mining enterprises in Swedish Lapland, all the people working on the sites used the same residential facilities regardless of their origin and thus formed a very close community. However, as time went by, social conflicts emerged and escalated in such a manner that when the mining community moved to Kvikkjokk, the ethnic dichotomy was present also in the residential arrangements and the Sámi people involved with the foundry lived away from the foundry site (for a more detailed discussion, see Nurmi n.d.).

Silbojokk was apparently a very close and partly isolated multiethnic community that formed a fertile ground for transcultural development. People who spent their everyday lives together learned a lot from each other more or less consciously. Such learning has been particularly important for the miners who moved to the site from farther south and hence were not familiar with the local environment and conditions. The best and most convenient way to adapt to the local setting would have been by learning from the locals, who had knowledge and experience and shared the same daily activities and premises. The bone and antler artifacts from Silbojokk indicate that such development took place. Roslund (1989a, 125–27) notes on a few occasions that the bone and antler artifacts from Silbojokk bear atypical elements compared to traditional Sámi handicrafts. The features noted appear either as the amateurish quality of the work, the mixing of different regional styles, or the use of decoration motifs very atypical of Sámi style. In contrast, the material includes examples of high-quality Sámi handicrafts as well. The even distribution of items among the foundry structures and the varying quality of the work—particularly the atypical decorative features—strongly indicate the existence of close and active everyday contacts between the Sámi and Swedish and German workers. The amateurish and atypical items could have been made by the Swedish and German workers, or the atypical decoration on these artifacts could have been adopted by the Sámi from the southern newcomers. In either case, the features bear elements of cultural adoption and reinterpretation.

In close interaction, cultural adaptation works in both directions. Since the beginning of European interest toward the natural and cultural conditions of the north in the seventeenth century, European imaginations have been fascinated by exoticism, aboriginality, and close-to-nature imagery and constructed the fixed stereotypical habitus of the non-European Sámi people, who were seen as primitive but romantic (for a more detailed discussion, cf. Naum 2016). However, Sámi society has also developed, and through contacts with outsiders, it has adopted material and cultural elements as a part of its life and worldview. The archaeological data of the Lycksele *timmerkåtan* provides a good illustrative example of the presence of "European" material culture in an everyday Sámi context. Lycksele Gammplatsen was an old Lapp marketplace on an island in the Ume river some 120 kilometers inland from the town of Umeå. In 1606, Gammplatsen became an official marketplace of the Crown, and during the seventeenth century, it grew into one of the most important marketplaces in Västerbotten. The Lycksele marketplace consisted of three residential blocks—*borgstad*, *finnstad*, and *lappstad*. *Borgstad* was for merchants from the town of Umeå, *finnstad* for peasant families, and *lappstad* for Sámi people (Rydström 2006, 2–5). The remains of the *timmerkåtan* were excavated in 1998–99. The building was a rectangular log cabin located in the *lappstad* area of the Lycksele marketplace. The building itself represented the typical permanent building type of the forest Sámi people and had a square log frame with an open hearth in the middle (Fjellström 1986, 230–41). The artifact assemblage from the building dates to the middle and latter half of the seventeenth century (Rydström 1999, 8).

The artifact assemblage of the *timmerkåtan* includes bronze sheet pieces and small metal fittings that represent the traditional Sámi material culture. Bone material was not documented during the excavations, but a few pieces of bone artifacts decorated in the south Sámi style were recorded as having been present in the assemblage (Rydström 1999, 2006). However, the rest of the material culture of the *timmerkåtan* consists of typical commercial everyday items of the period. Based on the assemblage, the Sámi population in the Lycksele region had easily adopted the use of clay tobacco pipes, glassware, and ceramic kitchen and table ware. In fact, the *timmerkåtan* assemblage includes items that would have been atypical finds even in urban or rural residential contexts of the same period. The assemblage includes pieces of glass tubes (e.g., VBM 4783:1) whose function has not been interpreted, as well as a section of a red earthenware artifact of unknown function (VBM 27092:120; Figure 4.4).

Figure 4.4. A piece of an unidentified, glazed, and bolus-decorated red earthenware item. The internal parts of the item have been carefully glazed as well. (Photograph by Susanne Sundström, courtesy of Västerbottens Museum, Umeå, Sweden.)

The item is a piece of a round earthenware tube that has a funnel-shaped piece attached. The funnel has a passage to the inside of the tube. The form of the piece suggests a candelabrum. The item is glazed and has underglaze *bolus* decoration. However, the item has also been glazed on the inside, which indicates that the interior part of the tube had to be resistant to liquids for some functional reason. Candelabrum or not, the presence of such a decorated and rare item in a Sámi dwelling gives us a very good perspective on the assimilation level of "European" material culture among the Sámi population in the Västerbotten region during the latter half of the seventeenth century.

Elements of Industrial Society

Naturally, a significant part of the archaeological finds from both sites consists of artifacts related to the mines and metal processing. Slag heaps surrounded the remains, and various smithy tools, often heavily worn and at the end of their use life, were common finds. Most of the tools and machinery at Silbojokk were transported to Kvikkjokk in 1661 (Bromé 1923, 253–68; Awebro 1989, 28). Thus, it is natural that less work-related items were found at Silbojokk. The tools of the miners, smelters, and smiths, as well as large machinery such as bellows, hammers, and furnaces, were not the only artifacts representing early industrialism at these early mining sites. The state also had another, more high-minded sociocultural agenda that it aimed to push in the context of the mining projects in the north. In the spirit of the times, the Kingdom of Sweden viewed the founding of mining sites as an opportunity to modernize and develop the northern region, ultimately aiming to integrate it more deeply within Swedish society. Thus, in the context of the mining projects, the state invested considerably in the improvement of local conditions and the local population. This, of course, was considered purely as one-way development from "primitiveness toward civilization" (cf. Naum 2017).

Most of the activity in the sphere of sociocultural "improvement" took the form of founding schools and churches at remote locations in Lapland. In a wider perspective, the "Swedification" of the north aimed to introduce the modern European worldview and its economic basis to the local population along with education and preaching. In an industrial environment, one element of this worldview was the industrial concept of time. To function efficiently, a complex system of different processes in different locations involving a considerable amount of people needs to be synchronized. The problem of synchronizing the activities and actions carried out in the mining enterprises in the north was a sore spot throughout the seventeenth century. This was mainly due to drastic differences in worldview, subsistence economy, and values between the European society and the northern peoples (cf. Symonds et al. 2015). Most of the preserved historical documents on this subject concern complaints and problems related to logistics and give the impression of lazy, unpredictable, and unreliable Sámi people who do not keep to agreements (e.g., Bromé 1923; Awebro 1983). However, the attitude of the foundry officers (at least some of them) toward the local people appears to have been contemptuous and highly colonialist. More importantly, it showed a lack of understanding the ideas and perspectives of the other.

The objective to incorporate the western concept of time into the local population and to control the operations expressed itself concretely in the form of devices that measure time—clocks and hourglasses. A clock is mentioned in the inventories of all three seventeenth-century mining sites (Naum 2017, 797. During the seventeenth century, clocks were not commonly used in northern Scandinavia even in an urban environment. They began to become common only by the end of the eighteenth century. The bells of churches and town halls had indicated the starting times of different events since the medieval period, but clocks showing the time were not introduced until the late eighteenth century. Privately owned clocks also appear more commonly in probate inventories from this period on (Symonds et al. 2015, 77).

Thus, the mining sites introduced clocks in the north about a hundred years before they were more commonly taken into use in northern society. The Silbojokk artifact assemblage includes pieces of an hourglass (Awebro 1989, 41). No traces of a clock were preserved there, but because all the usable materials and tools were moved to Kvikkjokk, it is likely that the clock mentioned in both the Silbojokk and Kvikkjokk inventories is, in fact, one and the same object. It is still not known what kind of clocks these early timepieces used in Lapland were. The map of the Kengis works drawn by Joris Denis in 1660 mentions a sundial in the middle of the yard of the Momma-Renstrierna manor (Figure 4.5). A star-shaped limestone sundial dating to the sixteenth or seventeenth century has also been found in the town of Tornio during construction works there (Kuokkanen n.d.; Figure 4.6).

The Kvikkjokk clock was definitely a mechanical clock and never left the site intact. Both hands of the clock were found during the excavations in the early 1970s (Figure 4.7). The clock had been dismantled and/or destroyed on site, and the parts had been dispersed. The hands were found far away from each other. The minute hand was located in the remains of the small warehouse right behind building A5. The tip of the hour hand was found in the remains of the foundry smithy

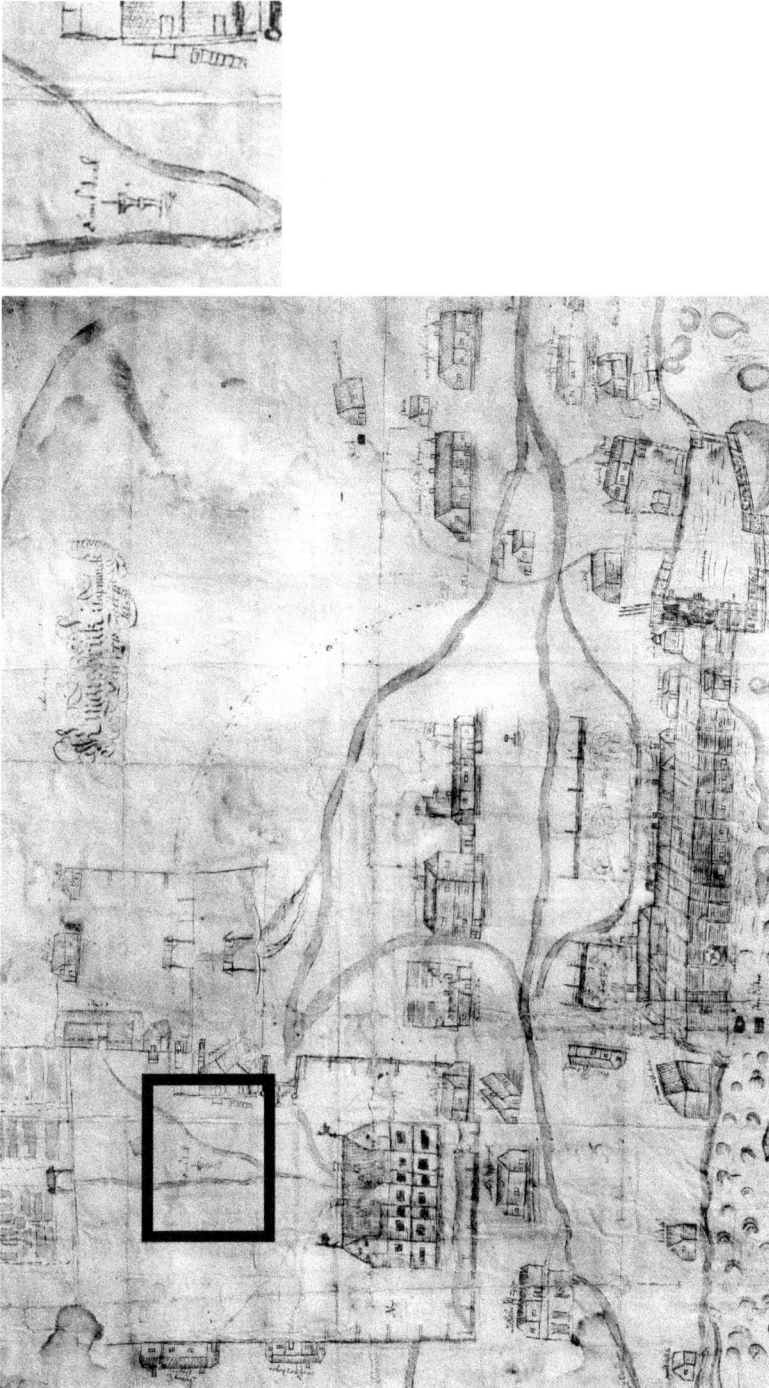

Figure 4.5. Map of the Kengis works in present-day Pajala, Sweden, drawn by Joris Denis in 1660, with enlarged section. (Image courtesy of Jernkontoret, Sweden; amendments by Risto Nurmi.)

(Figure 4.2). The meaning and introduction of time-showing clocks in industrial communities has been debated and discussed. The use of clocks has been considered as a phenomenon connected to the Enlightenment and the rise of factory-based production (Thompson 1967; Landes 1987; Symonds et al. 2015), but data from the seventeenth-century early mining enterprises indicates that the mining industry in Sweden had adopted the use of clocks already a century earlier. The expertise and experience required for the mining and refining of minerals was imported to Lapland from the large enterprises of the central Swedish mining districts—mainly from the Sala and Lövåsen silver mines (Bromé 1923, 68–70)—and the experts presumably brought the idea of controlled time and devices for controlling it with them to the north. How much the presence of clocks eventually influenced the daily life of the works and the worldviews and conceptions of the people related to it remains vague. Maybe the clocks were "tools of power" (Landes 1983; Lucas 2005, 75–76) rather than devices for actually organizing and synchronizing the operations of the works. After all, work in the early mines was carried out mainly as a sequence of tasks and followed annual economic cycles much like agrarian (cf. Landes 1987, 194) or even Sámi economies and conceptions.

Conclusion

The archaeological material from the early mining communities in Silbojokk and Kvikkjokk in Swedish Lapland forms a rich and still largely unutilized source for the study of early modern life in the north. This chapter introduced only a fraction of the available data and concentrated on a few case studies related to daily life and the use of material culture in the works. The ceramic assemblages of both works are abundant and provide a good overview of the food culture of the works. The interpretations based on ceramic finds are supported by the observations made on the basis of the antler artifacts, particularly the presence of numerous antler spoons at Silbojokk. Moreover, the antler artifacts form an important set of material for illuminating the sociocultural transculturation that occurred in the interaction between the locals and the newcomers.

The early mining enterprises in Swedish Lapland introduced many elements of European society, both material and social, into the sociocultural context of the north. However, the cultural adoption of material culture and ideas seems to have functioned in both directions within these interactions. Thus, we cannot really simply determine (and classify) the sociocultural background of people based on the presence of particular types of material culture and their contexts, but the data provides

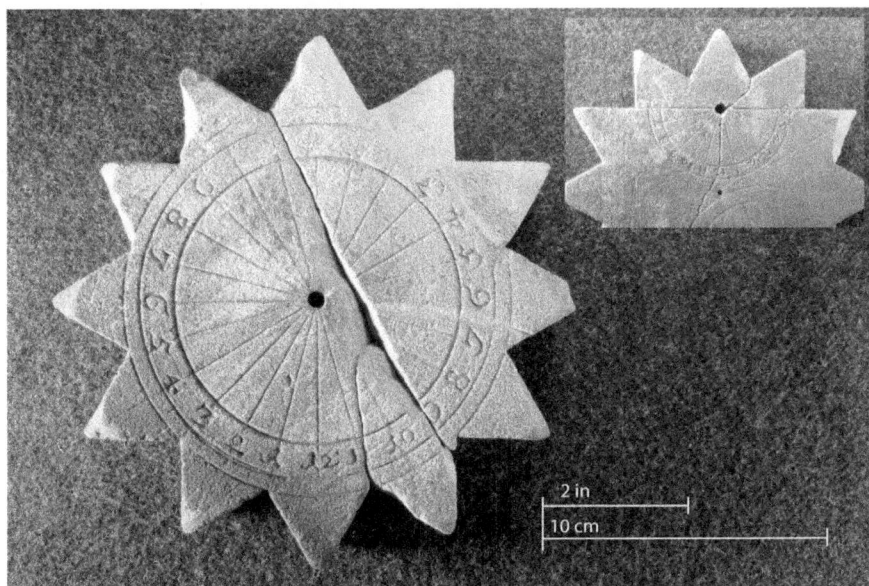

Figure 4.6. The star-shaped equatorial sundial from Tornio. This rare prestige item made of limestone dates to the sixteenth or seventeenth century. The immersed picture shows the winter-time display that has been incised on the back of the device. (Photograph by Susanna Kuokkanen.)

Figure 4.7. The hands of the Kvikkjokk clock. (Photograph by Risto Nurmi.)

plenty of information about the contacts and influences between people. At Silbojokk, Sámi presence and influence were obviously strong, and the Sámi interacted closely with the German and Swedish people, at least in some phases of the operation of the works. Sámi material culture has played an important role in the daily activities and catering of the works. This kind of evidence of close everyday interaction is no longer present at the Kvikkjokk works. According to historical documents, the Sámi still held an important role in the logistics of the works, like they did at Silbojokk, but contacts in residential contexts had decreased.

The common view of the relations between the mining enterprises and the local Sámi population in seventeenth-century Lapland tends to highlight the strong contradictions between them. An often-quoted citation describes how the local Sámi population from the region "ran away" over the border to Norway to avoid the burdensome duties at the works (e.g., Awebro 1983, 183–224; Nordin 2012, 156). However, this was only one part of the whole picture. Relations were clearly inflamed particularly during the leadership of Isak Tiock in the later phase at Silbojokk and the early years of the Kvikkjokk foundry, but in a wider perspective, the Sámi people also had a lot of personal interest and involvement in the works. For example, at the same time, the Kengis works did not have similar problems at such a scale. Sámi workers were hired continuously (Lindmark 1963), and the head of the Kengis works, Abraham Momma, even said that he favored Sámi over Swedes as workers, because he viewed them as more diligent (cf. Nordin and Ojala 2017).

Acknowledgments

I wish to acknowledge my gratitude to the following people and institutions, who have helped and supported me in the completion of this chapter: Jenny Widgren, the Antiquarian-Topographical Archive, the Swedish National Heritage Board, Norrbottens Museum, Västerbottens Museum, and the Academy of Finland.

Risto Nurmi is a Finnish archaeologist, who is currently a postdoctoral research fellow at the University of Oulu. Dr. Nurmi has specialized in historical archaeology and has studied the commercial development, behavioral urbanization, and early industrialization of Northern Fennoscandia. His current interests include the development of early medieval north, artifact biographies, and historical motorcycles.

References

Archival Sources

Västebotten's Museum archaeological collections (VBM)
Swedish National Heritage board online database (RAÄ).

Published Sources

Awebro, Kenneth. 1983. *Luleå silververk: Ett norrländskt silververks historia*. Luleå: Luleå kommun.

———. 1986. *Från malm till mynt: en historisk-metallurgisk studie om Nasafjäll*. Stockholm: Institutet för lappmarksforskning.

———. 1989. "Bebyggelsen vid Silbojokk åren 1635–1659." In *Silvret från Nasafjäll: arkeologi vid Silbojokk*, ed. Kenneth Awebro, Nils Björkenstam, Jan Norrman, Stig Petersson, Ylva Roslund, Sabine Sten, and Einar Wallquist, 31–50. Stockholm: Riskantikvarieämbetet.

———. 1993. "Tornionlaakson ruukintoiminnasta." In *Tornionlaakson Historia II, 1600-luvulta vuoteen 1809*, ed. Olof Hederyd and Yrjö Alamäki, 361–80. S.L.: Tornionlaakson kuntien historiatoimikunta.

Boudin, Hugh R. 2002. "Vallonutvandringen som religiös migration." In *Valloner: järnests* människor, ed. Anders Florén and Gunnar Ternhag, 75–82. Hedemora: Gidlunds Förlag.

Bromé, Janrik. 1923. *Nasafjäll: Ett Norrländskt silververks historia*. Stockholm: A.–B. Nordiska Bokhandeln.

Elfwendahl, Magnus. 1999. *Från skärva till kärl: ett bidrag till vardagslivets historia i Uppsala*. Lund: University of Lund.

Fagerwall, Britt-Inger, Esther Salomonsson-Juuso, and Brita Tervaniemi. 2006. *Kengis bruk, världens nordligaste järnbruk*. Bachelor's thesis, Institutionen för industriell ekonomi och samhällsvetenskap, Luleå tekniska universitet.

Fjellström, Phebe. 1972. "Saamelaisten kansantaide." In *Saamelaista kansantaidetta*, ed. István Rácz, 12–18. Helsinki: Otava.

———. 1986. *Samernas samhälle i tradition och nutid*. Stockholm: P.A. Norstedt and Söners Förlag.

Götlind, Anna. 2005. "Gruvnäringen." In *Signums svenska kulturhistoria, Renässansen*, ed. Jakob Christensson, 261–99. Lund: Bokförlaget Signum.

Heckscher, Eli F. 1963. *An Economic History of Sweden*. Cambridge, MA: Harvard University Press.

Herva, Vesa-Pekka. 2006. *Oulu Pikisaari, Historiallisen ajan kaivaustutkimus. 15.– 26.5.2006.* An unpublished excavation report. Oulu: Laboratory of Archaeology, University of Oulu.

Hildebrand, Karl-Gustaf. 1992. *Swedish Iron in the Seventeenth and Eighteenth Centuries: Export Industry before the Industrialization*. Stockholm: Järnkontoret.

Huhtelin, Timo. 2017. *Oulun Pikisaaren pitkä kivijalallinen ja multapenkillinen rakennus keramiikka-aineiston valossa*. Master's thesis, University of Oulu.

Hyttinen, Marika, and Titta Kallio-Seppä. In press. "They Were Here too: Women and Children in Industrial Communities." In _Oxford Handbook of Industrial Archaeology_. Oxford: Oxford University Press.

Hyttinen, Marika, Timo Ylimaunu, Titta Kallio-Seppä, and Paul R. Mullins. 2016. "Pien polttoa ja käsityöläisyyttä: materiaaliset muistot Oulun Pikisaaren Pikiruukkiyhteisöstä." In _Arkeologipäivät 2015, Teollisuusperintö and teknologiat ja niiden tutkimus_, ed. Piritta Häkälä, 27–41. Helsinki: Suomen arkeologinen seura.

Immonen, Visa. 2006. "Sámi Spoons as Artefacts of Ethnicity: Archaeological Reflections on an Ethnographic Artefact Group." In _People, Material Culture and Environment in the North: Proceedings of the 22nd Nordic Archaeological Conference, University of Oulu, 18–23 August 2004_, ed. Vesa-Pekka Herva, 42–51. Oulu: University of Oulu.

Itkonen, T. I. 1948. _Suomen lappalaiset vuoteen 1945, ensimmäinen osa_. Porvoo: WSOY.

Kent, Neil. 2014. _The Sámi Peoples of the North: A Social and Cultural History_. London: Hurst and Company.

Kuokkanen, Susanna. n.d. _Tornion Suensaaren_ tähdenmuotoinen aurinkokello. An unpublished manuscript in the possession of the author.

Landes, David S. 1983. _Revolution in Time: Clocks and the Making of the Modern World_. Cambridge, MA: Harvard University Press.

———. 1987. "The Ordering of the Urban Environment: Time, Works, and Occurrence of Crowds 1790–1835." _Past and Present_ 116: 192–99.

Lehto, Marja-Liisa. 1996. _Huvikaluja lapsille, vanhat suomalaiset lelut_. Helsinki: Tammi.

———. 2004. "Paijasta barbeihin: suomalaisten lelujen vaiheita." In _Leikin pikkujättilainen_, ed. Liisa Piironen, 374–83. Helsinki: WSOY.

Lindgren, Åsa. 2014. _Masugnsbyn LKAB:s dolomittäkt: Arkeologisk utredning, fastighet Masugnsbyn 2:3 och Masugnsbyn S:8, Kiruna kommun, Norrbottens län_. Rapport 2014: 19. Luleå: Norrbottens Museum.

———. 2015. _Silbojokk 2015: Arkeologisk räddningsundersökning av kyrka och kyrkogård inom Raä Arjeplog 368:1, Arjeplogs KRÖLM, Arjeplogs kommun, Lapplands landskap, Norrbottens län_. Rapport 2015: 12. Luleå: Norrbottens museum.

Lindmark, Albin. 1963. _Torneå lappmarks kopparbruk anno 1655–1780_. Svappavaara: Albin Lindmark Förlag.

Lindroth, Sten. 1955. _Gruvbrytning och kopparhantering vid Stora Kopparberg intill 1800-talets början, Del 1, gruvan och gruvbrytningen_. Uppsala: Almqvist and Wiksells boktrykkeri AB.

Ling, Hans, and Bo Annuswer. 1999. _Fördelning av fyndmaterial från arkeologisk undersökning av fornlämning nr 368, Arjeblog socken, Lappland_. Finds catalogue. Stockholm: ATA, Statens Historiska Museer.

Lucas, Gavin. 2005. _The Archaeology of Time_. London: Routledge.

Lundmark, Lennart. 2008. _Stulet land, svensk makt på Sámisk mark_. Stockholm: Ordfront.

Naum, Magdalena. 2016. "Between Utopia and Dystopia: Colonial Ambivalence and Early Modern Perception of Sápmi." _Itinerario_ 40(3): 489–521.

———. 2017. "The Pursuit of Metals and the Ideology of Improvement in Early Modern Sápmi, Sweden." _Journal of Social History_ 51(4): 784–807.

Nergård, Maj-Britt. 2002. "Louis de Geert et Consorts: En studie av liégiska entreprenörers etablering i Sverige under början av 1600-talet." In *Valloner— järnets människor*, ed. Anders Florén and Gunnar Ternhag, 47–65. Hedemora: Gidlunds förlag.

Nordin, Jonas M. 2012. "Embodied Colonialism: The Cultural Meaning of Silver in a Swedish Colonial Context in the Seventeenth Century." *Post-Medieval Archaeology* 46(1): 143–65.

———. 2015. "Metals of Metabolism: The Construction of Industrial Space and the Commodification of Early Modern Sápmi." In *Historical Archaeologies of Capitalism: Contributions To Global Historical Archaeology*, ed. Mark P. Leone and Jocelyn E. Knauf, 249–72. New York: Springer.

Nordin, Jonas M., and Carl-Gösta Ojala. 2017. "Copper Worlds: A Historical Archaeology of Abraham and Jakob Momma-Reenstierna and their Industrial Enterprise in the Torne River Valley, c. 1650–1680." *Acta Borealia* 34(2): 103–33.

Nurmi, Risto. n.d. "Mines of Transculturation: The Physical Adaptation and Acculturation of Early Mining Communities in the Seventeenth Century Lapland, Northern Sweden." An unpublished manuscript in possession of the author.

———. 2009. "The Others Among Us? Sámi Artefacts in a Seventeenth Century Urban Context in the Town of Tornio, Northern Finland." *Máttut—Máddagat: The Roots of Sámi Ethnicities, Societies and Spaces/Places*, ed. Tiina Äikäs, 68–87. Oulu: Giellagas Institute/University of Oulu.

———. 2011. *Development of the Urban Mind. An Object Biographical Approach: The Case study of the town of Tornio, northern Finland*. PhD diss., University of Oulu.

Ojala, Carl-Gösta. 2017. "Contested Colonial History and Heritage in Sápmi: Archaeology, Indigeneity and Local Communities in Northern Sweden." In *Archaeologies of "Us" and "Them": Debating History, Heritage and Indigeneity*, ed. Charlotta Hillerdal, Anna Karlström, and Carl-Gösta Ojala, 258–71. London and New York: Routledge.

———. 2018. "Encountering 'the Other' in the North: Colonial Histories in Early Modern Northern Sweden." In *Facing Otherness in Early Modern Sweden: Travel, Migration and Material Transformations 1500–1800*, ed. Magdalena Naum and Fredrik Ekengren, 209–28. Woodbridge: The Boydell Press.

Ojala, Carl-Gösta, and Jonas M. Nordin. 2015. "Mining Sápmi: Colonial Histories, Sámi Archaeology, and the Exploitation of Natural Resources in Northern Sweden." *Arctic Anthropology* 52(2): 6–21.

Rosén, Christina. 2004. *Stadsbor och bönder: materiell kultur och social status i Halland från medeltid till 1700-tal*. Stockholm: Almqvist and Wiksell international.

Roslund, Ylva. 1989a. "Den arkeologiska undersökningen." In *Silvret från Nasafjäll: arkeologi vid Silbojokk*, ed. Kenneth Awebro, Nils Björkenstam, Jan Norrman, Stig Petersson, Ylva Roslund, Sabine Sten, and Einar Wallquist, 71–132. Stockholm: Riskantikvarieämbetet.

———. 1989b. "Bebykkelseutvecklingen i Silbojokk enligt det historiska och det arkeologiska materialet." In *Silvret från Nasafjäll: arkeologi vid Silbojokk*, ed. Kenneth Awebro, Nils Björkenstam, Jan Norrman, Stig Petersson, Ylva Roslund, Sabine Sten, and Einar Wallquist, 185–94. Stockholm: Riskantikvarieämbetet.

———. 1992. "Silbojokk: A Place Founded by the Crown." In *Rescue and Research: Reflections of society in Sweden 700–1700 A.D.*, ed. Lars Ersgård, Marie Holmström, and Kristina Lamm, 252–70. Stockholm: Riksantikvarieämbetet.

Rydberg, Sven. 1979. *Stora Kopparberg: 1000 Years of an Industrial Activity.* Stockholm: Gullers International AB.

Rydström, Gunhild 1999. *Rapport över slutundersökning av kåtatomt, raä nr 343, Gammplatsen i Lycksele sn, Västerbottens län, Lappland, 1999.* Lycksele: Skogsmuseet.

———. 2006. *"Det äldsta Lycksele—Öhn: Rapport över genomgång och bearbetning av fyndmaterial från undersökningar åren 1949–2001, raä nr 343, Gammplatsen, lycksele socken, Lappland."* Excavation report. Lycksele: Skogsmuseet.

Sillanpää, Merja. 2000. *Happamasta makeaan: suomalaisen ruoka- ja tapakulttuurin kehitys.* Vantaa: Finfood.

Sipiläinen, Kirsi. 2003. "Pienoisaseita ja puunukkeja: leikin jäljet arkeologisessa aineistossa." In *Kaupunkia pintaa syvemmältä, arkeologisia näkökulmia Turun historiaan*, ed. Liisa Seppänen, 295–306. Turku: Suomen keskiajan arkeologian seura.

Skandfer, Marianne. 1996. *Čoarverbasttet: Sámiske hornskjeer fra middelalder til modern tid.* Master's thesis, University of Tromsø.

Sten, Sabine. 1989. "Husdjurshållning, jakt och fiske i Silbojokk: en osteologisk analys av djurben." In *Silvret från Nasafjäll: arkeologi vid Silbojokk*, ed. Kenneth Awebro, Nils Björkenstam, Jan Norrman, Stig Petersson, Ylva Roslund, Sabine Sten, and Einar Wallquist, 167–78. Stockholm: Riskantikvarieämbetet.

Symonds, James, Timo Ylimaunu, Anna-Kaisa Salmi, Risto Nurmi, Titta Kallio-Seppä, Tiina Kuokkanen, Markku Kuorilehto, and Annemari Tranberg. 2015. "Time, Seasonality and Trade: Swedish/Finnish—Sámi Interactions in Early Modern Lapland." *Historical Archaeology* 49(3): 74–89.

Talve, Ilmar. 1990. *Suomen kansankulttuuri.* Helsinki: Suomalaisen kirjallisuuden seura.

Thompson, Edward P. 1967. "Time, Work-discipline, and Industrial Capitalism." *Past and Present* 38(1): 56–97.

Vuorela, Toivo. 1975. *Suomalainen kansankulttuuri.* Helsinki: WSOY.

Wallerström, Thomas. 1976. *Silververket, Kvikkjokk, Jokkmokk sn, Lappland.* Excavation report. Luleå: Norrbottens Museum.

Chapter 5

"Not on Bread but on Fish and by Hunting"
Food Culture in Early Modern Sápmi

Ritva Kylli, Anna-Kaisa Salmi, Tiina Äikäs, and Sirpa Aalto

[T]hey [Sámi people] live not on bread but on fish and by hunting wild creatures …

> —Olaus Magnus, *A Description of the Northern Peoples*, 1555

Introduction

When Olaus Magnus was writing his *Description of the Northern Peoples* in the mid sixteenth century, he relied partly on what he himself had seen on his journey in the northern parts of Sweden and partly on what he had heard about the habits of the Sámi people. Olaus's statement that the Sámi live on fish and game meat reflects rather well how outsiders saw the Sámi way of living and food culture. His statement is not totally wrong, but it does oversimplify things. In the sixteenth century, the Sámi people lived in a large geographical area that stretched from the southwestern part of Norway to the Kola Peninsula, which means that the Sámi culture was not unified with regard to environment and sources of livelihood. The local Sámi food culture was affected not only by these factors, but also by the contacts the Sámi had with their Scandinavian or Finnic neighbors. Our hypothesis is that the Sámi food culture in areas where the Sámi encountered the Scandinavian or Finnic culture was hybridized, meaning that it was influenced by products that Scandinavians or Finns used.

We have examined and tested our hypothesis by comparing archaeo-logical data from various places in northern Fennoscandia with written sources from the sixteenth and early seventeenth centuries. The choice of this period is based on the fact that King Gustavus I of Sweden (reigned 1523–1560) developed a taxation system that produced a wealth of docu-ments known as Bailiff's Accounts. These documents are the best avail-able sources for investigating this matter.

The sixteenth and early seventeenth centuries offer an interesting point of departure for our investigation because the Crown was not the only party that had closer contacts with the Sámi. After the Reformation, which was headed in Sweden by Gustavus I during the sixteenth century (Ylikangas and Tarkiainen 2005), the Lutheran Church began its mission-ary work among the Sámi in earnest when it realized that the Sámi were not "proper Christians." Religion and food are closely related to each other, which can be seen, for example, in dietary rules concerning fast-ing and unclean food. Especially in the case of the Sámi ethnic religion, offering traditions and livelihood were intertwined: parts of the catch were often promised as offerings (Äikäs et al. 2009; Äikäs 2015). We have therefore also included archaeological data from various Sámi offering sites, which can cast light on what kind of (food) offerings were made.

The underlying theme of our research is thus as follows: how does the food culture of Scandinavians and Finns present itself in Sámi food culture? If it can be perceived, what elements of it were adopted by the Sámi and why?

Food historians have mostly been interested in the history of European and Western food cultures, while the food histories of national minorities have often been neglected (Claflin and Scholliers 2012). This reflects what is considered to be worthy of study. In cultural encounters, the cultural practices of both parties become altered, forming hybrid cultural forms, ambiguous third spaces, multiple identities, and new ways of using and creating material culture (Comaroff and Comaroff 1997; Gosden 2004; Johnson 2006; Naum 2010; Ylimaunu et al. 2014). Although the power relations in colonial situations, like the one that prevailed in northern Fennoscandia, are often simplified to dualistic terms such as domination and resistance, in reality, a wide variety of strategies have taken place in colonial societies (Shohat 1992; Lightfoot and Martinez 1995; Comaroff and Comaroff 1997, 22; Lindenfeld and Richardson 2010; Bergman and Edlund 2016; Kuusela, Nurmi, and Hakamäki 2016). Many of these strategies were played out in the small details of everyday life, such as food culture (Pavao-Zuckerman and DiPaolo Loren 2012; Kennedy and VanValkenburgh 2016). The examination of Sámi food culture can therefore contribute to the understanding of the complicated power relationships and cultural negotiations that took place in the encounters between the Sámi and the Scandinavians or Finns. It also provides a unique window into the everyday strategies the Sámi employed to negotiate their relationships with the Scandinavians and Finns.

Sources

Archaeological Data

Archaeological data on Sámi foodways consists of faunal assemblages, supported by pollen and macrofossil data. For the purposes of this chapter, we rely on previously excavated and published data from Sámi dwelling sites excavated in present-day northern Norway and Finland (Carpelan 1987, 2003; Hambleton and Rowley-Conwy 1997; Halinen 2009; Hedman, Olsen, and Vretemark 2015). We also compare this data with published pollen and macrofossil data (Bergman and Hörnberg 2015; Hörnberg et al. 2015) from Sámi dwelling sites, as well as published faunal data from sites visited or temporarily occupied by the Sámi, such as market places (Lahti 2006; Harlin 2007, 2009) and mining communities (Sten 1989). In addition, we compare the data with information provided by the stable isotope analysis of human remains (Fjellström 2011). The dietary information provided by the faunal, macrofossil, pollen, and stable isotope analysis is also compared with faunal assemblages from Sámi offering sites (Äikäs 2015; Salmi et al. 2018).

The archaeological sites discussed here are scattered around a vast area inhabited by various Sámi groups that rely on different modes of subsistence. In addition, the sites span a long period of time from ca. AD 800 to the eighteenth century. The data therefore does not allow us to produce a comprehensive description of the foodways of various Sámi societies in the course of a thousand years, but it does offer glimpses into several regions, supply networks, and interactions that shaped the food culture in those locations and beyond.

Written Sources

The Lapland that belonged to the Kingdom of Sweden in the sixteenth century was divided into administrative regions. We have examined the two northernmost regions, *Torne Lappmark* (Tornio Lapland) and *Kemi Lappmark* (Kemi Lapland), which were mostly inland areas (the northernmost parts of Finland, Sweden, and Norway) of the current Sápmi. The administrative centers of these Lappmarks were situated on the coast of the Gulf of Bothnia. The town of Tornio was founded in 1621 on an old market place from which trade excursions to Lapland could be carried out (Ylimaunu 2007). The area of Torne and Kemi Lappmarks is characterized by many lakes and large salmon rivers, but also mountains and fells. The written records concerning taxation—the so-called Bailiff's Accounts—from the sixteenth and seventeenth centuries are one of the few document-record series covering these areas. When King Gustavus I began to reorganize the administration and taxation, local bailiffs had to write detailed accounts of taxes collected from the Crown's subjects (Seppälä 2009, 9–25).

The Bailiff's Accounts, which began in the 1530s, are imperfect at some points, but they give us a glimpse of what kind of tax parcels the Crown was able to collect from the Sámi. This also ought to reflect their sources of livelihood and thus, indirectly, their food culture, as the taxes were collected in the form of natural products (Seppälä 2009, 208). Admittedly, these sources are one-sided and do not give a full picture of the Sámi food culture, but they reveal what kind of barter economy flourished between the Crown and its subjects. Combining all this information with narrative sources and archaeological data allows us to look at a fuller picture of the Sámi food culture.

Narrative sources consist of the book *Historia de Gentibus Septentrionalibus* (Description of the Northern Peoples, 1555), written by the Swedish author Olaus Magnus. The book was partly based on Olaus Magnus's ([1555] 1996, 212) own journeys, but he was also familiar with the texts of earlier European authors. We also use various accounts from the seventeenth century, such as Olof Tresk's atlas of Kemi and Torne Lappmarks, *Kartor över Kemi och Torne Lappmarker 1642 och 1643*. Tresk worked as a land surveyor and visited every village in the area during the first half of the seventeenth century. Johannes Schefferus' *Lapponia* ([1673] 1963) is also useful. Schefferus had many local informants, including clergymen who worked among the Sámi and knew about their living conditions. In addition, we refer to some earlier sources, such as medieval Icelandic sagas and ethnographic data from the nineteenth and twentieth centuries.

Meals of Fish and Game

Fishing was important for the Sámi who lived by the seaside, as well as for those living close to rivers and lakes. In fact, already in the Middle Ages, the Sámi living by the seaside in Finnmark were called "sedentary Finnar" (búfinnar) or fishermen.[1] In *Historia Norwegiae* (from ca. 1170), in turn, the anonymous author describes how the Sámi people were skillful hunters and how they moved following the game (*Historia Norwegiae*, 58–61). The author also mentions that the Sámi paid their taxes to the Norwegian kings in the form of squirrel and ermine furs. On several occasions, Olaus Magnus ([1555] 1996) mentions that the Sámi hunted different kinds of birds, for example.

The Bailiff's Accounts confirm that hunting was an important source of livelihood in Lapland. There were yearly records of squirrels, different kinds of foxes (such as white fox and red fox), otters, beavers, wolves, weasels, pine martens, lynxes, wolverines, wild reindeer, and bears (RA, KA). Altogether, the bailiffs had listed a considerable number of fur animals. According to these tax records, the Sámi specialized in different sources of livelihood, meaning that there was a separation of producers (of different resources) in the sixteenth century. Some of the villages produced a lot of game animals, while others produced a lot of fish. Fur trade flourished, and some Sámi started to focus more on hunting. Also, salmon and other kinds of fish had considerable importance as commodities. Some villages in Torne Lappmark produced a lot of lake fish, and the Bailiff's Accounts especially emphasize the significance of dried pike, which was an essential export product for the Swedish kingdom. Fish products were in high demand in Catholic Europe, as they were suitable for fasting on Fridays and consumption during Lent (Seppälä 2009, 136–37).

According to Olof Tresk (1928, 18), "the best and the biggest" village in all of Swedish Lapland was situated in Inari (which contained the winter village of Nukkumajoki, where Sámi families gathered in the wintertime). The Bailiff's Accounts contain both taxation and trade information from Inari from the sixteenth and seventeenth centuries. It seems that the Sámi saved the most valuable skins to be used as trade goods. The wealthy paid taxes at higher rates than the poor (1556, KA 4973). The most affluent Sámi of Inari might sometimes have paid their taxes with beaver skins, but it was not common. In 1594, a taxpayer named Aikia Tutiasson paid one beaver, twenty squirrel skins, and five pikes to the Crown. At the same time, most of the other taxpayers paid their taxes with pikes, squirrels, and sometimes also pine marten skins (KA 4987:10). In 1607, Sámi inhabitants of Inari sold to Swedish officials, among other things, the skins of fifteen beavers, five bears, three wolves, one wolverine, two male reindeer, and two red foxes. Beaver furs had become very fashionable during the sixteenth century. According to Eric Jay Dolin (2011), during the reign of Queen Elizabeth I (1558–1603), high-quality beaver hats were more and more desired throughout Europe, where they had become symbols of social status.

124 *Ritva Kylli, Anna-Kaisa Salmi, Tiina Äikäs, and Sirpa Aalto*

According to Olof Tresk (1928, 18), there were good opportunities for wild reindeer hunting and fairly good opportunities for beaver hunting in Inari. Tresk also praised the fishing waters of Inari, which produced so much fish that it could be exported to neighboring areas. Although many Sámi villages had good inland fishing waters, they also imported cod from the coast of the Arctic Ocean (RA 1578). On the basis of the taxation lists in the Bailiff's Accounts, even the inhabitants of Inari sometimes paid their taxes in the form of dried cod, which means that either they had contacts with coastal people or they went to the coast to fish themselves. In 1578, there was one taxpayer in Inari with fifteen squirrel skins, one reindeer skin, thirty pikes, and thirty *Bernfisk*, which means dried cod (KA 4985:67).

In 1555, Olaus Magnus (1996, 202) wrote that the Sámi paid the officials with "valuable pelts and many sorts of fish." All in all, fish was an important resource for many Sámi communities, but it was also a very important part of the Sámi diet. Samuel Rheen, who worked as a minister in Lapland during the seventeenth century, described the Sámi diet: "They make their meals of fish and game that they have hunted; they eat that in the winter and summer, in the autumn and spring." Johannes Schefferus ([1673] 1963, 301) also mentioned how frequently the Sámi ate fish during the sixteenth and seventeenth centuries. Fish was such an important commodity for the Sámi that, although it was often preserved by drying, it had also tied them to the global salt trade (STR).

Historical sources, then, focus mainly on tax and trade items. These items are also visible in the archaeological record. For example, skeletal representation and cut marks on pike bones suggest that pike was probably processed and dried for trade and taxation purposes but not necessarily consumed at dwelling sites in the Pasvik area (Hedman et al. 2015). Fur species, such as beaver, pine marten, wolverine, and bear also feature in some faunal assemblages from dwelling and offering sites (Carpelan 1987; Äikäs 2015; Salmi et al. 2018).

Archaeological finds also contain a wealth of information on subsistence activities and food procurement that are not visible in historical sources. Especially fowling and noncommercial fishing feature heavily in many of the faunal assemblages from Sámi sites. Depending on the seasons of use of the site, several species of waterfowl and grouse were encountered in the faunal assemblages from Sámi dwelling sites (Carpelan 1987; Lie 1992; Halinen 2009; Hedman et al. 2015), market places (Lahti 2006; Harlin 2007, 2009), and offering sites (Äikäs 2015; Salmi et al. 2018). At Juikenttä, a few bones of crane, great cormorant, and northern goshawk may indicate that the skins were used for making bags (Carpelan 1987) or that they were consumed for food (Itkonen 1948a, 507; 1948b, 36, 50, 370; Paulaharju 1961, 118–19).

Subsistence fishing is also visible in archaeological animal bone assemblages. In the faunal assemblages from dwelling sites near the Arctic seacoast, a variety of freshwater and marine fish species were identified (Lie 1992; Hedman et al. 2015). In the faunal assemblages from inland locations near lakes and rivers, bones of freshwater fish were identified (Halinen 2009). In the fish bone assemblages from market places in Markkina and Pappila, salmonid and cod bones were the most common finds, followed by pike and perch (Harlin 2007, 2009). Fish bones and scales were also found at two offering sites, namely Näkkälä and Taatsi in present-day Finland (Figure 5.1).

In the comparison of historical sources and bone finds from Sámi dwelling and offering sites, it is clear that the Bailiff's Accounts first and foremost reflect what the authorities considered valuable. Even though the Sámi often had the chance to decide their tax parcels independently (Vahtola 2003, 119), they also had to hunt and fish the products that the Crown and its authorities deemed useful. Archaeological data, on the other hand, provides information on subsistence hunting and fishing, revealing the importance of seasonal fishing and fowling in the Sámi food culture. It has to be noted, though, that archaeological assemblages

Figure 5.1. Perch bones found in the archaeological excavation in the Taatsi offering site. (Photograph by Anna-Kaisa Salmi.)

are also subject to bias. For instance, written sources indicate a wider significance of fish offerings than the bone finds testify to (Äikäs 2015, Figure 57). The *sieidi* (a type of Sámi offering site, often a large boulder unshaped by humans) of Koskikaltiojoen suu is known in both written sources and living oral tradition as a fish *sieidi* (Paulaharju, MV:KTKKA 1914; Paulaharju [1927] 1965), whereas excavations yielded bones of reindeer and wood grouse. Fish bones are small and fragile in comparison with mammal and bird bones, which is probably one of the reasons why they are underrepresented in archaeological assemblages. Other archaeological data, such as the stable isotope analysis of human remains from Rounala, testifies to a diet consisting of mixed marine and terrestrial resources (Fjellström 2011).

Reindeer Meat, "The Most Esteemed Delicacy"

Reindeer hides are mentioned in the Bailiff's Accounts concerning Kemi Lappmark since 1550. Hides were collected as tax parcel at a rate of approximately twenty hides per year until 1575. After that, the amounts increase, and the top year was 1582, when fifty-four reindeer hides were given to the bailiff (KA 4986). After 1585, the amounts decreased dramatically. The reason may be the war between Sweden and Russia (1570–1595), which may have affected the locals and disturbed tax collection. For example, some years are missing from the accounts. Wartime was also reflected in the amounts of products acquired by hunting. For example, between 1560 and 1580, there was first an increase in the amount of squirrel and pine marten furs. These amounts decreased towards the end of the sixteenth century.

Can we figure out how much reindeer meat was consumed by the Sámi or how reindeer husbandry developed just by investigating the Bailiff's Accounts? We have some information about reindeer herds owned by the Sámi in the latter half of the sixteenth century. In Torne Lappmark, some of the villages (or at least some individual Sámi in these villages) specialized in reindeer herding. The tax lists of Rounala from 1559, for example, included pike, pine martens, and wolverines, but one taxpayer had four reindeer skins among his tax parcels. In the same year, reindeer herds were also listed in the Bailiff's Accounts. According to the documents, a Sámi woman named Kirsin Jönsdåtter, who lived in Torne Lappmark, owned twenty-three male reindeer, fifteen female reindeer, and eight young reindeer calves (RA 1559:17).

In the beginning of the seventeenth century, the Swedish documents contain even more detailed descriptions of reindeer herds and the amount of reindeer. This was part of the politics of King Charles IX (1600–1611), who was interested in utilizing the resources that could be extracted from the northern areas of his kingdom (Kylli 2012, 34–35). The Crown's growing interest in reindeer herds is also reflected in the tax parcels. In Torne Lappmark, there were a lot of reindeer skins as tax parcels in the second half of the 1570s, and again starting from 1601. In 1576, the number of reindeer skins was fifty-four, and thirty years later, in 1606, the Sámi of Torne Lappmark paid 151 skins to the Swedish Crown. For the sake of comparison, in 1586 there were only twenty-eight reindeer skins listed. The Russo-Swedish War also hindered reindeer herding during the last decades of the sixteenth century. In the early years of the seventeenth century, many taxpayers in Torne Lappmark (for example, in Utsjoki) paid their taxes with money or with reindeer skins. The situation was different in Kemi Lappmark, where the Sámi focused more on fishing and hunting. The Inari Sámi, for example, had traditionally hunted a lot of wild reindeer and beavers and kept only a few reindeer themselves. In 1607, there were only twenty-nine male reindeer, twenty-eight female reindeer, and twenty reindeer calves in Inari (RA 1607:6).

If reindeer hides were paid as tax parcels and sold, we may assume that something was also done with the meat—it was most probably eaten by the Sámi. The Sámi were considered primitive by outsiders because of their cooking habits: they either dried or grilled reindeer meat (Steckzén 1964, 239). Among the archaeological finds from Nukkumajoki, there are fragments of cooking cauldrons (Carpelan 2003, 73), and also on the basis of written sources, the Sámi cooked their meals during the Early Modern period. In the 1670s, Johannes Schefferus ([1673] 1963, 300) wrote that the Sámi used to boil reindeer blood in water in order to make gruel. According to Samuel Rheen, this was a very common dish among the Sámi. Johannes Tornaeus ([1672] 1772, 59), who was in charge of the church services for the Sámi in Torne Lappmark, also described the reindeer-based diet of the Sámi living within his parish as follows: "The most esteemed delicacies of the Lapp are reindeer meat, bone marrow, reindeer tongue, cheese, and milk. The best cheese is made in the summer. The cheese made in the autumn has less fat. The Lapp conserves autumn milk in pots and reindeer stomachs with blueberries and crowberries, and allows it to freeze." Presumably the Sámi adopted the milking of reindeer from their sedentary neighbors, who kept cattle (Ingold 1980, 102).

Reindeer dominated all the archaeological animal bone assemblages, which testifies to the importance of reindeer meat in the Sámi diet and foodways. Because of the presence of two subspecies with similar skeletal morphology and overlapping size, it is usually impossible to identify wild and domesticated reindeer based on fragmentary archaeological bone finds. The reindeer bones discovered at the archaeological sites discussed in this chapter can therefore be derived from either wild or domesticated reindeer. The percentage of reindeer bones varied from ca. seventy to one hundred percent of number of identifies specimens (NISP) at different sites. Zooarchaeological data suggest that reindeer consumption patterns were generally similar at different Sámi dwelling sites. At all dwelling sites, mainly adult reindeer were slaughtered for food, with very few or no bones of juvenile, subadult, or old individuals (Hambleton and Rowley-Conwy 1997; Hedman et al. 2015). Both meaty and meat-poor body parts were present in the assemblages (Hambleton and Rowley-Conwy 1997; Hedman et al. 2015). This suggests that the reindeer were slaughtered and consumed locally. It also indicates that all reindeer body parts were utilized for food, which has been character-istic of the Sámi foodways also in later periods (Itkonen 1921; Soppela 2000). In the archaeological assemblages, also the splitting of metapodi-als, phalanges, and even upper limb long bones testifies to the intensive use of marrow (Hambleton and Rowley-Conwy 1997; Carpelan 2003). At market places, all body parts were present and the age profile was similar to that seen at dwelling sites (Lahti 2006; Harlin 2009).

Reindeer were the most common animals offered. Reindeer offerings began around the twelfth century and peaked around AD 1400–1600, which is probably related to the onset and intensification of reindeer pastoralism occurring at the same time (Äikäs 2015; Salmi et al. 2018). The reindeer age profiles from offering sites are heavily dominated by prime-age adults, and plenty of old individuals past ten years of age were offered as well. Of the skeletal elements, antlers and crania especially are common at offering sites, and their scarcity at dwelling sites may partly be due to the offering tradition (Hambleton and Rowley-Conwy 1997; Hedman et al. 2015). There is a description from the fifteenth century concerning Sámi offering of reindeer antlers in a lake, which attests to the habit in the Middle Ages (*Jämtlands och Härjedalens Diplomatarium*, 7). Split metapodials are also present in the faunal assemblages from offer-ing sites. This may indicate that reindeer were sometimes consumed at offering sites. Indeed, later ethnographic data indicates that sometimes people ate at the offering site, believing that the god was also fed as people were eating (Äimä 1903, 115; Collinder 1953, 171; Itkonen 1948b, 311; Paulaharju 1932, 18; Ravila 1934, 62, 85). The occurrence of burnt bone in the faunal assemblage from two sites (Koskikaltiojoen suu and Ukonsaari) may also indicate the use of fire for cooking the meat (Salmi, Äikäs, and Lipkin 2011; Äikäs 2015).

Again, historical sources focus mainly on reindeer hides as tax and trade items, with some insights into the use of reindeer meat in the Sámi diet. Archaeological finds, on the other hand, are a rich source of information on the role of reindeer meat and marrow in the Sámi food culture. In addition to indicating the overall importance of reindeer in the Sámi diet, archaeological bone finds also suggest how the reindeer carcasses were handled and prepared for food. The archaeological assemblages from offering sites also testify to the great importance of reindeer to the Sámi.

Bread and Butter—Hybridized or Colonial Diet?

The historical Sámi are often connected with reindeer herding, hunting, and fishing, but there are also indications of very early connections to agriculture and animal husbandry. In the medieval saga of *Ketils saga hœngs* (1950, 159), two Sámis come to meet Ketil's Norse friend Brúni to obtain butter from him. Although the saga itself cannot be considered to describe historical characters or events, this kind of description may refer to real-life encounters in the Middle Ages.

Bones of cattle and sheep or goat were identified in small numbers in faunal assemblages from dwelling sites in Norway (Hambleton and Rowley-Conwy 1997; Hedman et al. 2015). One of the ovicaprid bones from Brodtkorbneset in Pasvik was radiocarbon dated to AD 990–1155, making it the earliest evidence so far of livestock at a Sámi dwelling site (Hedman et al. 2015). Bearing in mind the small sample size, it seems that ovicaprids were slaughtered at the dwelling site, but it is not clear whether the animals were actually kept by the Sámi or whether the animals were traded live or as complete carcasses for consumption (Hedman et al. 2015).

At the market places in Markkina and Pappila, there were bones of cattle and sheep or goat (Lahti 2006; Harlin 2009). The livestock bones may be related to the foodways of the merchants from Tornio, but on the other hand, cattle and sheep were kept by the Sámi residing by the Teno River already in the eighteenth century (Itkonen 1948b, 194). Cow owners of the eighteenth century were listed, for example, in Lapland's taxation records. In 1776, there were seven (fisher) Sámi who owned altogether fourteen cows in Utsjoki (Figure 5.2). There were also thirty-four sheep in Utsjoki, which was inhabited entirely by the Sámi population (Nahkiaisoja 2016, 290). Moreover, in the seventeenth century, the reindeer-herding Sámi had sometimes traded live sheep and cattle to be butchered from the Sea Sámi (Hansen 2005, 177).

Bones of sheep or goat and cattle were also identified at offering sites in present-day Norway, Sweden, and Finland. Ovicaprid bones at offering sites date from the thirteenth century onwards. A dated cattle bone sample from Mørsviksbotn in Norway was modern (Salmi et al. 2018). The Sámi are associated with keeping goats also in the Icelandic sagas, which confirms the evidence seen in the archaeological finds[2].

According to Johannes Schefferus ([1673] 1963, 302), the Sámi ate mainly fish and meat, but also berries (such as cloudberries and lingonberries), wild celery (*Angelica*), and chopped pine bark (Figure 5.2). He did not mention grain, and wrote that "most Sámi did not know the use of bread and salt." However, pollen analysis suggests that the Sámi in interior northern Sweden cultivated cereals in the Late Iron Age and Medieval period (AD 800–1500) (Bergman and Hörnberg 2015; Hörnberg et al. 2015). In addition to cereals, other plants such as *Angelica archangelika* and pine inner bark were utilized for food (Bergman, Östlund, and Zackrisson 2004; Bergman and Hörnberg 2015).

It seems that Norwegian angelica (*Angelica archangelika*) was one of the key vegetables of the Early Modern Sámi diet. It was also exported to

Figure 5.2. Many Sámi families kept sheep and milking cows in Utsjoki and Inari. In the early 1900s, there were a lot of milk dishes, for example, in this Paulus Valle's house in Inari. The person in front is processing scots pine innerbark. (Photograph by T. I. Itkonen [Inari, Juutua, 1914], courtesy of Finno-Ugric Picture Collection, Finnish National Board of Antiquities.)

central Europe in the sixteenth century, as it was considered an important remedy in fighting the plague (Snellman 1996, 15–27). According to written sources, edible commodities were also imported from the south to Sápmi. Olaus Magnus ([1555] 1996, 201) mentions that the Sámi lived "not on bread" (but by fishing and by hunting); but, he also wrote about their merchandising: "But their gold comes into the business, a commodity that is utterly unknown among the race I am now describing; for valuable pelts, woollen and linen cloth, salt, corn... ." Olaus Magnus' information about exchanging commodities seems quite accurate when it is compared to the contents of the Bailiff's Accounts. According to them, furs were exchanged for fabrics, hemp, flour, bread, and salt—but also for money. In 1577, Per Jonsson, a Sámi from Rounala, exchanged one pine marten for twenty loaves of bread. Anders Jonsson, another Rounala Sámi, exchanged one beaver for hemp and flour, and also four red foxes for such commodities as butter, forty-five loaves of bread, flour, and an ax. In 1604, the skins of wolverines and wolves were exchanged for butter, wadmal, and so on (RA 1604:8). In the same year, the accounts contain information on transporting liquor to Torne Lappmark, which indicates that more and more new products entered the Sámi culture.

Additionally, many Sámi chose to take money as payment for their furs (instead of butter or flour). They were therefore able to make purchases, for example, in the market places on the coast of the Arctic Ocean. For example, the Sámi from Inari village visited these market places regularly. There were a lot of trading situations (which also might have affected the Sámi diet) that have not been registered in written sources at all. According to Olof Tresk (1928, 18), the Sámi products of Kemi Lappmark were very good and were exported to Sweden, Norway, and Russia. Written documents from Russia from the sixteenth or seventeenth century are not available to us, but there is sixteenth-century archaeological evidence of Russian trade contacts (the Grand Prince of Moscow Ivan Vasilyevich's coin from 1535–1547) with Nukkumajoki in Inari, for example (Carpelan 2003, 73). Swedish merchants also complained, in 1614, that the Sámi were used to selling their best furs on the coast of Norway (Fellman 1910, 457–60). Among the Nukkumajoki archaeological finds, there were also "fruit knives," which, according to Christian Carpelan (2003, 73), were made probably either in England or Holland and came to Nukkumajoki through the coast on the Arctic Ocean.

The Sámi actively tried to influence what kind of merchandise was brought to Lapland. According to the Bailiff's Accounts, sixteenth-century Sámi complained when the fur tradesmen did not come and buy their furs in the customary manner (Vahtola 2006). The Early Modern Sámi needed their trade connections. Even though reindeer meat was their delicacy, they also wanted to eat bread and butter. The flour may have been used, for example, for thickening blood gruels, as mentioned above (Itkonen 1948a, 261). The Sámi might have needed salt and flour also for ritual interaction with their gods. Olaus Magnus ([1555] 1996, 151) wrote in 1555 that the Sámi delivered to their deities "certain offerings comprising the bones of wild beasts and of great whales and fishes they have hunted." "The men of the North" had no incense, but according to Olaus Magnus, it was possible to "seek a favourable omen by means of grain, ground and salted." Olaus Magnus' texts are sometimes very accurate, but they also require strict source criticism and comparison with archaeological sources: there are no signs of offering salt, flour, or liquor, but these would probably not have left any signs in the archaeological record. All we can conclude is that according to written sources, salt, flour, and liquor were offered by the Sámi, but this cannot be attested in the archaeological finds.

Olaus Magnus ([1555] 1996, 201) described how unjust it was that business transactions in Sápmi were practiced "at the expense of simple folk" and how faithfully the Sámi carried on their commercial dealings. Later, however, Johannes Tornaeus ([1672] 1772, 64–65)—who worked as a pastor in Torne Lappmark and visited the area regularly—wrote a different kind of description of the Sámi trading skills: "In trading matters the Sámi are wise… if they learn what things cost in Stockholm, they want to have the same price." According to Tornaeus, the Sámi fixed prices unjustly, added water to dry fish to make it heavier, stretched reindeer hides, and so on. Especially the Norwegians, "poor creatures," were thoroughly fooled by the Sámi: when a reindeer died, a Sámi man carried the meat to Norway and said he had slaughtered it himself, and, in doing so, took good *riksdalers* (coins) and other decent goods. Traders imported goods, such as colored clothes, hemp, bread, butter, flour, salt, axes, and liquor, to Lapland and exported reindeer skins, red foxes, dry fish, and so on back to the cities. Olaus Magnus did not mention liquor in the context of Lapland in the mid 1500s. Tornaeus, in turn, mentions it, as liquor became a very valued commodity in the fur trade after the sixteenth century. According to Peter Sköld (1999), the use of spirits as offerings was a fairly late phenomenon, not starting until the seventeenth century.

Export products that entered the Sámi culture can be seen as one feature of colonialism from today's perspective. However, as Johannes Torneus's description shows, the Sámi were not necessarily just "victims" but also active players in the commercial field. This poses the question of how to define colonialism in the Sámi food culture. Fur animals and fish resources stimulated the colonization of the northern areas, and power asymmetries are also mirrored in the sixteenth-century Bailiff's Accounts. On the one hand, the Sámi actively adopted new products and enriched their food culture. Salt and other imported food products must have been valued by the Sámi because they were traded for highly valuable furs. On the other hand, liquor did not improve their lives when its consumption became excessive and addiction caused not just health problems, but also social problems.

At this stage, fur animals were very abundant in Lapland and sixteenth-century fashion still favored wearing furs. Great demand for reindeer products and dried pike had also affected the Sámi food culture. The situation was changing, however. In the 1640s, the Sámi of Kemi Lapland wrote a letter of complaint to Christina, Queen of Sweden. The Sámi were concerned because peasants from more southern provinces were now invading their fishing waters, which impoverished the local residents. They were also worried because the numbers of wild reindeer and other prey animals, birds, and fish had significantly decreased in Lapland (Fellman 1915, 201). Beaver skins and other furs were still exported from Lapland after the sixteenth century, but since the seventeenth century, they were more often exchanged for liquor and not so often for bread, butter, and salt. In this sense, we see that interaction between the Sámi and merchants was becoming asymmetrical: the merchants could take advantage of the addiction that liquor caused.

Conclusion

For a long time, it was thought that encounters between the Sámi and their neighbors—be they in the form of taxation or trade—consisted only of positive development from the Sámi point of view (Steckzén 1964, 268). In addition, these encounters were long thought to be one-sided, which shows only that the Sámi people have been considered passive bystanders who were influenced by their neighbors. One feature of this colonial thinking is that not much emphasis has been put on the idea that the Sámi food culture also affected their neighbors' food culture in the areas where different cultures encountered one another.

A changing food culture is one feature of colonialism. Swedish and Finnish authorities tried to control not only the lands they had occupied but also the food cultures of ethnic minorities. In narratives about the Sámi from the sixteenth to eighteenth centuries, their food culture consisting mostly of meat and fish was disdained because it lacked bread, which was considered to be the sign of civilized, sedentary living. However, bread and flour were already present in sixteenth-century archival sources, meaning that the local food culture was hybridized and the use of power was under constant negotiation. Sámi people actively shaped their own diets, but their food culture was also affected by the Swedish and Norwegian cultures which expanded into Sámi territories. The representatives of the Crown collected taxes, which they often got in the form of dried fish and furs. These tax items also feature in the archaeological record. Tax collecting itself may not have affected the food culture, but merchants who were keen to obtain Sámi products certainly did: they brought with them new products, such as flour, salt, and spirits.

Not just the Sámi were affected by these encounters. Change took place also in the other direction: according to the written sources, food products exported from the Sámi area (such as dried pike and Norwegian angelica) were also consumed in Early Modern Europe. The importance of processing dried pike is also visible in the archaeological record from Sámi dwelling sites. Moreover, the archaeological record from towns and agrarian settlements in northern Fennoscandia shows that reindeer meat was consumed also by the non-Sámi population, who may have bought whole reindeer or reindeer meat cuts from the Sámi (Salmi 2011). In addition, features that were later characteristic of the Sámi food culture, such as the longitudinal splitting of reindeer metapodials to consume the marrow, were shared between different social and ethnic groups in late Medieval and Early Modern northern Fennoscandia (Salmi et al. 2014).

It is often very difficult to find Sámi voices in the colonial archives produced by the church and the state (Stoler 2002, 98). Although the tax lists also reflect encounters at the local level, there is a risk that they portray the Sámi only as taxpayers and trading partners. During the early centuries, the state was not interested in what the Sámi might think, for example, of their own cultural identity—on the contrary, its aim was to maximize tax income and the prosperity of the kingdom (Axelsson 2011). Through the archaeological material, we can view the Sámi food culture more from the Sámi point of view (especially when excavations have been carried out at dwelling sites and offering sites, allowing us to shift our gaze out of the market places). Whereas the archival material of the sixteenth century tells first and foremost of the construction and use of power, archaeological finds from the same period provide very detailed information about the Sámi food culture—especially fishing, hunting, and reindeer herding.

Ritva Kylli is a university lecturer of Arctic and Northern History, and adjunct professor of Finnish and North European History at the

University of Oulu. She specializes in the study of food history. She has most recently concentrated on food, health, and environmental history of the Indigenous Sámi and Ainu peoples. In 2018, she was as a visiting researcher in the Arctic Research Center of Hokkaido University.

Anna-Kaisa Salmi is Associate Professor and Academy Research Fellow in Archaeology at the University of Oulu. With a specialization in zooarchaeology, her research focuses on human-animal relationships, reindeer domestication, and foodways in northern Fennoscandia. She has a special interest in the ways people interact and live with animals, and the roles animals play in human societies and histories. Her current research concentrates on human-reindeer relationships and reindeer domestication.

Tiina Äikäs is a postdoctoral researcher in archaeology at the University of Oulu and Docent in Archaeology at the University of Helsinki. She specializes in Sámi archaeology with a special interest in Sámi sacred places and their use from the Iron Age to contemporary times. She has also written about contemporary meanings and uses of heritage, and postcolonial archaeology.

Sirpa Aalto is an adjunct professor of Medieval Scandinavian History at the University of Oulu. She specializes in Old Norse literature as a historical source, and cultural contacts between Scandinavians and Sámi people in the Middle Ages. Her recent publications deal with the possible Sámi immigrants or Norwegians with Sámi background in medieval Iceland, and hunting as a livelihood in medieval Finland.

Notes

1. Sneglu-Halla þáttr, *Flateyjarbók* III, 1868, 422. The author of *Historia Norwegiae* tells how the Sámi went fishing with "Christians" and pulled a huge catch of fish from the depths into the boat (*Historia Norwegiae*, 2006, 62–63).
2. For example, a poem attached to *Haralds saga gráfeldar* from the 1230s reflects on bad harvest and weather. It mentions that the Sámi take their goats inside (Haralds saga gráfeldar, *Heimskringla* I, 1979, 221).

References

Archival Sources

Danish National Archives
The Sound Toll Registers, http://soundtoll.nl/ (STR): Vardø 1629
National Archives of Finland
The Old Collection of Accounts (KA) = Bailiff's Accounts
National Board of Antiquities (NBA)
Paulaharju, Samuli 1914. Inari. Seidasta. Haltioista. Taikoja. MV:KTKKA
The Swedish National Archives
Landskapshandlingar, Norrlands lappmarker (RA) 1556–1620

Published Sources

Äikäs, Tiina. 2015. *From Boulders to Fells—Sacred Places in the Sámi Ritual Landscape.* Translated by Sarianna Silvonen. Monographs of the Archaeological Society of Finland 5. Helsinki: Archaeological Society of Finland.

Äikäs, Tiina, Anna-Kaisa Puputti, Milton Núñez, Jouni Aspi, and Jari Okkonen. 2009. "Sacred and Profane Livelihood. Animal Bones from Sieidi Sites in Northern Finland." *Norwegian Archaeological Review* 42(2): 109–22.

Äimä, Frans. 1903. "Muutamia muistotietoja Inarin lappalaisten vanhoista uhrimenoista." *Virittäjä* 8: 113–16.

Axelsson, Per. 2011. "'In the National Registry, All People Are Equal': Sami in Swedish Statistical Sources." In *Indigenous Peoples and Demography: The Complex Relation Between Identity and Statistics*, ed. Per Axelsson and Peter Sköld, 117–33. New York: Berghahn Books.

Bergman, Ingela, and Lars-Erik Edlund. 2016. "Birkarlar and Sámi—Inter-cultural Contacts beyond State Control: Reconsidering the Standing of External Tradesmen (birkarlar) in Medieval Sámi Societies." *Acta Borealia* 33(1): 52–80.

Bergman, Ingela, and Greger Hörnberg. 2015. "Early Cereal Cultivation at Sámi Settlements: Challenging the Hunter-Herder Paradigm?" *Arctic Anthropology* 52(2): 57–66.

Bergman, Ingela, Lars Östlund, and Olle Zackrisson. 2004. "The Use of Plants as Regular Food in Ancient Subarctic Economies: A Case Study Based on Sami Use of Scots Pine Innerbark." *Arctic Anthropology* 41(1): 1–13.

Carpelan, Christian. 1987. "Juikenttä—keskiajan ja uuden ajan alun metsäsaamelainen yhteisö arkeologisen aineiston valossa." In *Saamelaiset. Sovinnolliset sopeutujat*, ed. Raili Huopanen, 62–76. Oulu: Lapin maakuntamuseo.

———. 2003. "Inarilaisten arkeologiset vaiheet." In *Inari: Inarin historia jääkaudesta nykypäivään = Aanaar*, ed. Veli-Pekka Lehtola, 28–95. Inari: Inarin kunta.

Claflin, Kyri W., and Peter Scholliers. 2012. *Writing Food History: A Global Perspective.* New York: Berg.

Collinder, Björn. 1953. *Lapparna: En Bok Om Samefolkets Forntid Och Nutid.* Stockholm: Forum.

Comaroff, John L., and Jean Comaroff. 1997. *Of Revelation and Revolution, Vol 2. The Dialectics of Modernity on a South African Frontier.* Chicago: University of Chicago Press.

Dolin, Eric Jay. 2011. *Fur, Fortune, and Empire: The Epic History of the Fur Trade in America.* New York: W. W. Norton & Company.

Fellman, Isak. 1910. *Handlingar Och Uppsatser Angående Finska Lappmarken Och Lapparne: 1.* Helsingfors: Finska litteratursällskapet.

———. 1915. *Handlingar och Uppsatser Angående Finska Lappmarken och Lapparne: 4.* Helsingfors: Finska litteratursällskapet.

Fjellström, Markus. 2011. *Stable Isotope Analysis and Ethical Issues Surrounding a Human Skeleton Material from Rounala in Karesuando Parish.* Master's thesis, Stockholm University.

Flateyjarbók III. 1868. Edited by G. Vigfússon and C.R. Unger. Christiania: P.T. Mallings bokforlag.

Gosden, Chris. 2004. *Archaeology and Colonialism. Cultural Contact from 5000 BC to the Present.* Cambridge: Cambridge University Press.

Halinen, Petri. 2009. "Change and Continuity of Saami Dwellings and Dwelling Sites from the Late Iron Age to the 18th Century." In *Máttut—Máddagat. The Roots of Saami Ethnicities, Societies and Spaces/Places,* ed. Tiina Äikäs, 100–15. Publications of Giellagas Institute. Oulu: University of Oulu.

Hambleton, Ellen, and Peter Rowley-Conwy. 1997. "The Medieval Reindeer Economy at Gæccevaj'njar'ga 244 B in the Varanger Fjord, North Norway." *Norwegian Archaeological Record* 30(1): 55–70.

Hansen, Lars Ivar. 2005. "Spesialisert reindrift eller kombinasjonsnæring?: reinholdet i Sør-Troms på 1600- og 1700-tallet." In *Fra villreinjakt til reindrift: Gåddebivdos boatsojsujttuj,* ed. Oddmund Andersen, Sven Donald Hedman, Inga-Maria Mulk, Kjersti Schanche, Ingrid Sommerseth, Kjell-Åke Aronsson, Johan I. Borgos et al., 165–83. Drag: Árran julevsáme guovdásj.

Harlin, Eeva-Kristiina. 2007. "Suomen puoleisen Tornion Lapin Markkinat." In *Peurakuopista kirkkokenttiin. Saamelaisalueen 10 000 vuotta arkeologin näkökulmasta,* ed. Eeva-Kristiina Harlin and Veli-Pekka Lehtola, 154–67. Publications of Giellagas Institute 9. Oulu: University of Oulu.

———. 2009. "The Possibilities of Osteology in Historical Sámi Archaeology. Life and Livelihood at the 18th-century Ohcejohka Sámi Market." In *Recent Perspectives on Sámi Archaeology in Fennoscandia and North-West Russia. Proceedings of the First International Conference on Sámi Archaeology, Rovaniemi, 19–22 October 2006,* ed. Petri Halinen, Mika Lavento, and Mervi Suhonen. Iskos 17: 121–32. Helsinki: Finnish Antiquarian Society.

Hedman, Sven-Donald, Bjørnar Olsen, and Maria Vretemark. 2015. "Hunters, Herders and Hearths: Interpreting New Results from Hearth Row Sites in Pasvik, Arctic Norway." *Rangifer* 35(1): 1–24.

Heimskringla I. 1979. Edited by Bjarni Aðalbjarnarson. Íslenzk fornrit XXVI-XXVIII. Reykjavík: Hið íslenzka bókmenntafélag.

Historia Norwegie I. 2006. Edited by Inger Ekrem and Lars Boje Mortensen, translated by Peter Fisher. Copenhagen: Museum Tusculanum Press.

Hörnberg, Greger, Lars Östlund, Olle Zackrisson, and Ingela Bergman. 2015. "Indications of Shifting Cultivation West of the Lapland Border: Multifaceted Land Use in Northernmost Sweden since AD 800." *The Holocene* 25: 989–1001.

Ingold, Tim. 1980. *Hunters, pastoralists and ranchers. Reindeer economies and their transformations.* Cambridge: Cambridge University Press.

Itkonen, T. I. 1921. *Lappalaisten Ruokatalous.* Hki: Société Finno-Ougrienne.

———. 1948a. *Suomen Lappalaiset Vuoteen 1945: 1. osa.* Porvoo: WSOY.

———. 1948b. *Suomen Lappalaiset Vuoteen 1945: 2. osa.* Porvoo: WSOY.

Jämtlands och Härjedalens diplomatarium I. 1943. Edited by K.-E. Löfqvist and R. Swedlund. Östersund: A.B. Wisénska Bokhandeln.

Johnson, Matthew. 2006. "The Tide Reversed: Prospects and Potentials for a Postcolonial Archaeology of Europe." In *Historical Archaeology,* ed. Martin Hall and Stephen W. Silliman, 313–31. Malden, MA: Blackwell.

Kennedy, Sarah A., and Parker VanValkenburgh. 2016. "Zooarchaeology and Changing Food Practices at Carrizales, Peru Following the Spanish Invasion." *International Journal of Historical Archaeology* 20: 73–104.

Ketils saga hœngs. 1950. Fornaldarsögur norðrlanda 2, Guðni Jónsson bjó til prentunar. Íslendingasagnaútgáfan, 149–81. Reykjavík: Prentsmiðjan Edda h.f..

Kuusela, Jari-Matti, Risto Nurmi, and Ville Hakamäki. 2016. "Co-existence and Colonisation: Re-assessing the Settlement History of the Pre-Christian Bothnian Bay Coast." *Norwegian Archaeological Review* 49(2): 177–203.

Kylli, Ritva. 2012. *Saamelaisten kaksi kääntymystä: Uskonnon muuttuminen Utsjoen ja Enontekiön lapinmailla 1602–1905.* Helsinki: SKS.

Lahti, Eeva-Kristiina. 2006. "Bones from Sápmi: Reconstruction of the Everyday Life of Two Ancient Saami Households." In *People, Material Culture and Environment in the North. Proceedings of the 22nd Nordic Archaeological Conference,* ed. V. Herva, 284–95. Oulu: University of Oulu.

Lie, R. 1992. "Appendix 4: Faunal Remains from the 1984 Research." In *The Varanger Saami. Habitation and Economy AD 1200–1900,* ed. Knut Odner, 193–94. Oslo: Scandinavian University Press.

Lightfoot, K.G., and Antoinette Martinez. 1995. "Frontiers and Boundaries in Archaeological Perspective." *Annual Review of Anthropology* 24: 471–92.

Lindenfeld, D.F., and Miles Richardson. 2010. "Introduction. Beyond Conversion and Syncretism." In *Beyond Conversion and Syncretism: Indigenous Encounters with Missionary Christianity, 1800–2000,* ed. D.F. Lindenfeld and Miles Richardson, 1–24. New York: Berghahn Books.

Nahkiaisoja, Tarja. 2016. *Saamelaisten maat ja vedet kruunun uudistiloiksi: Asutus ja maankäyttö Inarissa ja Utsjoella vuosina 1749–1925.* Oulu: Oulun yliopisto.

Naum, Magdalena. 2010. "Re-emerging frontiers: Postcolonial Theory and Historical Archaeology of Borderlands." *Journal of Archaeological Method and Theory* 17(2): 101–31.

Magnus, Olaus. [1555] 1996. *A Description of the Northern Peoples, 1555,* edited by Peter Fisher, Peter Godfrey Foote, John Granlund, and Humphrey Higgens. Ashgate Publishing Ltd.

Paulaharju, Samuli. 1932. *Seitoja ja seidan palvontaa.* Helsinki: SKS.

———. 1961. *Kiveliöitten kansaa Pohjois-Ruotsin suomalaisseuduilta.* Porvoo: Werner Söderstöm.

———. [1927] 1965. *Taka-Lappia*, 2nd edition. Porvoo: Werner Söderström Osakeyhtiö.

Pavao-Zuckerman, Barnet, and Diana DiPaolo Loren. 2012. "Presentation is Everything: Foodways, Tablewares, and Colonial Identity at Presidio Los Adaes." *International Journal of Historical Archaeology* 16: 199–226.

Ravila, Paavo. 1934. *Reste Lappischen Volksglaubens.* Helsinki: Suomalais-ugrilainen seura.

Salmi, Anna-Kaisa. 2011. "Riistaa, kalaa ja konttiluita—Pohjois-Suomen maaseudun ruokakulttuurista n. 1400–1700 AD." In: *Harmaata näkyvissä—Kirsti Paavolan juhlakirja*, ed. Janne Ikäheimo and Risto Nurmi, 221–36. Oulu: Oulun yliopisto.

Salmi, Anna-Kaisa, Tiina Äikäs, and Sanna Lipkin. 2011. "Animating Rituals at Sámi Sacred Sites in Northern Finland." *Journal of Social Archaeology* 11(2): 212–35.

Salmi, Anna-Kaisa, Tiina Äikäs, Marte Spangen, Markus Fjellström, and Inga-Maria Mulk. 2018. "Tradition and Transformation in Sámi Animal Offering Practices." *Antiquity* 92(362): 472–89.

Salmi, Anna-Kaisa, Annemari Tranberg, Mirva Pääkkönen, and Risto Nurmi. 2014. "Becoming Modern—Hybrid Foodways in Early Modern Tornio, Northern Finland." *International Journal of Historical Archaeology* 18(3): 489–512.

Schefferus, Johannes. [1673] 1963. *Lapponia eli Lapin maan ja kansan uusi ja todenmukainen kuvaus.* Translated by Tuomo Itkonen. Rovaniemi: Lapin tutkimusseura.

Seppälä, Suvianna. 2009. *Viljana, nahkoina, kapakalana: talonpoikien maksamat kruununverot Suomessa vuosina 1539–1609.* Helsinki: SKS.

Shohat, Ella. 1992. "Notes on the 'Post-Colonial.'" *Social Text* 31/32: 99–113.

Sköld, Peter. 1999. "Seime staembe. Brännivinet i den samiska religionen." *Oknytt* 20(1–4): 63–84.

Snellman, Eeva. 1996. *Väinönputki Oljenkortena.* Rovaniemi: Arktinen keskus.

Soppela, Päivi. 2000. "Poro ravinnonlähteenä." In *Siiddastallan: Siidoista kyliin: Luontosidonnainen saamelaiskulttuuri ja sen muuttuminen*, ed. Jukka Pennanen and Klemetti Näkkäläjärvi, 92–95. Oulu: Pohjoinen.

Steckzén, Birger. 1964. *Birkarlar och Lappar: En Studie i Birkarleväsendets, Lappbefolkningens och Skinnhandelns Historia.* Kungl. Vitterhets historie och antikvitets akademien, Historiska serien 9. Stockholm.

Sten, S. 1989. "Husdjurshållning, jakt och fiske i Silbojokk—en osteologisk analys av djurbenen." In *Silvret från Nasafjäll: Arkeologi vid Silbojokk*, ed. K. Awebro, N. Björkenstam, J. Norrman, S. Petersson, Y. Roslund, S. Sten, and E. Wallquist, 167–78. Stockholm: Riksantikvarieämbetet.

Stoler, Ann Laura. 2002. "Colonial Archives and the Arts of Governance." *Archival Science* 2: 87–109.

Tornæus, Johannes. [1672] 1772. *Prostens och Kyrko-herdens i Tornå Mag. Johannis J. Tornæi Beskrifning, öfwer Tornå Och Kemi Lappmarker. Författad. År 1672.* Helsinki: Helsingin yliopiston kirjasto.

Tresk, Olof. 1928. *Kartor över Kemi och Torne Lappmarker 1642 och 1643: Av Trycket Utg. Och Tillägnade K. B. Wiklund På 60-årsdagen 15 Mars 1928 av Vänner.* Stockholm: S.l.

Vahtola Jouko. 2003. "Saamelaiset Inarin kansa 1550–1660." In *Inari: Inarin Historia Jääkaudesta Nykypäivään = Aanaar*, ed. Veli-Pekka Lehtola, 114–33. Inari: Inarin kunta.

———. 2006. "Oravainen, Niilo Niilonpoika (n. 1520–1597)." In *Suomen kansallisbiografia 7: Negri–Pöysti*, ed. Matti Klinge, 362–64. Studia biographica 3(7). Helsinki: SKS.

Ylikangas, Heikki, and Kari Tarkiainen. 2005. "Kustaa Vaasa (1496–1560)." In *Suomen kansallisbiografia 5: Karl–Lehtokoski*, ed. Matti Klinge, 565–69. Studia biographica 3(5): Helsinki: SKS.

Ylimaunu, Timo. 2007. *Aittakylästä kaupungiksi: Arkeologinen tutkimus Tornion kaupungistumisesta 18. vuosisadan loppuun mennessä*. Rovaniemi: Pohjois-Suomen Historiallinen Yhdistys.

Ylimaunu, Timo, Sami Lakomäki, Titta Kallio-Seppä, P. R. Mullins, Risto Nurmi, and Markku Kuorilehto. 2014. "Borderlands as Spaces: Creating Third Spaces and Fractured Landscapes in Medieval Northern Finland." *Journal of Social Archaeology* 14(2): 244–67.

Chapter 6

Landscapes of Resilience at the
Cut Bank Boarding School, Montana

William A. White III and Brandi E. Bethke

Introduction

On a brisk July day in Browning, Montana, two researchers from the University of Arizona's Bureau of Applied Research in Anthropology (BARA)—Maria Nieves Zedeño and William White—took a break from conducting research to attend the 2016 Blackfeet Tribal Junior Rodeo. They watched Blackfeet youth try their luck at one of the most dangerous sports in the world. During the bronc busting competition, the announcers took time to acknowledge several of the former rodeo champions in attendance. The banter between announcers included a salutation to Truman "Mouse" Hall, a Blackfeet Tribal member and champion saddle bronc rider who was inducted into the Montana Pro Rodeo Hall of Fame in 2014. A few days earlier, Mouse shared his memories of attending the Cut Bank Boarding School during the 1950s with BARA researchers. While the Blackfeet are legendary for their horsemanship, Mouse said he learned much about managing livestock while living at the boarding school. This interview was fresh in the researchers' minds as they listened to the announcers' jovial banter: "Back in the day, cowboys like Mouse didn't have to walk to school. They just lassoed and broke whatever bronc they found along the road and rode it the rest of the way to school." Of course it was a joke, but tribal elders like Mr. Hall are the personification of one of the most difficult and emotional parts of Native American history.

The Cut Bank Boarding School Archaeological Site (24GL0302) is located on the Blackfeet Indian Reservation in Glacier County, Montana, just north of the town of Browning (Figure 6.1). A multicomponent site, this location is part of a much larger landscape that was first used by the Blackfeet people, before European American contact, as a hunting ground and campsite. Following the forced resettlement of the once nomadic Blackfeet people in the 1880s, the site was incorporated into their reservation territory. In 1905, this location was transformed into a boarding school campus for Native Americans living on the Blackfeet Indian Reservation. Today, it remains a tribally administered boarding school for tribal youth from disadvantaged households. Through the lens of archaeology, archival research, and the recorded memories of those who attended the school, this chapter demonstrates how the Blackfeet people are actively reclaiming and reinterpreting this continually used landscape—and its elements of contested, difficult memories—as well as their own resilience through trying periods.

Assimilation and Indian Boarding Schools on the Blackfeet Indian Reservation

Histories and archaeologies of Native American boarding schools fall within a grey area of subjectivity partially because of the varied experiences of former students but also because of the diversity of the

Figure 6.1. Overview of Cut Bank Boarding School historic property survey area in 2016. (Figure by William A. White III.)

administration found in the various schools across the United States. Researchers, many of whom are not Native American, must perform a balancing act to depict the extreme effects of the US government's explicit goal of assimilation of Native communities while also accurately recording the individual experiences of former students. Those who experienced it are the ones who can unpack the complicated impacts of the boarding school system.

Following the demise of the bison populations in the Northwestern Plains in the 1880s, a period of government dependency and resettlement ensued due to the necessary acceptance of government housing and food. Native people were more willing to accept dependence as their reservations slipped deeper into poverty (Child 1998). Central to resettlement efforts by the United States government were programs of forced assimilation that sought to restrict or eliminate traditional Blackfeet practices and adopt a more European American lifestyle. To facilitate this task, Congress and the Indian Bureau adopted a suite of education policies aimed at transforming Indian conceptions of life, culture, and relationship to the earth. Across the country education programs aimed at young children had become integral to the campaign to assimilate Native people into "mainstream" American society since administrators believed educating Native American children to accept European American cultural values from a young age was the easiest path to assimilation (Adams 1995; Szasz 1999, 8). In addition to basic grammar and arithmetic, boarding schools would emphasize vocational training.

An ancillary goal to gross assimilation was the idea that students should be taught skills that would allow them to survive off the reservation because government officials wanted graduates to leave the reservations. It was believed this would reduce Indian dependence upon the Federal government while simultaneously destroying their cultural connection to traditional lands and ways of life (Adams 1995). Thus, from its conception, the boarding school system was dedicated to teaching Native children how to manage livestock, grow vegetables, and execute all the activities necessary to operate a small farmstead. Emphasizing Western traditions, education, and morals while omitting traditional ways was central to accomplishing the government's goal of inculcating Blackfeet children into an idealized image of European America. The entire boarding school concept emphasized these virtues of self-reliance, strict gender roles, and scientific household management (Child 1998).

On the Blackfeet Reservation, a major part of this program was the creation of residential schools that removed children from their homes (Dempsey 1978, 26). Children would be assimilated more easily, it was thought, if they were removed from the influence of adult family members in their homes and communities. During the first half of the twentieth century, attending government boarding schools was a contentious issue on the Blackfeet Reservation and many families tried to resist them (McFee 1972). However, the widespread poverty of the Blackfeet people that resulted from the demise of the bison, forced settlement, and repression of traditional lifeways encouraged some parents to agree to send their children away from their homes. Many Blackfeet households were characterized by a lack of material and financial resources available to raise children. The severalty and allotment of Blackfeet lands was advertised as a means to provide agricultural property, but many families were unable to subsist on their allotments. By the early twentieth century, therefore, a number of Blackfeet families were subsisting on government rations and there was little stable employment (Cloud 1932). Boarding schools were seen as a way children could get food, shelter, and clothing—things many parents could no longer provide.

Providing a modern education to Blackfeet children posed numerous problems for government administrators. With an area larger than the state of Rhode Island, building enough day schools and buses to provide for the sparse population was not cost-effective. During the early 1900s, not all Blackfeet children had access to school. In 1911, 366 of 655 school-aged children were not attending school (Baker 1911). In 1915, 631 of the 950 school-aged children were still not in school (Ellis 1915). Expanding the boarding school system was advertised as a more economical and efficient way of providing education on the reservation (Baker 1911). As a result, there were several attempts to create boarding schools on the Blackfeet Reservation. However, the Blackfeet Reservation lacked sufficient educational facilities even well into the twentieth century. From 1883 to 1884, a short-lived boarding school was established on Badger Creek, about twenty-five miles west of present-day Browning, Montana. The Catholic Church established the Holy Family Mission School in 1890 a few miles from Browning in the Two Medicine River Valley. This school was better attended and had 120 students by 1893 (Matson 1893). Perhaps motivated by the success of the Mission School, a second government boarding school opened on Willow Creek in 1892. This substantial facility was composed of dormitories and a heating system along with a ten-acre farm and infrastructure for livestock. Despite this investment, the school on Willow Creek fell into disrepair. A catastrophic fire in 1897 destroyed the boy's dormitory, but the Willow Creek School continued operations until plans were approved for the Cut Bank Boarding School in 1904 (Montana Memory Project 1899).

History of the Cutbank Boarding School

Construction on the Cut Bank Boarding School began in 1905. The school opened on 18 October 1906. A substantial, modern facility, the first buildings at the school were made of brick and designed to serve seventy-five students, however, eighty-seven were enrolled in the first term (Dare 1906). The school was designed on the same regimented system commonly used in other Indian boarding schools across the country. School activities took place on a rigorous schedule. Students were instructed in tasks and allotted a period of time in which to complete them. Boy students were made to learn how to manage a small-scale ranch or farm. Girls were expected to learn basic homemaking skills like sewing, cooking, and cleaning. At the Cut Bank School, older boys managed livestock and the school's agricultural fields. The kitchen and sewing rooms were where girls learned what it was believed would help them be good homemakers. During the early twentieth century, this was not unusual and vocational training was part of regular public education. The Montana public school curriculum, for example, also included vocational and homemaking courses (McFatridge 1911). However, at the Cut Bank School, labor was also used to support the institution since administrators hoped that this school would prosper and become self-sustaining (Gaymond 1905). The Cut Bank School, therefore, became yet another element in this larger campaign to acculturate Native America into an idealized version of European American ranchers, farmers, and housewives.

Both students and school administrators had significant obstacles to overcome from the start. While it was well-attended, the Cut Bank School was underfunded. This caused persistent difficulties for administrators and teachers, especially as the facility aged. The school had fallen into disarray within ten years of its founding. A Blackfeet Indian Agent controlled the school, and by 1914 he was under investigation for charges of corruption, partially associated with the mismanagement of school funds and supplies. United States inspectors were sent to the Blackfeet Indian Reservation to investigate the case. The school housed 150 pupils at that time and consisted of "two two-story brick dormitory buildings, one one-story brick school building, one two-story employees' quarters, a pump house and a laundry building" (Linnen and Cook 1915, 33). Strewn with ashes and trash, investigators could clearly see the dormitories had not been cleaned for an extended period of time. Sanitation was in neglect. Toilets, which were heavily used and had not been cleaned for an unknown period of time, were in "a very filthy condition" (Linnen and Cook 1915, 34–35). The children themselves showed signs of neglect. They complained that they did not have enough to eat and frequently left the table hungry (Linnen and Cook 1915, 41). The school lacked facilities for sick children. Worst of all, investigators discovered that, while the school had been receiving its supplies, they had been hoarded by the agency and were not distributed to the teachers, pupils, or employees (Linnen and Cook 1915, 12). This investigation clearly revealed that the Blackfeet Agency had failed to provide for the boarding school students. The superintendent was removed from his position soon after the report's publication in 1915 and conditions somewhat improved thereafter.

By 1916, the school buildings had been repaired and the children no longer complained about their food or hunger. Investigators reported: "It is safe to say that conditions are improved from fifty to seventy-five percent over those which obtained on said reservation a little over a year ago" (Linnen 1916). Nevertheless, persistent budgetary shortfalls led the school's physical plan to continue to deteriorate. During the 1920s, the Office of Indian Affairs officials were clearly aware of the poor condition of Indian boarding schools across the United States, but they stated this was not solely due to underfunding. Deficiencies among school administrators and staff were blamed for the decay of these facilities (Office of Indian Affairs 1926). The task of making these schools successful was left to understaffed, underfunded administrators.

With the onset of the Great Depression, government funding was slashed across the board and dependent facilities like Indian boarding schools were prime targets for budget cuts. On 30 June 1934, the Cut Bank Boarding School was closed temporarily due to budget cuts and its facilities and property reverted to tribal control. The dormitory buildings were still to be occupied by older students. Younger children were to be sent to day schools in the newly established Montana State Public School District No. 9, which serviced the Blackfeet Reservation (Montana Memory Project 1934a, 1934b). Public School District No. 9 was supposed to be supported by public taxes, but the reservation had trouble raising enough money to keep all the schools in the district in operation. The Cut Bank School was back in action by 1938 (Montana Memory Project 1937).

By the 1940s, the Cut Bank Boarding School was expanded to eight grades and complemented other schools in District No. 9. The vocational program at the Cut Bank School was considered exemplary. A well-kept and productive dairy herd was maintained and the facilities appeared to be in good order (Thompson 1943). The Bureau of Indian Affairs (BIA) had planned to redevelop the boarding school, which included building a new school plant and expanding the school to twelfth grade (McBride 1944). It is unknown how much of this plan was initiated as the school only went up to eighth grade in the 1950s. During this time, the Cut Bank School continued to be a vocational institution that maintained livestock herds and an irrigated garden while simultaneously providing a basic, public school-quality education to its students.

The Cut Bank Boarding School focused on providing an education for students from broken homes and poor family conditions during the 1950s and 1960s. It remained an agricultural and vocational institution at that time. The school continued to maintain its garden, livestock, domestic science, and machine repair programs. It still went only to the eighth grade at that time, so graduates had to go elsewhere if they wanted to continue their education. In the 1970s, the school curriculum abandoned agricultural training to focus on academics. The working farm was abandoned sometime in the 1970s and the physical plan has been upgraded throughout the years.

Revisiting the Cut Bank Boarding School

Today the Cut Bank Boarding School facility remains in transition. Another round of construction from 2013 to 2014 brought a new dormitory building that was constructed in the same place where several other school buildings have existed in the past. These activates became the impetus for new research at the Boarding School site that was conducted from 2013 to 2016 through a collaborative partnership between the Blackfeet Tribal Historic Preservation Office (THPO) and Bureau of Applied Research in Anthropology (BARA) at the University of Arizona. This project focused on the history of this landscape, emphasizing the long time-depth of its occupation. Reclaiming precontact heritage through archaeology is another way the Blackfeet people are reconnecting with this long-used space for their own cultural uses. These efforts, which included a combination of archival research, ethnographic fieldwork, building recordation, and zooarchaeological analysis, provide insight into the ways the Blackfeet people have experienced this landscape as a source of persistence in the face of change. In this way, this work moves away from a colonialist narrative of specific policies that enabled the boarding school system to exist to provide a richer understanding of the meaning and effect of this process on Native people.

Precontact Landscape

Archaeological evidence suggests that the area encompassing the Cut Bank Boarding school has a long history of occupation by Blackfeet ancestors prior to its reappropriation as a boarding school campus. To date, two archaeological projects have been conducted at the site to explore the precontact use of the area. The first excavations at the nearby bluff slope and adjacent floodplain were conducted by Thomas Kehoe over three field seasons in 1952, 1958, and 1959 (Kehoe 1967). Through the analysis of diagnostic artifacts, lithic debris, and large quantities of bison remains, Kehoe (1967) identified several general periods of occupation within the project area, including the use of the area as a temporary camp and hunting ground during the Middle Precontact period (ca. 150 BC–450 AD) and its seasonal use as a bison hunting and processing complex and camp site during the Late Precontact period (ca. AD 500–1700). In the Late Precontact period the site was occupied seasonally for short periods of time during which several large bison drives took place (Kehoe 1967, 73, 89–90). Plains and Prairie side-notched points were recovered from these bone-bed layers, suggesting that these kill events date to some-time during the Old Women's phase (AD 1300–1700), which is generally understood as the ancestors of the Blackfeet people (Kehoe 1967, 42; Peck 2011, 405–45). At least one additional kill episode occurred in the area following these large-scale hunting activities, but this activity was repre-sented by very little bone and no diagnostic artifacts, possibly suggesting the use of horse-mounted hunting and packing techniques at this time.

Recent excavations at the site occurred in 2013 when the Blackfeet THPO administered and conducted archaeological testing prior to constructing a new classroom facility. These excavations revealed the existence of an extensive bone bed and processing site, thus expanding what was known about Blackfeet use of this landscape for bison procurement during the Precontact period (Bethke 2016). Bison were the single most significant resource for northwestern Plains people for over a millennium. They were important not only as sources of food and raw material, but there is also ample evidence that bison were at the core of their belief systems, serving as an organizing principle of social, ceremonial, and religious life (Ewers 1958; Grinnell 1962; Schaeffer 1978; McClintock 1999). Hunting commu-nities exploited bison in the prairies of the northwestern Plains from the terminal Pleistocene to the late nineteenth century (McHugh 1972; Lott 2003). For the ancestral Blackfeet people bison hunting was primarily practiced communally in the systematic, landscape-scale method of using drivelines, jumps, pounds, and corrals, which helped the hunters achieve the goal of killing hundreds of animals at once (Brink 2008, 67; Cooper 2008, 296; Zedeño and Anderson 2010). The zooarchaeological analysis of these excavations supports the notion that the Boarding School Site was part of this large-scale communal hunting complex that dominated this region during the Late Precontact period (e.g., Forbis 1962; Quigg 1978; Vickers 1991; Peck 2004; Brink 2008; Cooper 2008; Zedeño, Ballenger, and Murray 2014). Therefore, the Blackfeet invested heavily in this location as a resource procurement and culturally significant site up until and possibly following European American Contact.

Historical Landscape

In addition to these precontact activities, the 2013 excavations also revealed more information about the site's historic use. Cattle remains discovered at the site provide direct archaeological evidence of beef-rationing practices known from the historic and ethnographic record (Bethke 2016). Beef rationing for the reservation took place at the Agencies located in Browning and in other reservation communities. However, beef for the Cut Bank Boarding School was raised and butchered on site for consumption by students and staff. From the limited faunal remains positively identified to cow it is believed these animals were being raised, butchered, rationed, consumed, and the remains discarded at the site. Metal-saw marks associated with deer remains suggest that these animals were hunted during the area's use as a boarding school. Similarly, the single butchery mark along with metal staining witnessed on the elk rib recovered from the site suggests that this animal was also hunted during this period (Bethke 2016). While it is impossible to tell exactly who at the boarding school was hunting these animals, ethnographic work by Zedeño and collaborators suggests that the hunting of game animals became an important activity for the Blackfeet people during the historic period not only in terms of subsistence but also as a cultural extension of previous hunting activates associated with bison (Reeves 2003; Zedeño 2013; Zedeño, Murray, and Murray 2015, 12). The results of this investigation suggest that this practice, at least in some capacity, extended to those living at or within the vicinity of the Cut Bank Boarding School.

A building inventory and ethnographic survey of the site was conducted in 2016 as a continuation of resource management activities associated with the 2013 excavations. Archival research yielded a cache of audio cassettes containing thirteen oral histories with Blackfeet boarding school students recorded in the 1980s. Additionally, a site tour was conducted in 2016 at the boarding school with a Blackfeet elder who attended the school in the 1950s. Interviews with former students of the Cut Bank Boarding School did not recall their experiences being particularly violent, as has been noted at other Indian boarding schools, but they do recall that their education there had a mission—teach them the ways of European Americans. English-language lessons were central to the education taught at the boarding schools on the Blackfeet Reservation. Repetition was key to learning English at the boarding school. Former students recall writing and saying the same words repeatedly until they had been memorized (Long Time Sleeping 1978). In a 1978 interview, Blackfeet tribal members Louie Fish, who attended boarding school in the 1930s, recalled that he did not speak English well when he started at the Cut Bank Boarding School in the 1920s. He said that he was spanked with a ruler or forced to stand in the corner whenever he spoke Blackfeet (Fish 1978). Learning English was important to being able to function in the European American world, but administrators also understood its role in assimilation. The Blackfeet language was a connection to traditional thought and culture. Replacing their traditional language was more than just teaching students a valuable skill. It was believed to be a way of erasing the traditional knowledge needed to keep their culture alive.

Students became accustomed to labor during their stay at the school. Tasks were designed to teach students how to manage a small farm or household and to find work off the reservation in hopes that they would no longer have to rely on resources provided by the US Government. Student labor was also used to support the school. Labor was allocated by sex and age. Older children did heavier work and girls primarily did tasks indoors like laundry and kitchen work. Students hauled coal, carried water, washed dishes, sewed, and did laundry (Long Time Sleeping 1978; Sherman 1978). Managing livestock was also a central job. A student in the 1920s and 1930s, Albert Sherman (1978) recalls that students milked cows in the morning and evening. The milk was hauled to the kitchen in buckets where the cream was separated so butter could be made. Students also fed the pigs with kitchen scraps (Sherman 1978). Several students helped the school's cook in the kitchen where bread was baked in large ovens, other courses were cooked in large pots, and dishes were washed (Sherman 1978).

Several former students credit these chores, along with the formal education they gained at the boarding school, with helping them survive in a non-Native world as adults. These graduates subverted governmental pressures to assimilate by successfully raising families, remaining gainfully employed, and staying on the reservation. It is by becoming upstanding members of the Blackfeet tribe that students were able to strengthen their community and provide for its perseverance. Students took what they learned at the boarding school and applied it in their daily lives as adults. For example, Lucy Owl Rattler (1978) got married after leaving the Holy Mission Boarding School on the Blackfeet Reservation. As a homemaker on a tribal allotment, she managed livestock, harvested alfalfa, and took care of household tasks. During the Great Depression, she took a job sewing at a Works Progress Administration workshop housed at the Cut Bank Boarding School. After the Depression, she supplemented her income by working as an itinerate farm laborer with other family members in Washington State where she trimmed trees and harvested fruit.

"Mouse" Hall is another example of how the boarding school experience failed to acculturate the Blackfeet. Born in 1940, Hall attended the boarding school from 1945/46 until 1954 when he transferred to the Carlisle Industrial School in Flandreau, South Dakota. Hall recalls the boarding school as a rigid but fair place. Students received clothing, regular meals, and a basic education in exchange for their labor. Separated by gender, approximately thirty to forty children lived in each dormitory. Students were awake at 6 a.m. every day and had about thirty minutes to wash up before reporting to breakfast. Classwork started right after breakfast and lasted until lunch. Chores began after lunch. Breaks for playing and sports were interspersed throughout the day. Hall understands that his experience is not the same as that of all the children who attended the Cut Bank School, but he accredits it as a place that brought stability and discipline to a youth that was trying to make his way on the Blackfeet Reservation (Hall, pers. comm., 2016). As an adult, Hall became a champion bronc rider for the Professional Bull Riders (PBR) Association. He held several jobs before using what he learned in vocational schools like Cut Bank and Flandreau to start a trail riding business out of East Glacier, Montana. Despite his age, Hall still manages this business today.

The twentieth century was a time of great change for the Blackfeet. Their society was not static and, in response to assimilation pressures and economic hardships, those who remained on the reservation had to change aspects of their lives to adjust to ever-changing conditions. Building an educational system on the reservation was part of this change. The Federal government or religious organizations supported the first schools on the reservation. By the 1930s, the reservation had its own public-school system centered around day schools. Day schools have become the preferred institutional vehicle, but they have not fully replaced boarding schools on the Blackfeet Reservation. School curriculum has also changed during the twentieth century. Boarding schools on the reservation were initially designed to teach vocational skills while also providing for their own maintenance. In addition to the dormitories and classroom buildings, these facilities also contained gardens, pastures, barns, a bakery, laundry, a coal-powered steam plant, and other major infrastructure. Most of these infrastructural elements were abandoned or removed as the school's mission changed during the 1970s to focus more on academics and less on vocational training.

Changes in the Blackfeet educational system are reflected in the physical landscape of the boarding school campus. A building survey was designed to chronicle the historical use of this area as a boarding school and it was conducted as part of the 2016 archaeological fieldwork. A total of fifteen buildings older than fifty years in age were documented along with two archaeological features, all of which were associated with the school's operation between 1905 and the 1960s (White, Zedeño, and Edwards 2017). Facilities at the Cut Bank Boarding School have changed dramatically since its construction. New buildings have replaced older ones as allowed by funding and necessity (Figure 6.2). For its early years, the school was a combination of a working farm, educational establishment, and domestic place where employees and students lived in an institutional community. Its buildings have served both domestic and functional roles.

Existing buildings represent three phases of the school's development. A gymnasium, two log cabin-style houses, a nondescript brick shed, and a garage were all constructed prior to the 1930s and are the oldest standing structures at the school. Aside from the gymnasium, which does not meet BIA building codes, all of these historical buildings are still in use by the Blackfeet today. Ten Ranch-style houses built between the 1930s and 1960s are from the second phase of construction, which was part of the post-World War II redevelopment of the school by the Federal government. Houses at the school remain tribal housing and are still

Figure 6.2. Overview of remaining historical buildings juxtaposed against modern school buildings, view northwest. (Photograph by William A. White III.)

occupied by the Blackfeet. The main school building and newer buildings constructed since the 1960s represent the most recent iteration of the school. Buildings associated with the school's earliest period, the 1900s and 1910s, have been demolished.

Buildings show the progression of the material plan that was used to facilitate the educational process. Each of these phases involved the demolition of older buildings to make way for new construction. None of the original buildings from 1905 exists on the site. Archaeological excavations also show that the entire historical site has been built upon a precontact bison-processing site. It remained a resource procurement site while the school farm was in operation, but this ended when the school's farm ceased operation. The construction and evolution of the school buildings represent another iteration of Blackfeet land use in this location.

Understanding the Cut Bank Boarding School Landscape

Interpretations of the recent work at the Cut Bank Boarding School is rooted in anthropological conceptions of landscape. In the last thirty years there has been a large body of research that has sought to incorporate a definition of landscape that is inclusive of the social and symbolic inter-actions between people and environments in which they live (Scheiber and Clark 2008, 5). These works highlight the importance of agency, memory, and practice in order to better understand how "landscape" is perceived, constructed, and experienced by human groups (Ashmore and Knapp 1999). Instead of focusing on purely the ecological aspects of landscape, these studies have expanded to include studies of ritual and sacred places, links among people, pathways and places, identity formation, and the way in which people connect to the land in order to create and maintain a sense of place within their daily lives, even in the face of dramatic cultural change (Basso 1996; Zvelebil 1997; Scheiber and Clark 2008; Oetelaar and Oetelaar 2006; Zedeño and Bowser 2009; Oetelaar 2016). Cultural landscapes, therefore, represent a shared history of a given community that celebrates the lives of past and present indi-viduals by ascribing memory to physical space (Colwell-Chanthaphonh, Ferguson, and Anyon 2008, 62).

As this research has shown, the space occupied by the Cut Bank Boarding School encompasses a landscape that has been occupied by Blackfeet people for thousands of years. The precontact component at this site attests to the deep time-depth of Blackfeet interaction with this place as a bison-hunting landscape (an activity that defined what it meant to be Blackfeet). With the advent of European American encroachment into the region and the forced resettlement of the Blackfeet people, this traditional landscape was transformed into the physical embodiment of the non-Native world—a place where colonizers attempted to erase all traces of traditional Blackfeet society. This change can be read from the landscape at the Cut Bank Boarding School site. Indeed, extant buildings, historical archaeological resources, and the memories of those who attended the school remain as physical and emotional manifestations of this government-sponsored facility that attempted to acculturate the Blackfeet into another way of life. Blackfeet culture and lifeways changed dramatically. The educational process exemplified by the boarding school facilitated this change. However, not everything was lost. The Blackfeet continue to use this landscape to strengthen their community, despite the extensive transformation of this space and its people throughout time. While the Cut Bank Boarding School site was viewed as a vehicle of assimilation by government administrators, for many Blackfeet people the redefined landscape was a place for resisting assimilation efforts.

As a landscape of resilience and resistance, the Cut Bank Boarding School chronicles the shared human experience of generations of Blackfeet. Their memories have been ascribed to this place and archaeological excavations have extended this memory into the precontact past. Oral histories and archival documents show how an attempt at de jure assimilation was unsuccessful. Students and parents seized the chance for an education because they understood this would help their children compete in a European American–centric world. Many students used what they learned to find employment after graduation. Their resilience was strengthened by attending school. This made them better able to help their nation push back against colonization by finding gainful employment, raising families, and starting businesses. As the leaders of this project, the Blackfeet continue to shape narratives of their own past through cultural resource management and archaeology. Archaeological remains and buildings are material residues of this process.

This work has also shown how both the Blackfeet and non-Native government administrators have reimagined this place. Although the nature of activities taking place here have changed dramatically since the bison-hunting days, the Cut Bank Boarding School continues to serve the Blackfeet people. Today, it is administered by the tribe, teaches State of Montana curriculum, and primarily serves underprivileged children. The ways students used their education to become better tribal citizens and the reshaping of the colonialist landscape to suit the needs of the tribe today are just some of the many ways the Blackfeet people were able to negotiate Indigenous resistance to colonization. Expanding our understanding of the relationship between the Blackfeet people and the site to include not only its historic occupation but also its long-term use history as a bison hunting complex and modern educational center aids in significantly revising our understanding of the boarding school experience from an Indigenous perspective, thereby acknowledging "individual and community-specific historical realities" (Ferris 2009, 1).

Conclusion

Across the United States, American Indian boarding schools were an integral part of the United States government's efforts to acculturate Native Americans with the explicit goal of destroying Native American culture. The negative effects of these damaging programs on the Blackfeet people should not be discounted. When the Cutbank Boarding School was constructed the Blackfeet were still reeling by the changes wrought by the arrival of European Americans. Their lifeways had changed dramatically. Their buffalo-oriented economy was no longer tenable. The Federal government was exerting substantial pressure on the Blackfeet to relinquish their traditional ways and follow the mainstream into a Eurocentric society. Proscription of traditional cultural practices and confinement in the reservation and in the boarding school instilled fear and distrust. Worst of all, attempts to eradicate the Blackfoot language by forcing children to speak English only contributed to the erosion of cultural identity. Oral histories recall how the Blackfeet language was suppressed by teachers because it was perceived as an unnecessary skill and understood to be an effective means of destroying traditions. In addition, the remote location of the Blackfeet Indian Reservation presented tremendous obstacles to efficient communication between Indian agents and the Federal government, which lead to the mismanagement and poor maintenance of the school. It also prevented the government from direct oversight of Indian agents' policies and practices, which in some cases led to corruption and injustice. Archival research reveals Blackfeet students suffered during the earliest years of the school. Economic shortcomings plagued the school throughout its operations. In order to survive, administrators relied on student labor to keep the facility open.

Yet, at the same time, recent research suggests that at least some graduates of the Cut Bank Boarding School used what they learned to become valuable tribal members, strengthening themselves and their community. Through conversations with those tribal members that were students at the Cut Bank Boarding School we can better understand the complexity of their situation. Families on the reservation sent their children to the boarding school because poverty made it difficult for them to provide for their children. As is the case with archaeologies of other disenfranchised communities, poverty is not the main narrative that the Blackfeet focus on when it comes to interpreting this boarding school (Matthews 2011). To them, this is a place of persistence and survival. Many parents realized that their children would have to learn how to survive in European American society. At the school, students received room, board, clothing, and learned skills that would serve them after graduation as laborers and homemakers in the non-Native world. In this way, the boarding school continued to provide for tribal members.

The goal of tribal members, therefore, was to provide for Blackfeet survival, not to become like European Americans. At best, Western education was seen a useful tool—something that could be turned against the oppressors even though it was designed to eradicate traditional ways. While it may appear that those who graduated were acculturated completely into non-Native society through their education, oral histories suggest the opposite. Those that remain on the reservation used this education to benefit the tribe through their industry and resilience. Designed to acculturate Blackfeet children into Western society, the school taught students how to understand European American ways and they used this knowledge to strengthen their community. Their memories explain one instance when the acculturation process was coopted and transformed into a bulwark against colonization.

Thus, for the Blackfeet people the Cut Bank Boarding School is a testament of their resilience, serving as an example of how government attempts to assimilate Native children though education were not totally successful. Conventional studies of the boarding school experience craft a narrative that these institutions were vehicles for destroying Native culture. However, most of these narratives fail to reconcile the fact that the history of Indigenous people is one of survival and resistance (Ferris 2009, 29–30). Rather than obliteration, Indigenous people adapted to harsh conditions imposed by outside forces, maintaining as much of their culture as they could. Our work at the Cut Bank Boarding School suggests this process was complicated. Age, gender, personality, family situation, and tribal history all influenced the boarding school experience. While each individual's experience differed, the austerity, work ethic, and education helped at least some graduates survive and thrive in a rapidly encroaching non-Blackfeet world.

The history of the Cut Bank Boarding School is only the recent manifestation of Blackfeet traditions on a landscape that has been used by their ancestors for thousands of years. The precontact archaeological materials and the constantly changing physical footprint of the school are testaments to the longevity of the Blackfeet in this place. The use and physical place of the Cut Bank Boarding School has changed over its long occupation. These changes over the years have left their mark on the archaeology and architecture of this site. For the Blackfeet people, however, the Cut Bank School today represents a continually occupied landscape that for over two millennia has been a place for learning how to survive.

Acknowledgments

We are thankful for all the support received from the Blackfeet Tribe and the kindness of Blackfeet consultants, especially "Mouse" Hall, who generously shared their knowledge and concerns regarding the landscape and resources of the Cut Bank Boarding School. This project would not have been a success without the dedication of John Murray and Virgil Edwards of the Blackfeet Tribal Historic Preservation Office. Their tireless work and support helped further this research. Additional assistance and generosity from the rest of the Blackfeet Nation and local community of East Glacier, Montana made us feel at home while doing fieldwork and research. We thank you all.

Dr. William A. White III is an assistant professor of anthropology at the University of California, Berkeley. His research focuses on racialization and racism in the American West during the historical period inferred from the built environment, material culture, archival documents, and oral histories.

Dr. Brandi E. Bethke serves as Laboratory Director and Research Faculty at the Oklahoma Archeological Survey, University of Oklahoma. Her research focuses on understanding interactions between humans, animals, and the landscape in the North American Plains from the late precontact period to the present day through the integration of zooarchaeology, ethnohistory, computer modeling.

References

Adams, David Wallace. 1995. *Education for Extinction: American Indians and the Boarding School Experience, 1875–1928*. Lawrence: University of Kansas Press.
Ashmore, Wendy, and Bernard A. Knapp. 1999. "Archaeological Landscapes: Constructed, Conceptualized, Ideational." In *Archaeologies of Landscape: Contemporary Perspectives*, ed. Wendy Ashmore and A. Bernard Knapp, 1–31. Oxford: Blackwell.

Baker, Fred A. 1911. Inspection Report of Normal Instructor Fred A. Baker, 4 December 1911. Central Classified Files 1907–1939 Blackfeet Agency 150 Record Group 75—Box 33 Folder 106246-1-1911 Blackfeet 150. Document on file at Montana State Library, Helena.

Basso, Keith H. 1996. "Wisdom Sits in Places: Notes on Western Apache Landscape." In *Senses of Place*, ed. Steven Feld and Keith H. Basso, 53–90. Santa Fe: School of American Research Press.

Bethke, Brandi. 2016. *Analysis of Vertebrate Faunal Remains from the 2013 Excavations at the Cut Bank Boarding School, Site 24GL302, Blackfeet Indian Reservation, Glacier County, Montana*. Bureau of Applied Research in Anthropology, School of Anthropology, University of Arizona.

Brink, Jack W. 2008. *Imagining Head-Smashed-In: Aboriginal Buffalo Hunting on the Northern Plains*. Edmonton: AU Press.

Child, Brenda J. 1998. *Boarding School Seasons: American Indian Families, 1900–1940*. Lincoln: University of Nebraska Press.

Cloud, Henry Roe. 1932. Inspection Report of Indian Field Service Representative Henry Roe Cloud, 20 April 1932. Central Classified Files 1907-1939 Blackfeet Agency 150, 151 Record Group 75—Box 37, Folder 21991-1932 Blackfeet 150. Document on file at Montana State Library, Helena.

Colwell-Chanthaphonh, Chip, T. J. Ferguson, and Roger Anyon. 2008. "Always Multivocal and Multivalent: Conceptualizing Archaeological Landscapes in Arizona's San Pedro Valley." In *Archaeologies of Placemaking: Monuments, Memories, and Engagement in Native North America*, ed. Patricia E. Rubertone, 59–80. Walnut Creek: Left Coast Press.

Cooper, Judith Rose. 2008. *Bison Hunting and Late Prehistoric Human Subsistence Economies in the Great Plains*. PhD diss., Southern Methodist University.

Dare, J. Z.1906. Annual Report of the Commission of Indian Affairs. Central Classified Files 1907–1939 Blackfeet Agency. Document on file at Montana State Library, Helena.

Dempsey, Hugh A. 1978. "One Hundred Years of Treaty Seven." In *One Century Later: Western Canadian Reserve Indians Since Treaty 7*, ed. Ian A. L. Getty and Donald B. Smith, 20–30. Vancouver: University of British Columbia Press.

Ellis, C. L. 1915. Letter to Cato Sells, Commissioner of Indian Affairs, 18 March 1915. Central Classified Files 1907–1939 Blackfeet Agency 150 Record Group 75—Box 33. Folder 32216-1914 Blackfeet 150. Document on file at Montana State Library, Helena.

Ewers, John C. 1958. *The Blackfoot: Raiders on the Northwestern Plains*. Norman: University of Oklahoma Press.

Ferris, Neal. 2009. *The Archaeology of Native-Lived Colonialism: Challenging History in the Great Lakes*. Tucson: University of Arizona Press.

Fish, Louie. 1978. Interview with Louie Fish. Audio recording on file with the Blackfeet Tribal Historic Preservation Office, Browning, Montana.

Forbis, Richard G. 1962. "The Old Women's Buffalo Jump, Alberta." *National Museum of Canada Bulletin* 180: 56–123.

Gaymond, George A. 1905. Annual Report of the Commissioner of Indian Affairs. Central Classified Files 1907–1939 Blackfeet Agency. Document on file at Montana State Library, Helena.

Grinnell, George B. 1962. *Blackfoot Lodge Tales: The Story of a Prairie People*. Lincoln: University of Nebraska Press.

Kehoe, Thomas F. 1967. "The Boarding School Bison Drive Site." *Plains Anthropologist Memoir* 4: 12–35.

Linnen, E. B. 1916. Inspection Report of E. B. Linnen, Chief Inspector, The Blackfeet Indian Reservation, Montana, 3 February 1916. Central Classified Files 1907–1939 Blackfeet Agency 150 Record Group 75—Box 34, Folder 119979-1915 Blackfeet 150. Document on file at Montana State Library, Helena.

Linnen, E. B., and F. S. Cook. 1915. Investigation Report of Affairs on the Blackfeet Indian Reservation, Montana. United States Indian Service Chief Inspector E. B. Linnen and Special Agent F. S. Cook, 9 January 1915. Central classified files 1907–1939 Blackfeet Agency 150 Record Group 75—Box 33, Folder 30650-1915 Blackfeet 150. Document on file at Montana State Library, Helena.

Long Time Sleeping, Walter. 1978. Interview with Walter Long Time Sleeping. Audio recording on file with the Blackfeet Tribal Historic Preservation Office, Browning, Montana.

Lott, Dale F. 2003. *American Bison: A Natural History*. Los Angeles: University of California Press.

Matson, W. H. 1893. Report of Blackfeet Agency. Sixty-Second Annual Report of the Commissioner of Indian Affairs. Government Printing Office, Washington, DC. Pages 171–177. Document on file at Montana State Library, Helena.

Matthews, Chris. 2011. "Lonely Islands: Culture, Community, and Poverty in Archaeological Perspective." *Historical Archaeology* 45(3): 41–54.

McBride, F. H. 1944. Letter from Superintendent F. H. McBride, 9 October 1944. Central Classified Files 1907–1939 Blackfeet Agency 800 Record Group 75—Box 294, Folder 42804-36 Blackfeet 800. Document on file at Montana State Library, Helena.

McClintock, Walter. 1999. *The Old North Trail: Life, Legends and Religion of the Blackfeet Indians*. Lincoln: University of Nebraska Press.

McFatridge, Arthur E. 1911. Letter to commissioner of Indian affairs, 22 July 1911. Central classified files 1907–1939 Blackfeet Agency 150 Record Group 75—Box 33. Document on file at Montana State Library, Helena.

McFee, Malcolm. 1972. *Modern Blackfeet: Montanans on a Reservation*. Lincoln: University of Nebraska Press.

McHugh, Tom. 1972. *The Time of the Buffalo*. Lincoln: University of Nebraska Press.

Montana Memory Project. 1899. Report of Superintendent of Blackfeet School, Blackfeet Agency Boarding School, 30 June 1899. Document on file at Montana State Library, Helena.

_____. 1934a. Minutes of the Blackfeet Tribal Business Council, 14 March 1934. Central Classified Files 1907–1939 Blackfeet Agency 054 Record Group 75—Box 15, Folder 46597-1934. Document on file at Montana State Library, Helena.

_____. 1934b. Minutes of the Blackfeet Tribal Business Council, 11 September 1934. Central Classified Files 1907–1939 Blackfeet Agency 054 Record Group 75—Box 15, Folder 46597-1934. Document on file at Montana State Library, Helena.

_____. 1937. Memorandum from the assistant to the commissioner sent to various OIA divisions, 3 February 1937. Central Classified Files 1907–1939 Blackfeet

Agency 341 Record Group 75—Box 215, Folder 9085-1936 Blackfeet Part B 341. Document on file at Montana State Library, Helena.

Oetelaar, Gerald A. 2016. "Places on the Blackfoot Homeland: Markers of Cosmology, Social Relationships and History." In *Marking the Land: Hunter-Gatherer Creation of Meaning in their Environment*, ed. William Lovis and Robert Whallon, 45–66. Routledge, New York.

Oetelaar, Gerald A., and D. Joy Oetelaar. 2006. "People, Places, and Paths: The Cypress Hills and the Niitsitapi Landscape of Southern Alberta." *Plains Anthropologist* 51: 375–97.

Office of Indian Affairs. 1926. Office of Indian Affairs Circular No. 2265, 12 October 1926. Central Classified Files 1907–1939 Blackfeet Agency 150 Record Group 75—Box 34, Folder 48633-1926 Blackfeet 150. Document on file at Montana State Library, Helena.

Owl Rattler, Lucy. 1978. Interview with Lucy Owl Rattler. Audio recording on file with the Blackfeet Tribal Historic Preservation Office, Browning, Montana.

Peck, Trevor R. 2004. *Bison Ethology and Native Settlement Patterns during the Old Women's Phase on the Northwestern Plains*. BAR International Series 1278. Oxford: Archaeopress.

———. 2011. *Light from Ancient Campfires: Archaeological Evidence for Native Lifeways on the Northern Plains*. Edmonton: Athabasca University Press.

Quigg, J. Michael. 1978. "Winter Bison Procurement in Southwestern Alberta." *Plains Anthropologist* 23: 53–57.

Reeves, Brian O. K. 2003. *Mistakis: The Archaeology of Waterton-Glacier International Peace Park*. Archaeological Inventory and Assessment Program, 1993–1996. Denver, CO: National Park Service, Intermountain Region.

Schaeffer, Claude E. 1978. "The Bison Drive of the Blackfeet Indians." *Plains Anthropologist* 23: 243–248.

Scheiber, Laura L., and Bonnie J. Clark. 2008. *Archaeological Landscapes on the High Plains*. Boulder: University Press of Colorado.

Sherman, Albert. 1978. Interview with Albert Sherman. Audio recording on file with the Blackfeet Tribal Historic Preservation Office, Browning, Montana.

Szasz, Margaret Connell. 1999. *Education and the American Indian: The Road to Self-Determination since 1928*, 3rd ed. Albuquerque: University of New Mexico Press.

Thompson, Samuel H. 1943. Letter to the Commissioner of Indian Affairs from Commissioner of Indian Affairs Samuel H. Thompson, 8–10 April 1943. Central Classified Files 1907–1939 Blackfeet Agency 803 Record Group 75—Box 298 Folder 34292-38 Blackfeet 803. Document on file at Montana State Library, Helena.

Vickers, J. Roderick. 1991. "Seasonal Round Problems on the Alberta plains." *Canadian Journal of Archaeology* 15: 55–72.

White, William A. III, Marìa Nieves Zedeño, and Virgil Edwards. 2017. *Historical Architecture and Archaeology Assessment of the Cut Bank Boarding School Facility, Glacier County, Montana*. Prepared for the Tribal Historic Preservation Office, Blackfeet Tribe, Browning. Tucson: Bureau of Applied Research in Anthropology, University of Arizona.

Zedeño, Marìa Nieves. 2013 "To Become a Mountain Hunter: Flexible Core Values and Subsistence Hunting among Reservation-Era Blackfeet." In *The Archaeology and Historical Ecology of Small Scale Economies*, ed. Victor D. Thompson and James C. Waggoner Jr., 141–63. Gainesville: University Press of Florida.

Zedeño, Marìa Nieves, and Derek Anderson. 2010. "Agency and Politics in Hunter-Gatherer Territory Formation." *Revista de Arqueologia* 23: 10–28.

Zedeño, Marìa Nieves, Jesse A. B. Ballenger, and John R. Murray. 2014. "Landscape Engineering and Organizational Complexity among Late Prehistoric Bison Hunters of the Northwestern Plains." *Current Anthropology* 55: 23–58.

Zedeño, Marìa Nieves, and B. J. Bowser. 2009. "The Archaeology of Meaningful Places." In *The Archaeology of Meaningful Places*, ed. B.J. Bowser and Marìa Nieves Zedeño, 1–14. Salt Lake City: University of Utah Press.

Zedeño, Marìa Nieves, Wendi Field Murray, and John R. Murray. 2015. "Central Places in the Backcountry: The Archaeology and Ethnography of Beaver Lake, Montana." In *Engineering Mountain Landscapes: An Anthropology of Social Investment*, ed. Laura L. Scheiber and Marìa Nieves Zedeño. Salt Lake City: University of Utah Press.

Zvelebil, Marek. 1997. "Hunter-gatherer ritual landscapes: spatial organization, social structure and ideology among hunter-gatherers of northern Europe and western Siberia." *Analecta Praehistorica Leidensia* 29: 33–50.

Chapter 7

Conflicts in Memory and Heritage

Dakota Perspectives on Historic Fort Snelling, Minnesota

Katherine Hayes

Introduction

There can be no indifference by a people for a place they regard as the site of both genesis and genocide (Waziyatawin 2008). The public site of Historic Fort Snelling is so regarded by many Indigenous Dakota people whose histories are deeply and painfully embedded there. Working there as a university-based researcher and archaeologist (drawing upon archival and archaeological collections) has taught me a great deal about Dakota perspectives on archaeology and historic preservation, which most regard as colonialist enterprises. More than any other site in the region, Fort Snelling epitomizes the lessons of settler colonial studies for archaeologists about the vivid relevance and active struggle over historical memory and interpretation by Native people. According to this framework, settler societies are grounded in the elimination of the Native, and this logic of elimination is enacted through *ongoing* structures and processes, rather than temporally delimited events (Wolfe 2006). These processes may include physical genocide but also are enacted in cultural and social destructions, like boarding schools, outlawed religious practices and languages, relocation/removal, and adoption. Settler refusals to recognize land dispossession as an ongoing assault rather than an event relegated to an alienated past is one of the mechanisms by which they destroy indigeneity in order to replace, and to justify continued occupation of stolen land (Tuck and Yang 2012;

Vimalassery, Hu Pegues, and Goldstein 2016). In this sense, archaeologies of (settler) colonialism must encompass not simply the historic past but also the contemporary present in the conflicts of representation and sovereignty.

Public heritage sites are ideal case studies of how this process occurs within the realm of historical memory. As with any historical narrative, site excavation, preservation, and interpretation are undertaken by stakeholders who choose what counts significantly as evidence and create explanations that contribute to a coherent perspective. That perspective is not always multivocal, for many reasons; archaeologists and heritage professionals are most often in their positions because they come from some background of privilege, and racial and ethnic diversity is low in these fields. Their social standpoints inform the interpretations, which are then reified as truth in their presentation to public audiences. The identity of largely white and privileged professionals also relies upon not knowing or recognizing that privilege, especially as it relates to land disenfranchisement. Yet, as with archives, archaeological collections often contain traces of diverse and complex histories of disenfranchisement, traces which go unrecognized by researchers who are not attuned to such circumstances.

In this chapter I will draw upon Dakota perspectives expressed either in published or otherwise public venues which clarify their perspectives on both historic colonial sites and contemporary colonialist practices of appropriation and erasure. In some sense, contributing this chapter is a form of appropriation, in that I am describing a context that is much larger than my own research, drawing on others' voices, to explore how it structures my own work. This is not to suggest that I work outside of these conversations, merely that I have elected not to draw upon sentiments expressed to me personally given that that work is still very much in progress and it is not appropriate at this time to write specifically about it. Sentiments made public are at least acknowledged to be open to all by those who made them, and very often they have been offered up in an attempt to edify and elicit understanding. Thus I feel my appropriation is at least meant to extend that education, and as a non-Native (settler) scholar I cannot claim these arguments in my own voice. From these general and specific public comments I have come to better understand the potential effects of my research on incarceration at the site of Fort Snelling, and I have reshaped the approach that I take moving forward.

In the chapter that follows, I begin with the context and broad history of the site. I next explore a controversy which occurred locally over an artistic interpretation of Dakota history and which has significant lessons for archaeological interpretation. I then return to consider the site of Fort Snelling and some of the particular aspects of its history, with Dakota perspectives on how that history is and should be remembered. I will explore if and how it is possible to bring a sense of justice for Dakota people in the management and public interpretation of the site.

"It Presents a Pleasing and Beautiful View": Bdote Mni Sota

Historic Fort Snelling is located at the juncture of two major rivers, the Mississippi and the Minnesota, in the region west of the Great Lakes (Minnesota, USA; Figure 7.1). This confluence (*bdote* in the Dakota language) is regarded as one of places of emergence or origin of Dakota peoples. Both oral tradition and archaeological study have indicated the deep history of Indigenous occupation in the area (Gibbon 2003, 2012; Westerman and White 2012). Their history is marked by migrations and interactions with many people; in more recent history, Native groups from further east began migrating in, pushed by European colonization, while very small numbers of European missionaries, traders, and military began to appear as well. These early interactions with both migrating Ojibwe and European peoples were marked by an ebb and flow of relationships, constantly negotiated, and with little effort given to "permanent" settlement. But in 1820 the American military chose to build a frontier fort on the bluffs overlooking the confluence of the rivers. The construction marked the onset of settler colonialism and the displacement of the Dakota. It is the telling of this history that most concerns Dakota peoples today.

The period between 1820 and 1862 was characterized, from the Dakota perspective, by an unceasing struggle to negotiate a peaceful coexistence with settlers. Although the frontier fort was ostensibly built to guard against British re-incursion and to establish relations with Dakota and Ojibwe people, settlers regarded it as a foothold into large land and resource acquisitions. The Dakota were pressured to agree to a series of treaties, in 1830, 1837, 1851, and 1858, the latter of which was the same year that the territory was declared a state. Each treaty ceded more land and each saw its terms broken by the federal government; some Dakota language scholars have argued that the treaties were based on a fundamental misunderstanding wherein the Dakota believed that they were leasing the land to the Americans (Westerman and White 2012, 173–79). The terms included the provision of food and other essential materials necessitated by the restrictions of Dakota bands to smaller and smaller reservations, but federal officials repeatedly failed or were

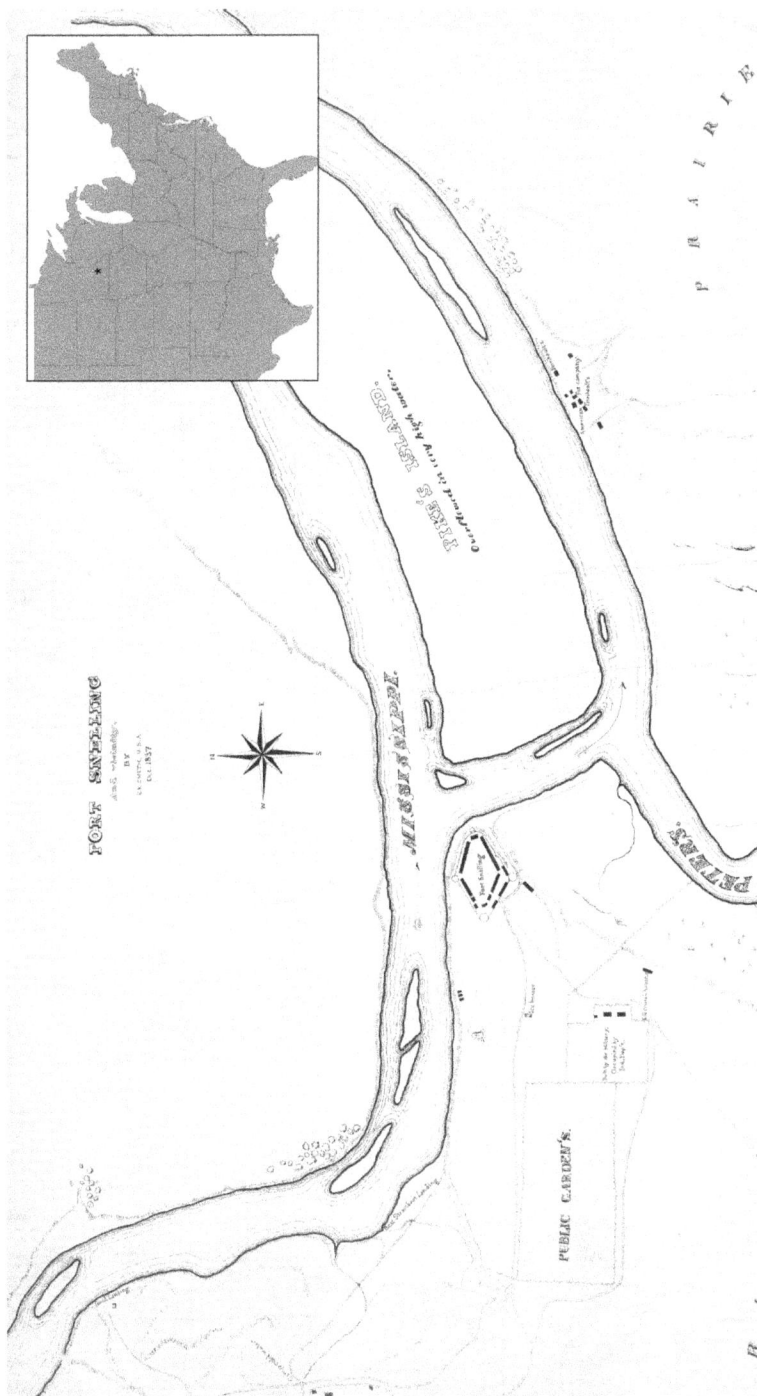

Figure 7.1. Location of Fort Snelling (diamond-shaped compound south of the Mississippi River) as detailed on an 1837 military map. Protected nearby settlements, such as the Indian Agency and the American Fur Company, are included. Inset marks location within the US. (Original map is in the collections of the National Archives; scanned copy is courtesy of the Minnesota Historical Society.)

delayed in the delivery of these promised supplies. Though reluctant to engage in a war they saw as futile, Dakota leaders saw that their families were starving to death, and that their state of life was unsustainable. In 1862, not long after Minnesota was established as a state, Dakota people engaged in war against the settlers. The Dakota were defeated, three hundred warriors condemned to death, nearly 1,700 non-combatants confined to a concentration camp at Fort Snelling, and all Dakota people were declared exiled from the state by the governor. While the number of condemned warriors was reduced to thirty-eight by the president, their execution in Mankato still stands as the largest mass execution in US history. In the spring of 1863, after suffering the loss of hundreds of prisoners to disease and poor conditions, the remaining Dakota prisoners at Fort Snelling were transported out of the state (Waziyatawin 2008; Westerman and White 2012; DeCarlo 2016).

This short and brutal history demonstrates easily why Dakota people would hold strong feelings about Fort Snelling. Those feelings would be compounded by the archaeology and historic preservation at the site beginning in the 1950s. Although a number of Dakota people had returned to the area (there are currently four federally recognized Dakota tribes in the state) and there was a substantial urban American Indian community residing close by in Minneapolis, the thoughts and perspectives of those communities were not included in the process. The military base had changed in function and expanded in use until its decommissioning in 1946, by which time most of the original fort structures had been demolished. Despite these significant changes, preservation efforts were focused on recapturing the earliest appearances of the fort (Johnson 1970). The Minnesota Historical Society, which acquired the property and underwrote this work, pursued the nostalgic valuation of the frontier past as an origin story. Ironically, this is an origin story for white settlers, and it clearly depends upon the disappearance of Native people. In this fashion, preservation contributes to the settler colonial project of eliminating the Native (Wolfe 2006), culminating in a reconstructed frontier fort which resolutely ignored the genocide in its interpretation.

Before I more fully engage the Dakota peoples' perspectives on the preservation and archaeology of this site of colonial genocide, I wish to first take a detour into a related case which highlights the ethics and sensitivities of how historical trauma is represented. This work is ongoing at Fort Snelling, but the case of the Walker Art Center's *Scaffold* sculpture in 2017 holds crucial lessons to be learned from Dakota people about what is at stake.

Scaffold: Art or Appropriation?

In May of 2017, the Walker Art Center, an internationally-recognized contemporary art museum in Minneapolis, was preparing to reopen its outdoor sculpture garden. This beloved portion of the museum had been expanded and numerous new large-scale sculptural works had been acquired for it, in addition to an "artist-designed mini-golf" area. One of the new sculptures was Sam Durant's *Scaffold* (2012), a massive wood and metal construction meant to evoke a series of historic executions, including the mass hanging of the thirty-eight Dakota men in 1862. Durant's aim was to provoke dialogue about inequities and capital punishment, and the Walker director, Olga Viso, also hoped it would be provocative (Viso 2017). Before the installation was even complete, the sculpture's distinctive representation was noticed, and a protest by Dakota community members, other American Indians, and sympathetic allies sprang up outside the fence around the sculpture garden.

Some of the protesters brought art supplies and encouraged those who gathered to create signs and messages about the scaffold sculpture. These messages are instructive: "Remember Their Names: 38+2"; "Feels Like 1862—Execution is Not Art"; "Art Celebrating Mass Murder of Our Ancestors and Family Ahead"; "Not Your Story" (Sawyer 2017). A somewhat more graphic sign read "$200.00 for scalp of artist" with material resembling a hank of hair attached. Other messages referenced the mismatch of the sculpture, which did somewhat resemble playground equipment and was intended to be walked on, with the seriousness of the history it indexed: "Come! Let your children run & play on this replica of a mass murder site." The juxtaposition of the sculpture to the artist-designed mini-golf seemed also to underline the observation that the institution was making light of this devastating history. In contrast, several Dakota protesters spoke of how the initial sight of the scaffold had caused visceral emotional responses (LeMay 2017; Regan 2017; Specktor 2017).

The director of the Walker Art Center posted a statement online expressing her sorrow and regret that the sculpture had caused such pain, and that she had failed to reach out to the Dakota community prior to installing the sculpture. Her open letter noted, "There is no doubt that what we perceived as a multifaceted argument about capital punishment on a national level affecting a variety of communities across the US may be read through a different lens here in Minnesota. We also acknowledge that the artist's intent to create a work meant 'as a space of remembering' may be misread" (Viso 2017). The differences in perception of the role of art to evoke memory and provoke discussion are fairly stark, deriving from the specificity of Dakota historical memory, which settler descendants, however sympathetic, are unlikely to recognize on their own. As Mona Smith, an artist of Dakota descent, was quoted in one media piece, "Any Dakota person would have suggested the pain triggered by this work. ... Perhaps next year they'd like to do a sculpture on the holocaust ovens?" (Regan 2017).

Though criticized for a process started too late, the Walker Art Center leadership and the artist, Sam Durant, proceeded to engage in a series of meetings with representatives, including elders, of Dakota communities both in and beyond the state. Community members themselves also held closed meetings to discuss their thoughts and responses. Though the specific discussions are not public or published, the result was an agreement to dismantle the sculpture, and both the physical pieces and the intellectual property rights of the art were given to community representatives to do with as they decided most appropriate. The decision ultimately was to bury the physical remains at an undisclosed location (Eldred 2017).

While much could be made of the parallels between this case and the still-fraught process of archaeological material repatriation and reburial, I would like to focus more upon what was being communicated by Dakota protestors about historical memory. I hear two entangled messages in their public statements which are quite relevant for the representation of history at Fort Snelling. The first is to point to a fundamental lack of knowledge among settler descendants about colonialist history and the impacts upon contemporary Native people. This is one of the clearest demonstrations of how colonialism is perpetuated, by the attempted erasure of Native lives—if not a physical erasure then a documentary one. It is a problem of education. While the 1862 US-Dakota War is now incorporated into the public school system's standards, most adults educated in that system continue to be unaware of the history, and are thus prone to misunderstanding Dakota activism (Wastvedt 2017). Even if they are aware of the historical events including the mass execution, they may not know how the impacts of the events have resonated through generations: exile from homeland, the stigma of Indian identity enforced through boarding schools and assimilation programs, the loss of language and community, all compounded by the labeling of their ancestors as criminals. This point is made in a number of comments and stories from Native activists who see building historical awareness in non-Native populations as an endless task (LeMay 2017; Regan 2017; Wastvedt 2017).

As an example of the erasure of such history in settler consciousness, one published anecdote observed an older white man expressing outrage at the perceived threat of violence he saw in the "$200 reward for scalp of the artist" sign (Specktor 2017). This man was likely using the stereotype of "savage Indians" who practiced scalping, a prevalent and popular trope, as his referent. As Ed LaBelle, a Dakota descendant, has noted, "[the war] stamped us with that stigma that we're nothing but a bunch of savages" (MNHS, US-Dakota War Oral History Project interview). In fact, historic sources document the practice of *settlers* to pay for the scalps of Native people in the wake of the war. For example, a man was noted in a newspaper report, not long after the Dakota War, for turning in "a large scalp-lock of [a] slain savage, and was paid the bounty of $200 offered by the Governor for such an achievement" (*Saint Paul Pioneer*, 4 February 1864). Such reports indicate not only the incidence of such violence, but that there was a state-sanctioned policy encouraging it.

The second message is that these histories cannot simply be replaced in social consciousness as a decontextualized historical fact; rather, the history needs to be told with or through Native perspective. Despite the sincere, social-justice oriented motives of the artist and the institution, protesters indicated that this was not their story to tell. For some this is another instance of cultural (or historical) appropriation (Specktor 2017). Yet, this is no simple question of control over a narrative, given that the narratives are deeply painful, and it is the affective content of the history which is lost when told by someone non-Native, or even non-Dakota. In order to overcome the ingrained stereotypes that settler descendants hold, it is often necessary to more thickly contextualize the history, and to trace its effects. The concept of *historical trauma* is not easily transmitted to populations who not only have no experience of it, but also have a fair degree of privilege derived from the same conditions which sustain generational trauma for others. Moreover, numerous Native activists spoke specifically about the long and problematic history of representation of Native people by non-Native historians, educators, and artists. This is a more pervasive problem within cultural heritage professions and institutions in the United States, which have a very poor record of diversity and inclusion (AAM 2011; Dichtl and Townsend 2009; SAA 2011; Mellon Foundation 2015).

"It's a Place of Shame": Dakota Perspectives on Fort Snelling

The history indexed in the scaffold sculpture is intimately connected to Fort Snelling and elicits similarly strong sentiments. Families of those executed Dakota men were either exiled following a difficult winter imprisonment at the military base or fled from the area; and two Dakota soldiers captured in early 1864 (Sakpe and Wakanozanzan) were incarcerated and publicly executed at the fort in late 1865 (as fully detailed in the *Saint Paul Pioneer*, 12 November 1865). Until recently, these areas have not been systematically researched. While site signage and interpretive programming provided by the Minnesota Historical Society does touch upon these aspects of the history at the fort, there is little in-depth consideration.

As the Walker sculpture controversy indicates, Dakota descendant communities seek both broad public awareness of their history and to have their perspective on that history represented. At Fort Snelling, both of these are largely missing from the preserved and reconstructed landscape. When the military base was decommissioned, the remaining property (ironically, referred to in documents as the "military reservation") was distributed among multiple state and federal entities including the National Park Service (NPS), the Veterans Administration (VA), the Minnesota Department of Natural Resources (MnDNR, or state parks), and the Minnesota Historical Society (MNHS). While the location at the top of the bluff where the first military fort was built is owned and managed by MNHS, the location of the post-1862 War concentration camp, where Dakota families were imprisoned awaiting expulsion from the state, is managed by MnDNR. These two organizations have very different approaches to remembering history.

The MNHS approach included the complete excavation of all of the original fort's buildings excepting the two which remained standing. This is accounted as the largest archaeological project ever undertaken in the state, and one which contributed to the planned reconstruction of the site to its 1820s frontier-era appearance (Fridley 1956; Callendar 1957; Johnson 1970). The preservation staff focused their reconstruction efforts on the accurate representation of the building fabric and construction of that initial period, and thus largely ignored the artifact assemblage which related to later building use and demolition. The bulk of this assemblage remains unanalyzed, demonstrating the priorities of preservation at that time: buildings, not people. The reconstruction of the landscape also was guided by a distinctly narrow vision of the past that should be represented, meaning that several extant historic buildings which were built in the later nineteenth century were demolished. This included the military prison in which Wakanozanzan and Sakpe, the two later-captured Dakota soldiers, were incarcerated (*Saint Paul Pioneer,* 26 September 1865).

Public programming at the reconstructed fort focused on military life within the walls, and was more circumspect about the Native populations surrounding the fort in its earliest years and persecuted by soldiers in later years (Figure 7.2). Arguably, the very structuring of fortifications and the remains of provisions within the fort were shaped by the

Figure 7.2. Entrance to the reconstructed "frontier-era" Fort Snelling (top). Interpretive sign outside the reconstruction discussing the mass incarceration of Dakota peoples following the 1862 US-Dakota War (bottom). Although some aspects of Dakota history are now included, the focus of interpretation at the site is given to the functioning of the military itself. (Photographs courtesy of John M. Matsunaga.)

military's relationship with Dakota people who lived (until removal and exile) throughout the surrounding lands. Moreover, extensive archival materials indicated the difficult and sometimes violent history of interactions between the military and the surrounding Native communities. Yet the choices made by MNHS staff, during the early years of the fort as a public heritage site, about what to preserve in the landscape, and what to interpret for the public, continued the work of settler colonialism by marking Native peoples as a ghostly, passively disappearing presence rather than active contributors to the site's history (Tyson 2013). As historian Bruce White wrote in expressing the concern with the effects of the reconstruction:

> The fundamental fact about the fort—as reconstructed and as interpreted—is that it is a fortress and that for many years since its reopening, when you walked into the fort you went through a gate, and often there was an interpreter there, dressed as a soldier, guarding that gate. The reconstructed fort created a logic of its own. One could try to give a different message inside the fort, but what did the fort itself say when no one was speaking? What did the mere presence of the fort say? The message was a military message and it told the story of the colonial conquest of the 19th century. (White 2009)

This seems to stem in part from an unwillingness to confront painful histories in any significant way, guided by the notion that visitors do not want to hear it and interpreters are reluctant to make them uncomfortable (Simon 2011; Miron 2014). In a parallel example, staff updated the interpretive programming ten years ago to include information about enslaved African Americans at the fort, but ethnographic observation showed that staff members would discuss this in-depth only when visitors showed interest. And unfortunately, most visitors seemed to avoid the question altogether (Tyson 2013, 160–65). Beyond similar attempts to update interpreter programs, there remains little in the reconstructed physical landscape which confronts or engages visitors with the deep Dakota history of the site.

By comparison, the MnDNR-managed Fort Snelling State Park below the fort, where the concentration camp for Dakota non-combatants was located, demonstrates a rather different approach to representing Dakota history. There are no attempts at reconstruction, only commemoration. One permanent monument stands near the visitor center made of wood in contrast to the imposing stone of the reconstructed fort and is not meant to stand as a literal replica of a historical structure (Figure 7.3). The park manager has maintained relationships with a wide network of descendant Dakota people—some of whom are descended from the

Figure 7.3. Commemorative monument honoring the incarcerated Dakota people in Fort Snelling State Park (MnDNR) (top). Ceremonially placed markers behind monument (bottom). Biannual pilgrimages are made by descendant communities and allies to remember those incarcerated. (Photographs courtesy of John M. Matsunaga.)

wider diaspora of exiles—as a means of sharing the decision-making authority regarding commemorative work (Larry Peterson, pers. comm. 2016). For example, within the monument sits a circular carved slab of pipestone, considered sacred material, inscribed with the names of the incarcerated and exiled bands of Dakota; the piece was commissioned by and made by descendants (MNHS, US-Dakota War Oral History Project interview, Ray Owens).

Memory is also performed differently in this place, being a location for ceremonies and community gatherings, and as embodied remembrance. Regular pilgrimages trace the route of the Dakota prisoners, and remember their names by leaving markers up to and in the state park (Wilson 2006). They are little more than sticks with a hand-written name and tied with ribbons, ultimately ephemeral and thus demanding that the process be repeated in order not to forget. These markers are visible in various states of decay in the state park, denoting the active, ongoing presence of Dakota people in this place (on performative memory see e.g., Connerton 1989; Bowman and Pezzullo 2010). No archaeology has been undertaken in the area where the concentration camp was constructed, though there has been minimally invasive survey based on a shared desire between descendant communities and park managers to identify the boundaries and burial locations of the estimated three hundred who died while incarcerated (Terrell and Terrell 2016).

The key difference in representing history between these two areas of Fort Snelling is the active voice of the Dakota people, deriving from collaborative rather than consultative relationships forged by the managing agencies. A series of demonstrations and writings by Dakota scholars and activists in the years leading up to the 2012 sesquicentenary remembrance of the US-Dakota War referenced both locations, but the ire and demand for change focused upon MNHS and the Fort Snelling reconstruction, up to and including demands that the reconstruction be torn down (Waziyatawin 2008). In light of this, the organization has initiated a number of efforts to seek and be more inclusive of Dakota perspectives on the site (DeCarlo 2016). One of the earlier efforts included the US-Dakota War of 1862 Oral History Project, in which interviewers asked both Dakota and settler descendants how the war should be remembered.

Dakota responses to these questions highlighted the lessons discussed above: the need for broad, common education and for historical context which may offer a sense of restorative justice. Though few used the language of genocide, many respondents drew parallels to the World War II holocaust. On the pointed question regarding the preservation or destruction of the current reconstructed landscape, however, responses were mixed. For example:

I think if anything, it should be preserved. But along with that the whole story should be told beginning with the government's manipulated treaties to their violations and broken promises of treaty rights, to coercing the Indians into a war, to travesties of justice and the mockery of military tribunal trials of sometimes innocent warriors, and the execution of 38 warriors, (at least one who was executed by mistake), and then the exile of an entire nation of Dakotas from their homeland. I think that Fort Snelling should be preserved as a tribute or memorial to the innocent Dakotas who spent a devastating winter there before finally leaving their beloved homeland forever. If you burned it down and bulldozed it under, they would just build some business over it and the history would be underground. Today, there are some who are trying to convince the people that the German Holocaust never happened. But the death camps are still there to prove it and a Holocaust Museum is located in Washington, DC to tell the story. Thousands of visitors from throughout the world visit the museum every year and learn what really happened. The Jewish people don't want people to forget what happened to their ancestors. (MNHS, US-Dakota War Oral History Project interview, Elden Lawrence, 12 April 11)

For Clifford Canku, physical reminders of this history seem unwarranted:

I think the most important thing is to tell the truth. About how the land was swindled from us as Dakota people. It's shameful. It's a place of shame that should be corrected in whatever way, in our modern sense of justice. What can we do? That's the message I get every time the spirits come, is that we need to clean up our act. And that Fort is a sham. It's a Fort whose history is shameful. And so, its use is no longer applicable to us today. Maybe a historical marker could be placed there, and just tear it down. (MNHS, US-Dakota War Oral History Project interview, Clifford Canku, 10 June 11)

A number of interviewees also touched upon the long-term impacts of the war in terms of trauma and of a one-sided historical representation. Such representations of the war and subsequent exile as justified do significant work in service of settler colonialism by portraying the nearly complete loss of Dakota land as an issue which need not be addressed in the present. Contemporary Dakota voices unsettle and problematize those embedded ideals, reminding us of broken treaties as context.

I think that the war was very unfortunate for our people. It stamped us with that stigma that we're nothing but a bunch of savages. We're a bunch of killers. We killed five hundred settlers. That's the way they want to look at it. But my vision of it is, we did it for survival. We did it to get something to eat, to feed our children. I don't condone the atrocities they did to the white people. That should never have happened but it did. (MNHS, US-Dakota War Oral History Project interview, Ed LaBelle, 7 June 12)

I think the native people should, they should remember it. We should teach our kids. And I'd like to hope to think that there's people out there that aren't so judgmental that they could know all the history. They only hear a part of it. They don't hear the whole thing and they judge us by that. (MNHS, US-Dakota War Oral History Project interview, Myron Taylor, 28 June 12)

Dakota interlocutors were also asked about their family connections. These individuals represented the breadth of the exiled Dakota diaspora, some living in Minnesota but many in South Dakota, where incarcerated families were relocated, or in Canada, where other communities fled to. Most noted family connections across wide areas, indicating how the war dispersed and disconnected communities. The consequences of those disconnections from family and homeland were clearly articulated by Clifford Canku.

To us Dakota the beginning of despair is if you don't know who you are. In other words, we're like trees. If we don't know our roots, in terms of who we are, and how we are connected from the very beginning—to creation, and to God, and to the land, and to the space and time in which we live—that's more important than what we are, which is the tree. So I think that in a sense, a lot of our young people are committing suicide because they lack the basic necessity of their identity—and that's the roots, the root part. If you don't have no roots, the tree falls. And it dies. (MNHS, US-Dakota War Oral History Project interview, Clifford Canku, 10 June 11)

The voices of Dakota descendant scholars and activists have had an effect on the Historical Society's approach to preserving and interpreting the site. Recognizing the multiple contemporary stakeholders who have pressed for acknowledgement of the 1862 War and other historical events and figures, the MNHS site joined the International Coalition of Sites of Conscience in 2011, seeking ways to more directly engage its difficult history to address social justice goals (DeCarlo 2016). Scholars of heritage tourism point to numerous contemporary examples of how MNHS might choose to move forward in addressing what has been referred to as "dark" or "dissonant" heritage (Light 2017), particularly through models of shared authority and co-creation with Indigenous communities (Lemelin et al. 2013). A notable recent example may be found in the National Park Service's interpretive work at the Colorado site of the Sand Creek Massacre, long remembered by settler society as a "battle" which absolved the military of fault. The newly created NPS site acknowledges, through broad inclusion of memory and historic sources, that instead a horrific and unwarranted attack by the military on an undefended group of Cheyenne and Arapahoe people left 150 dead (Kelman 2013). In these cases and more, it should be acknowledged that commitments to include

Indigenous voices is admirable, but a long way from decolonization and recognition of sovereignty.

In 2017, on the anniversary of the removal of the incarcerated Dakota from the state, MNHS sponsored the first annual Dakhóta Wówičakhe Wóyakapi Omníčiye (Dakota Truth-Telling Gathering), with both public and closed events organized by descendant communities (Xaykaothao 2017). Over the course of four days, Dakota people gathered at Fort Snelling and spoke openly and emotionally about what the place meant to them, and what they hoped would happen to change their relationship to that place. Many called for open access: to the place, to a voice in decision-making, and importantly for archaeologists, to the collections. Attending one of the public events, I was moved to hear elders speak of grave concerns that items of medicine (sacred objects) remain unidentified in the archaeological collections, items which required care that the curators lacked the cultural knowledge to provide. Participants also spoke of a need to know where significant events occurred, like the incarceration and execution of Sakpe and Wakanozanzan in 1864–65. These questions and concerns are a reminder to me, as a researcher, of the privileged access I enjoy, and the ethical responsibilities I hold to those whose history I study.

Lessons Learned from the Dakota

The site of Fort Snelling—recently renamed Fort Snelling at Bdote by MNHS—holds many lessons for us, not least of which is that archaeologies of colonialism are never simple research contexts in which to work. The experience of the MNHS in creating a public heritage site without inclusion of Dakota voices and perspectives is instructive, and one which will continue to unfold as they work to address the damage done by reconstructing a very material sign of settler colonialism. The same circumstances which make the history of Fort Snelling so painful for Dakota people also makes the process of collaboration and shared decision-making so difficult: from this place, families and communities were torn apart, scattered widely to places of relocation and refuge across state and international borders. To pursue research and interpretation on Fort Snelling in an ethical fashion requires first educating ourselves on what is at stake in this history, then taking the time to hear the voices from as many of those communities as possible. We must acknowledge that the processes of erasure of Native history, a key component in the structure which keeps settler colonialism in place, has impacted settler and Native scholars alike. We can only benefit by engaging in the research together to address the erasure.

But we also need to acknowledge that this research and interpretation is not solely for the education of white settler society. To act as though it does, reifies the sense of settler replacement of the Indigenous, as the inheritor and sole audience for knowledge. Instead, I understand the Dakota insistence that *"we are still here"* means that they have the sovereign right to tell their own history, as those most impacted by the historical circumstances under study. The *Scaffold* sculpture was meant to educate settler society, and was viewed, like hate speech, as harmful. I hear in the comments made by descendants that the historical conditions of incarceration (which I study) and the aftermath still cause pain. Why should the public edification of white audiences take priority over considering the way Dakota descendants want audiences to understand it? Though we more routinely engage in "collaboration," I would argue that reshaping how we listen to and work with our Indigenous stakeholders goes beyond the contemporary ethical standards we practice with regards to any descendant community, to constitute a direct challenge to settler colonialism. As we do so, we contribute to expressions of Indigenous sovereignty.

As a member site of the International Coalition of Sites of Conscience, the interpretation at Fort Snelling at Bdote should contribute to social justice movements. This means prioritizing those goals over institutional aims, whether they are the fiscal aims of the historical society or the publication aims of researchers at an academic institution. There are many opinions from the Dakota communities about what should happen to the site of Fort Snelling, but all agree that this place witnessed the attempted destruction of their people. We must respect their need to reclaim their own history there.

Katherine Hayes is an associate professor of anthropology and an affiliate member of the American Indian Studies Department at the University of Minnesota, Twin Cities. Her early work focused on archaeologies of colonialism in the US northeast (New York and Minnesota). More recently she has studied the roles of memory and forgetting in settler colonialism, particularly as they manifest in archaeological epistemology and heritage representations. She is a co-founder of the Heritage Studies and Public History graduate program at the University of Minnesota, which aims to increase diversity, inclusion, and equity in these professional fields.

References

AAM. 2011. *The Museum Workforce in the United States, 2009*. American Association of Museums report, Washington DC.

Bowman, Michael S., and Phaedra C. Pezzullo. 2010. "What's so 'Dark' about 'Dark Tourism'? Death, Tours, and Performance." *Tourist Studies* 9(3): 187–202.

Callendar, John M. 1957. "An Archaeologist Explores the Site of Old Fort Snelling." *Minnesota History* 35(8): 365–67.

Connerton, Paul. 1989. *How Societies Remember*. Cambridge: Cambridge University Press.

DeCarlo, Peter. 2016. *Fort Snelling at Bdote: A Brief History*. St. Paul: Minnesota Historical Society Press.

Dichtl, John, and Robert B. Townsend. 2009. "A Picture of Public History: Preliminary Results from the 2008 Survey of Public History Professionals." *Public History News* 29(4). Retrieved 18 June 2015 from https://www.historians.org/publications-and-directories/perspectives-on-history/september-2009/a-picture-of-public-history.

Eldred, Sheila M. 2017. "Dakota Plan to Bury, Not Burn, 'Scaffold' Sculpture." *The New York Times*, 1 September, C3.

Fridley, Russell W. 1956. "Fort Snelling, from Military Post to Historic Site." *Minnesota History* 35(4): 178–92.

Gibbon, Guy. 2003. *The Sioux: The Dakota and Lakota Nations*. Oxford: Blackwell.

———. 2012. *Archaeology of Minnesota: The Prehistory of the Upper Mississippi River Region*. Minneapolis: University of Minnesota Press.

Johnson, Loren. 1970. "Reconstructing Old Fort Snelling." *Minnesota History* 42(3): 82–98.

Kelman, Ari. 2013. *A Misplaced Massacre: Struggling over the Memory of Sand Creek*. Cambridge: Harvard University Press.

LeMay, Konnie. 2017. "'Scaffold' Sculpture Taints Memory of Dakota 38, Prompts Protests." *Indian Country Media Network*, 30 May. Retrieved 28 November 2017, from https://newsmaven.io/indiancountrytoday/archive/scaffold-sculpture-taints-memory-of-dakota-38-prompts-protests-Y7In_G55pkSVY_cVWKF33g/.

Lemelin, Raynald H., Kyle Powys Whyte, Kelsey Johansen, Freya Higgins Desbiolles, Christopher Wilson, and Steve Hemming. 2013. "Conflicts, Battlefields, Indigenous Peoples and Tourism: Addressing Dissonant Heritage in Warfare Tourism in Australia and North America in the Twenty-first century." *International Journal of Culture, Tourism and Hospitality Research* 7(3): 257–71.

Light, Duncan. 2017. "Progress in Dark Tourism and Thanatourism Research: An Uneasy Relationship with Heritage Tourism." *Tourism Management* 61: 275–301.

Mellon Foundation. 2015. Art Museum Staff Demographic Survey. Andrew W. Mellon Foundation.

MNHS, US-Dakota War Oral History Project. Interviews with Clifford Canku, Ray Owens, Judith Anywaush, Ed LaBelle, Elden Lawrence, and Myron Taylor. Retrieved 30 November 2017 from http://collections.mnhs.org/voicesofmn/index.php/10002746.

Miron, Rose. 2014. "Sacrificing Comfort for Complexity: Presenting Difficult Narratives in Public History." History@Work blog, National Council on Public History. Retrieved 24 April 2017 from http://ncph.org/history-at-work/sacrificing-comfort-for-complexity/.

Regan, Sheila. 2017. "After Protests from Native American Community, Walker Art Center Will Remove Public Sculpture." *Hyperallergic*, 29 May. Retrieved 28 November 2017, from https://hyperallergic.com/382141/after-protests-from-native-american-community-walker-art-center-will-remove-public-sculpture/.

SAA. 2011. *Report on the 2010 Member Needs Assessment Survey*. Rockville, MD: Association Research, Inc.

Sawyer, Liz. 2017. "After Outcry and Protests, Walker Art Center Will Remove 'Scaffold' Sculpture." *Star Tribune*, 28 May. Retrieved 28 November 2017, from http://www.startribune.com/walker-will-take-down-controversial-sculpture-after-protests/424820003/.

Simon, Roger. 2011. "A Shock to Thought: Curatorial Judgment and the Public Exhibition of 'Difficult' Knowledge." *Memory Studies* 4(4): 432–49.

Specktor, Mordecai. 2017. "Offensive Art." *The Circle*, 1 June. Retrieved 28 December 2017 from http://thecirclenews.org/index.php?option=com_content&task=view&id=1486&Itemid=39.

Terrell, Eva B., and Michelle M. Terrell. 2016. *Native American Context Statement and Reconnaissance Level Survey Supplement*. Shafer, MN: Two Pines Resource Group.

Tuck, Eve, and K.Wayne Yang. 2012. "Decolonization is not a Metaphor." *Decolonization: Indigeneity, Education & Society* 1(1): 1–40.

Tyson, Amy M. 2013. *The Wages of History: Emotional Labor on Public History's Front Lines*. Amherst: University of Massachusetts Press.

Vimalassery, Manu, Juliana Hu Pegues, and Alyosha Goldstein. 2016. "Introduction: On Colonial Unknowing." *Theory and Event* 19(4). Retrieved 6 April 2017 from https://muse.jhu.edu/article/633283.

Viso, Olga. 2017. "Learning in Public: An Open Letter on Sam Durant's *Scaffold*." *Walker Art Center Magazine News*, 26 May. Retrieved 28 December 2017 from https://walkerart.org/magazine/learning-in-public-an-open-letter-on-sam-durants-scaffold.

Wastvedt, Solvejg. 2017. "History We Don't Teach: Mankato Hangings an Uneasy Topic for MN Schools." *Minnesota Public Radio News*, 9 June. Retrieved 28 November 2017 from https://www.mprnews.org/story/2017/06/08/mankato-hangings-an-uneasy-topic-for-minnesota-schools.

Waziyatawin. 2008. *What Does Justice Look Like? The Struggle for Liberation in Dakota Homeland*. St. Paul: Living Justice Press.

Westerman, Gwen, and Bruce White. 2012. *Mni Sota Makoce: The Land of the Dakota*. St. Paul: Minnesota Historical Society Press.

White, Bruce. 2009. "Tearing Down Fort Snelling: Why It Makes Sense." MinnesotaHistory.net, 11 April. Retrieved 28 December 2017 from minnesotahistory.net/wptest/?p=1339.

Wilson, Waziyatawin A., ed. 2006. *In the Footsteps of Our Ancestors: The Dakota Commemorative Marches of the 21st Century*. St. Paul: Living Justice Press.

Wolfe, Patrick. 2006. "Settler Colonialism and the Elimination of the Native." *Journal of Genocide Research* 8(4): 387–409.

Xaykaothao, Doualy. 2017. "Dakota Gather at Fort Snelling to Recall Ancestors' Exile." *Minnesota Public Radio News*, 10 May. Retrieved 28 November 2017 from https://www.mprnews.org/story/2017/05/08/dakota-truth-telling.

Chapter 8

Discussion: Colonialism Past and Present
Archaeological Engagements and Entanglements

Carl-Gösta Ojala

Archaeologists working in Indigenous contexts with historical archae-ologies of colonial encounters are facing many challenges, and the archaeological engagements and entanglements with colonialism give rise to a multitude of questions. How can archaeology engage with colonial histories, which are still painful and traumatic, in fruitful and ethically sustainable ways? How can archaeologists relate to Indigenous communities who are affected by these histories? What new perspectives can archaeology bring forth, and how can archaeology contribute to cur-rent discussions on colonialism past and present?

Addressing these issues, we must never forget that we are dealing with histories of conquest, violence, oppression, exploitation, reloca-tion, assimilation, discrimination, racism, appropriation and erasure of culture, language, history, and heritage—histories with very real con-sequences and effects on the social, cultural, and economic lives and the well-being and health of Indigenous communities today. However, this volume also acknowledges another dimension of these histories, which is about Indigenous agency and Indigenous strategies for resistance and survival through times of great pressure and change.

Today, many Indigenous groups in different part of the world are actively working to reclaim their own histories and to have their rights as Indigenous peoples recognized and respected. Indigenous groups in many places are no longer silent, and they oppose and protest against colonial structures in society, also in archaeology and heritage management. It is within this field of tension that the present volume is situated. The focus of this volume is on "Indigenous perspectives on historical archaeology of colonialism," which brings it right into the heart of tension and contestation.

The chapters in this volume explore various aspects of colonial encounters, discussing case studies from North America, the Sámi regions in northern Europe, and Australia, attempting to trace and analyze Indigenous perspectives and agency. Using archaeological, historical, and oral sources, the authors emphasize the complexities and dynamics of colonial encounters and relations.

Based on the discussions in the chapters of the volume, and a case study concerning contested colonial history and heritage in the Sámi areas in northernmost Europe, I will discuss some aspects of this field of tension, highlighting some of the challenges as well as possibilities involved in the archaeological engagements and entanglements with colonialism both past and present.

Tracing Indigenous Perspectives

The theme of tracing Indigenous perspectives and voices in historical archaeologies of colonial encounters can be seen from two perspectives. Firstly, it is a matter of tracing Indigenous experiences in the historical records, written, material, and oral. Secondly, it is about Indigenous voices, experiences, power, and control in the archaeological research and heritage management today.

The field of historical archaeology has for some time been engaged with issues of colonial encounters, and scholars have debated the possibilities of locating and interpreting Indigenous agency and alternative experiences in the archaeological source material in colonial contexts (e.g., Silliman 2005, 2010; Naum and Nordin 2013a; Ferris, Harrison, and Wilcox 2014; Cipolla and Hayes 2015; Naum and Ekengren 2018; cf. also Äikäs and Salmi, in the Introduction to this volume).

The challenges in tracing Indigenous perspectives are testified by several of the authors in this volume. It is especially difficult to find Indigenous voices, experiences, and perspectives in colonial archives and written sources compiled by non-Indigenous authorities. The authors look to archaeology and archaeological materials, with the hope that archaeological approaches can bring forth Indigenous perspectives and provide more detailed insights into the dynamics of colonial identities and relations.

But the contributors also put forth cultural landscape approaches and oral historical approaches as ways of finding new, more nuanced, narratives about the past and the connections between past and present. Another central theme of the volume is the reinterpretation and rereading of sources—written, material, spatial, and oral—from new perspectives.

Many of the chapters discuss the study of material culture as a way of finding Indigenous perspectives. Central themes concern object biographies: the trade and exchange, use and reuse, and origins and movements of material objects. In their introduction to the volume *Rethinking Colonial Pasts through Archaeology*, Neal Ferris, Rodney Harrison, and Matthew A. Beaudoin discuss the development of "colonized-centric" perspectives in archaeological interpretations, which have "tended to arise from an examination of the processes of daily quotidian life, domestic residence, and prosaic materiality, in other words, those recursive social practices of the everyday that encompass much of how an individual, family, and community negotiate and experience life" (Ferris, Harrison, and Beaudoin 2014, 11). However, the interpretation of material culture and sites in colonial contexts are not all straightforward and uncomplicated, and there are many challenges in understanding the presence and agency of Indigenous groups through studies of material culture. As Stephen Silliman writes: "The difficulty in recognizing Indigenous people in distinctly colonial settings of the past lies in the fact that artifacts and spaces in colonial worlds are fraught with ambiguity, alternative functions, and multiple users" (Silliman 2010, 32). Many scholars have in recent years questioned the simple binary categories of "colonized" and "colonizer" and have called for more complex notions and understandings of relations and identities in archaeological studies of colonial encounters in different historical contexts (e.g., Horning 2007; Harrison 2014; Hayes and Cipolla 2015). Studying the ambiguities of material culture and spaces in colonial contexts, Stephen Silliman argues:

> [A]rchaeologies of colonialism must pull back from origins and taxonomies of cultural identities or artifacts that commemorate rather than complicate colonialism and instead refocus more on the practices, labors, and relations that tend to be hidden or simply assumed in traditional histories and representations. If not, then we may perpetuate the notion that those who are hard to see and those who are unnamed and limited in power are those who matter the least in history. (2010, 50)

I will return to the second perspective, that of Indigenous voices, power, and control in archaeology and heritage management, after a review of the perspectives of the seven chapters in this volume.

Perspectives from North America, Sápmi, and Australia

From different perspectives and with case studies from different locations, the contributors in this book explore aspects of colonial encounters and Indigenous perspectives on colonial histories and relations. One uniting aspect is the wish to explore the potential of archaeology to tell *other* stories, beyond the established historical narratives that have often excluded, marginalized, or misrepresented Indigenous experiences.

Violence—of different kinds—is a central element of most colonial histories and encounters in different parts of the world. LisaMarie Malischke (Chapter 3) explores the violent and tragic history connected with the Fort Saint Pierre in the Yazoo Bluffs region, near present-day Vicksburg in Mississippi, in the United States, which was established by the French in 1719 and was destroyed by an alliance of local Indigenous groups in 1729. The chapter illustrates the local consequences of larger-scale geopolitics and competition between the French and English colonial powers, in which the changing relations of the colonial powers and alliances with various Indigenous groups—the classical "divide-and-rule" strategy—affected the Native intergroup relationships and led to disastrous consequences. Furthermore, Malischke's chapter exemplifies the difficulties of tracing the Indigenous perspectives in colonial contexts. The history of Fort Saint Pierre and the relationship between the French colonists and the local Indigenous populations, as well as the changing Native intergroup relations and power struggles, are based to a large extent on French written sources and narratives through the colonists' eyes. However, Malischke argues that results from archaeological investigations at Fort Saint Pierre can present some insights into the history from an Indigenous perspective, recognizing Indigenous presence and influence at the Fort and the, at times, peaceful interactions between the French inhabitants and local Indigenous groups.

Several of the authors argue that in the everyday material culture and interactions, Indigenous strategies for coping, negotiation, resistance, and survival can be traced. Ritva Kylli, Anna-Kaisa Salmi, Tiina Äikäs, and Sirpa Aalto (Chapter 5) explore Sámi food culture in colonial contexts, as a way of tracing Indigenous perspectives on colonial histories and relations. In the colonial encounters, the authors argue, Sámi groups used a wide variety of strategies, many of which were performed in the small details of everyday life, such as in the food culture:

> Examination of Sámi food culture can therefore contribute to the understanding of the complicated power relationships and cultural negotiations that took place in the encounters between the Sámi and the Scandinavians or Finns. It

also provides a unique window to the everyday strategies the Sámi employed to negotiate their relationships with the Scandinavians and Finns. (Kylli et al., Chapter 5)

The historical sources focus mainly on taxation and trade products, which easily leads to a picture of the Sámi merely as taxpayers and trading partners, while the archaeological material has the potential to tell more detailed and varied histories about Sámi diets and foodways. In many of the early modern narrative sources, the Sámi were considered primitive and uncivilized because of their food culture, which was conceived as different from the Scandinavian food norms. Many of these sources convey a simplified and stereotypical view of Sámi food culture. However, in the archaeological material, for instance from dwelling and offering sites, it is possible to see a more nuanced picture, which includes influences on Sámi diet and cooking habits from Scandinavian and Finnish groups. Food products were also exported from the Sámi areas, such as dried fish, reindeer meat, and the plant *Angelica archangelica*, and consumed in early modern Europe, and the authors emphasize that the Sámi were not passive bystanders in these processes but actively shaped their own diets and the trading of food products, and that influences on food culture went in both directions.

Risto Nurmi (Chapter 4) also discusses objects of everyday life in colonial contexts. He focuses mainly on the early modern communities at the silver works at Silbojokk/Silbbajåhkå and Kvikkjokk/Huhttán in the Sámi areas in northern Sweden (in the mountainous regions of present-day Norrbotten County), trying to evaluate the interaction between different sociocultural groups, and the agency and participation of the local Indigenous Sámi groups in the mining projects of the Swedish state in the seventeenth and early eighteenth centuries. Nurmi also emphasizes the active participation of the Sámi in the mining enterprises, and that the narratives about the maltreatment and exploitation of Sámi forced labor in the mines and metal works in the North were only one side of this history. Furthermore, he underlines the problems of interpreting the material culture at these colonial sites in dualistic ethnic terms (Sámi or non-Sámi), as material influences worked in both directions at these sites.

In Chapter 1, "The Sounds of Colonization," Madeline Fowler, Amy Roberts, and Lester-Irabinna Rigney discuss the importance—past and present—of the bells at Point Pierce Aboriginal Mission Station/Burgiyana in South Australia. The authors explore the importance of sound—and who controls the sonic space—in the colonial past and its implications today: a much-needed reminder of the importance of senses and emotions in colonial encounters. Their chapter illustrates how contested sites and objects can have many different, even conflicting, meanings for the local populations today. In this case, the continuing bell ringing at Point Pearce/Burgiyana represents different notions and emotions at the same time. For some members of the local Indigenous community, the bell ringing represents a counter-memory to the earlier "bell hegemony," strengthening local identity and community as the bell ringing is no longer controlled by the colonizers, while for others, it is a troublesome reminder of the painful colonial history.

Chapter 6 by William A. White III and Brandi E. Bethke deals with the history and heritage of Cut Bank Boarding School, located on the Blackfeet Indian Reservation in Glacier County, Montana, in the United States. As with other similar institutions in the United States, and elsewhere in the world, the Cut Bank Boarding School is connected with many painful and traumatic memories. The boarding schools were used as instruments to assimilate Indigenous children and eradicate their Indigenous cultures and languages. However, to many of the local Blackfeet community, the boarding school is also a place of persistence, resilience, and survival, "serving as an example of how government attempts to assimilate Native children through education were not totally successful" (White and Bethke, Chapter 6). Acknowledging the complexity of this history and that the experiences of the boarding school vary among individuals, White and Bethke point to examples of how Western education was seen by some as a useful tool to resist and combat oppression and strengthen the local community—and how the tool of the oppressors could be turned against them. In their study, as well as in the study presented by Fowler, Roberts, and Rigney (Chapter 1), oral histories play a central role—being one of the prime ways of understanding Indigenous perspectives on colonialism in the past and the present.

Mission and conversion work form an integral part of many Indigenous colonial experiences, with deep and long-lasting legacies, which is acknowledged by several of the authors. The mission and conversion work represent one dimension of colonialism, which not only affects the land and bodies but also the minds and souls of the colonized. Religion and colonization is the theme of Chapter 2 by Inga-Maria Mulk and Tim Bayliss-Smith. They discuss the changing religious beliefs and practices of Sámi communities in Northern Fennoscandia (the northern parts of Norway, Sweden, Finland, and northwestern Russia) in a long-term perspective. Focusing on archaeological material from Sámi sacrificial sites, as well as Sámi burials and rock art, they analyze the changing religious practices, especially offering practices, in the context of colonial contacts, which influenced new religious ideas and rituals. Mulk and Bayliss-Smith problematize the concept of religious conversion, and argue that religious change usually takes place slowly, with different stages and effects in different communities:

> Using the concept of religious "syncretism" we suggest that the *lived religion* of the Sámi was the outcome of a long process of blending and fusing of different religious traditions, following cultural interchange with Finnish, Karelian, Russian, and Scandinavian neighbors, both Pagan and Christian. (Mulk and Bayliss-Smith, Chapter 2)

Mulk and Bayliss-Smith also emphasize the importance of cultural landscape approaches, in order to capture the holistic nature of Sámi cosmology. The authors demonstrate that Sámi offering practices continued even after the intensive mission and conversion work by the Scandinavian Lutheran churches in the seventeenth century—and indeed many old sacrificial sites are still visited and respected by local Sámi people today. In the context of this volume, the continuing but transformed sacrificial practices can be seen as an example of Indigenous coping, negotiation, and resistance in a period of great external pressure and internal social, cultural, and religious change.

In Chapter 7, "Conflicts in Memory and Heritage," Katherine Hayes addresses challenges involved in archaeologies of colonialism, including collaboration, taking for her point of departure the heritage site of Fort Snelling in Minnesota in the United States. Hayes' chapter importantly points out the difficulties of "collaboration" in highly sensitive and traumatic historical contexts. Hayes explores the consequences of the failure to collaborate with the local Indigenous people, and the failure to include Indigenous voices, in the heritage projects at Fort Snelling, which is closely connected with the traumatic history of colonial violence, dispossession, and dislocation of the Dakota people. These failures add to the notions of many local Indigenous people of archaeology and heritage resource management as colonial enterprises. "To pursue research and interpretation on Fort Snelling in an ethical fashion requires first educating ourselves on what is at stake in this history, then taking the time to hear the voices from as many of those communities as possible," Hayes writes. "But," she continues, "we also need to acknowledge that this research and interpretation is not solely for the education of white settler society. To act as though it does, reifies the sense of settler replacement of the Indigenous, as the inheritor and sole audience for knowledge" (Hayes, Chapter 7). Considering the theme of this volume, Hayes' study is a critical reminder of the importance of understanding the nature of the connections between past and present and the different ways of relating to the past, as well as the power relations involved in heritage projects.

The study, furthermore, points to the need to problematize "collaboration," and to recognize the importance of "safe spaces" controlled by those concerned for dealing with the long-term and severe consequences of traumatic colonial histories.

Contested Colonial History and Heritage in Sápmi

Several of the chapters discuss issues dealing with Sámi history, from historical archaeological perspectives. In the following, I will discuss some aspects of the contested colonial history and heritage in the Sámi areas which illustrate the interconnections between past and present, and the ongoing legacies of colonialism in society today.

Sápmi, the present-day traditional core settlement and cultural area of the Indigenous Sámi population, stretches across state boundaries in the northern areas of Norway, Sweden, Finland and the Kola Peninsula in Russia. Divided by the modern state boundaries, Sámi groups have for a long time struggled for recognition of their land and cultural rights. The conditions for, and the status of, Sámi communities vary between the different states, and here I will primarily focus on what is today the Swedish part of Sápmi.

From the sixteenth century, the Swedish kingdom actively strived to incorporate the Sámi areas in the North. This process of colonial expansion was further accelerated from the early seventeenth century. There is a long history of extractive industries in Sápmi, which has had profound impacts on the Sámi communities (and which has been described as "extractive violence" by Kristina Sehlin MacNeil [2017]). The Sámi areas are rich in natural resources, and the expectations of finding great new wealth from the exploitation of natural resources was one of the strongest driving forces behind the colonization of the Sámi areas in present-day inland northern Sweden. From the early seventeenth century until today, extractive industries, in particular the mining of metal ores, have been a central component in the colonial expansion of the Swedish state in the Sámi areas (Hansson 2015; Ojala and Nordin 2015; Nordin and Ojala 2017).

The question of the Sámi responses to the early modern mining has often been framed as a matter of *either* conflict *or* collaboration, but more recent research has underlined that this history should not be viewed in such a simplified manner. Instead, researchers have emphasized Sámi agency and the varying and changing responses and strategies to deal with external pressure and exploitation as well as internal social change (Ojala and Nordin 2015; Nordin and Ojala 2017; cf. also Nurmi, Chapter 4).

However, internal Sámi politics and conflicts in connection with early modern mining have not been explored in any detail in earlier research. In the background, old notions that Sámi culture and history is homogeneous, static, and unchanging are still alive (cf. Ojala 2009).

Recent plans for new mines in the Sámi areas have been met with strong protests from Sámi and environmentalist groups (Gärdebo, Öhman, and Maruyama 2014; Ojala and Nordin 2015; Liliequist and Cocq 2017). The recent mining boom in Sápmi, which has put much pressure on Sámi communities and reindeer herding, adds to other large-scale extractive industries in the Sámi areas such as hydroelectrical- and wind-power (see Lawrence 2014; Össbo 2014).

One of the most important cases of protest and conflict has concerned the plans for a new iron mine at Gállok outside Jokkmokk/Jåhkåmåhkke in Norrbotten County, with large-scale Sámi protests. Another current case concerns the planned mine on Nasafjäll, on the Norwegian side of the border. Silver was discovered in Nasafjäll in 1634, which was the starting point for the Swedish mining activities in Sápmi (Nordin 2015; Ojala and Nordin 2015; cf. also Nurmi, Chapter 4). There are several accounts from the seventeenth century of the bad treatment of the local Sámi population in Nasafjäll, who were at times forced to work for the mine, especially in transportation, and Nasafjäll has in many ways become a symbol for colonial oppression of the Indigenous Sámi population. In the protest movement today against the new mine, histories and memories of the early modern mining at Nasafjäll have been activated.

Another current issue concerns Sámi cultural rights and control over cultural heritage management (see, e.g., Ojala 2009; Xanthaki et al. 2017), in which debates on repatriation play an important part. In the seventeenth and eighteenth centuries, parallel with state and industrial colonialism and the Lutheran mission, the practice of collecting Sámi material culture also developed. There was great interest in the Sámi people and their material culture among collectors in Scandinavia and Europe. Especially sacred objects, such as the Sámi drums, were highly sought-after by collectors around Europe. As part of the Lutheran mission in the Sámi areas and the campaigns against all traces of non-Christian Sámi religious beliefs and practices, the use of the Sámi drums was forbidden in Sweden under threats of serious punishment, even the death penalty. A large number of drums were confiscated in the seventeenth and eighteenth centuries by the Swedish state and church, and many others were destroyed, along with other sacred objects and sacred sites. As a result, several of the sacred Sámi drums ended up in museum collections and private collections in Scandinavia and other parts of Europe (Nordin and Ojala 2015, 2018). The drums that have survived in different museum collections have become important symbols of Sámi identity and culture before colonization and the Christian mission and have been at the center of repatriation debates.

As with the history of natural resource exploitation, recent research has complicated the understanding of the missionary processes in Sápmi, focusing on Sámi agency and the use of different strategies to cope with the external pressure from missionaries and clergymen (Rydving 1995). Sámi individuals were not only victims of oppression in these historical processes, some individuals also participated in the conversion and were allies with the missionaries. There were also several Sámi who became clergymen or had other important official positions in society (Rydving 2010; Rasmussen 2016b). Additionally, some researchers have recently pointed to the need to reconsider the old narrative of the missions and Christian conversion of the Sámi as starting only in the seventeenth century, and have emphasized the importance of contacts between Sámi groups and Scandinavian Christian groups during the Middle Ages (Lundmark 2016; Rasmussen 2016a; Wallerström, Segerström, and Nordström 2017; cf. also Mulk and Bayliss-Smith, Chapter 2).

One especially controversial issue has concerned the collections of Sámi human remains, collected as part of early anatomy and craniological and racial biological research in the nineteenth and early twentieth centuries (for more on the histories of collecting Sámi human remains, see Ojala 2009, 2016). Demands for repatriation and reburial of Sámi human remains in collections have been put forth by Sámi activists in all of the four states in Sápmi. However, the situation concerning Sámi influence and control over cultural heritage matters vary greatly among the different states. In Norway, the Sámi Parliament has part of the responsibility for Sámi heritage, including the right to control the anatomical collections of Sámi human remains (Holand and Sommerseth 2013), but in Sweden the Sámi Parliament lacks the power to decide on these matters. There have been several cases of reburial of Sámi human remains in Norway, Sweden, and Finland (Harlin 2008; Ojala 2009; Svestad 2013), and there are several ongoing cases being discussed. It should also be noted that Swedish museums have repatriated human remains to Indigenous groups in other parts of the world, such as Australia, New Zealand, Hawaii, and French Polynesia.

In the discussions on Sámi cultural rights, international law plays an important role, which has repeatedly been pointed out by Sámi activists and the Sámi Parliaments. The United Nations Declaration on the Rights of Indigenous Peoples, from 2007, which contains several statements declaring the cultural rights of Indigenous peoples, including the right to the repatriation and reburial of their ancestral human remains, is especially important. This declaration has, however, not yet been implemented in Swedish heritage management practices.

In recent years, there has been a development of community-based collaborative projects in the Sámi areas, involving both professional archaeologists and local communities (see, e.g., Norberg and Fossum 2011; Ljungdahl and Norberg 2012; Barlindhaug 2013; Norberg and Winka 2014). Many of these initiatives have taken place in the South Sámi area in Sweden and Norway—an area in which the Sámi historical presence has been contested in earlier historical research as well as in several recent court cases. Several Sámi villages have been sued by land owners claiming that the Sámi villages do not possess traditional rights to reindeer herding on their lands. In the court cases, archaeologists have taken part as expert witnesses and archaeological arguments have been used in the court proceedings. However, these conflicts over land rights, with severe consequences for the local Sámi reindeer herding communities, have also led to an increasing interest in archaeology as a way of exploring local history, which has been the basis for the development of collaborative participatory archaeological projects in the region.

In all of these conflicts, the understanding of the colonial histories and the historical relationships between the Swedish state and the Sámi people are central. These conflicts over land and cultural rights clearly show that colonialism in Sápmi is not only about the past, but also about the present.

The very notion of a colonial history in Sápmi is contested. This relates to a more general reluctance to acknowledge and deal with the colonial past of the Scandinavian states (Fur 2013; Naum and Nordin 2013a, 2013b; Ojala 2017, 2018). In Sweden, knowledge of the colonial history in Sápmi, and its consequences (or continuation) in present-day society, is limited amongst the general public, although there has been increasing attention to these issues in Swedish public debates and mass media in the last few years. There is thus a great need to discuss the colonial histories and relations in Sápmi, and the legacies today—discussions in which archaeology could play an important role in exploring alternative dimensions and stories, and in opening up some of the homogeneous entities that earlier research has constructed.

In this field of tension, archaeologists face many challenges. How should archaeologists act in these contested situations? How should archaeologists relate to contested heritage sites such as the Nasafjäll mine? How should sacred objects, such as the Sámi drums that were confiscated by the Swedish authorities, be treated? How should a historical archaeology of colonial encounters in Sápmi be structured and work? Whose perspectives will be given space in the new narratives produced by archaeologists and whose voices will be heard?

Indigeneity and Indigenous Archaeology

Indigeneity is a central concept in discussions on Indigenous perspectives in and on the past, closely connected with notions of colonialism. It is a complex and multidimensional concept, with contested definitions (Niezen 2003; see also contributions in Hillerdal, Karlström, and Ojala 2017).

One of the complexities of indigeneity lies in the politics of categorizing and managing people's (read minorities' and Indigenous peoples') identities, and the division of people into categories of being more or less "real" and "authentic." The realities of Indigenous peoples are inevitably affected by the colonial powers' divisions and categorizations, which shape official, popular, and scholarly imaginations, and furthermore often channel financial support and the acceptance of rights, for example: in North America concerning federal or government recognition of Indigenous groups (cf. Lawrence 2004; Lightfoot 2005), in the Nordic countries concerning Sámi identity criteria (Beach 2007; Åhrén 2008), and in the Russian Federation concerning the status of "Indigenous small-numbered peoples" (Donahoe et al. 2008; Berg-Nordlie 2015). Archaeology, as well as other academic fields such as ethnography and anthropology, have been part of the historical, and present, constructions of indigeneity in different parts of the world.

Indigenous archaeology is an archaeological field which is growing in importance globally, and which is closely connected to the colonial past and present experienced by Indigenous groups, and the entanglements of archaeology with colonial attitudes, practices, and categorizations. Therefore, Indigenous archaeology—as an ethnopolitical movement and an academic field—is highly relevant to the theme of this volume. Today, there is an extensive collection of scholarly work on Indigenous archaeology (see, e.g., Smith and Wobst 2005; Watkins 2005; Atalay 2006; Bruchac, Hart, and Wobst 2010; Phillips and Allen 2010; McNiven 2016; Hillerdal et al. 2017; cf. critical discussions in Smith 2012), including personal accounts on the experiences of "being and becoming Indigenous archaeologists" (Nicholas 2011). However, Indigenous archaeology is not a unified, homogeneous field, but rather a movement with strong global connections and many local specificities and variations.

For the proponents of Indigenous archaeology, it strives to be a decolonizing practice, and a means for Indigenous empowerment and self-determination in archaeology and heritage management, as well as an instrument for the promotion of Indigenous voices and experiences in archaeology—aiming to transform archaeological theory and practice.

In her article "Indigenous Archaeology as Decolonizing Practice," Sonya Atalay stresses that a decolonizing archaeology:

> ... must include topics such as the social construction of cultural heritage, concerns over revitalization of tradition and Indigenous knowledge, issues of ownership and authority, cultural and intellectual property, and the history and role of museums, collections and collecting. (Atalay 2006, 302)

Indigenous archaeology can be seen as part of a more general post-colonial critique. The—not entirely trouble-free—relationships between Indigenous archaeology and postcolonial critique and theory have been discussed by scholars in recent years (see, e.g., Preucel and Cipolla 2010; Byrd and Rothberg 2011; cf. Spangen, Salmi, and Äikäs 2015 on Sámi archaeology and postcolonial theory).

Much of the focus in Indigenous archaeology approaches has been on community-based and community-initiated research, with participatory and collaborative methodologies (see Atalay 2012; Colwell 2016; Nicholas 2017)—ways of doing research that do not only consider academic inter-ests and standards, but also take seriously the perspectives, interests, wishes, and priorities of local and Indigenous communities.

One important theme in Indigenous archaeology has concerned repa-triation and reburial debates, which have to a large extent influenced the general perception of Indigenous archaeology and have an extensive body of literature (among many others, see Fforde, Hubert, and Turnbull 2002; Gabriel and Dahl 2008; Ojala 2009; Tythacott and Arvanitis 2014; Colwell 2017). Another important dimension, which was mentioned earlier in this chapter, is the recognition of the limits of archaeological approaches and collaboration, and the need to develop "safe spaces" for Indigenous individuals and groups to discuss and deal with troubled and traumatic histories.

It has been debated whether Indigenous archaeology should be seen as a field of its own, separate from archaeology in general, or whether it should be integrated into general archaeology. Sonya Atalay has argued that, "Indigenous archaeology is not only for and by Indigenous people but has wider implications and relevance outside of Indigenous com-munities." Indigenous archaeology, in her words, "provides a model for archaeological practice that can be applied globally as it calls for and pro-vides a methodology for collaboration of descendent communities and stakeholders around the world" (Atalay 2006, 292). George Nicholas has also argued that "rather than working to develop Indigenous approaches to archaeology separate from others, we should be trying to incorporate them within the discipline" (Nicholas 2010, 233). Failing to do so could, in his view, lead to isolation and marginalization, as well as significantly limit "the potential contributions of archaeology as a more representative and responsible discipline and constrain its continued intellectual growth" (Nicholas 2010, 233).

Indigenous archaeology often carries a more or less radical critique of traditional archaeology and cultural resource management, which are often seen as part of colonial ideas and practices. As a kind of "counter-archaeology," it challenges the power relations of archaeology and traditional ways of doing archaeology—challenges which should be taken seriously in all kinds of archaeology, not only in Indigenous contexts.

Colonialism Past and Present: Ways Forward

The discussions in the chapters in this volume emphasize the complexities of colonial relations and the connections between the past and present, and raise many new questions about the archaeological engagement and entanglement with colonialism. Discussing these questions is relevant not only in Indigenous contexts but everywhere within archaeology.

The theme of the book also raises questions about the roles and responsibilities of archaeology and archaeologists, and about the power relations involved in archaeological research. Issues such as the archaeologist as an activist and as an active participant in current debates in society (see, e.g., McGuire 2008; Stottman 2010; Tarlow and Nilsson Stutz 2013; Atalay et al. 2014) are important to discuss in more depth. There is a need to discuss the roles of archaeologists in relation to local and Indigenous communities, as well as in the academic world and contemporary society. Whose voices and perspectives will be heard in archaeology, and whose archaeological voices and perspectives will be heard in society?

Taking up the challenges posed by the Indigenous archaeology movement—to be more engaged, sensitive, relevant, representative, and ethically sustainable in archaeology—in the end, is much about the politics of archaeology. What do we want to achieve with our engagements? What do we want to change? Who do we want to convince? Furthermore, how to do archaeology is also a matter of priorities. For contract and rescue archaeology it is to a large extent about a lack of resources, which can limit efforts to collaborate and include local and Indigenous perspectives. For academic archaeology, it is also a matter of the priorities of individual researchers in relation to publishing demands and criteria for promoting academic careers, which do not always value collaborative approaches and contact with descendant communities.

This volume contributes to discussions about the present importance of the past and the ways in which we study and understand past encounters in colonial contexts. Hopefully, the contributions in the volume will inspire and stimulate continued discussions on these issues.

One of the greatest potentials of archaeology in our contemporary world, as I see it, is to explore the politics of connections between the past and present, and to trace other perspectives, voices, and experiences than those represented in the general historical narratives. By engaging with past as well as present ongoing colonialism, historical archaeologies of colonial encounters have an important role to play in contemporary society. As the chapters in this volume testify, to do this means encountering many challenges, but also many opportunities to work for change in our world.

Acknowledgments

I would like to thank the editors Tiina Äikäs and Anna-Kaisa Salmi for the invitation to write this discussion chapter. The chapter has been written as part of the research project *Collecting Sápmi: Early modern globalization of Sámi material culture and Sámi cultural heritage today*, which has been funded by the Swedish Research Council (421-2013-1917).

Carl-Gösta Ojala is a researcher in archaeology at the Department of Archaeology and Ancient History at Uppsala University. His main research interests include Sámi history and archaeology; Russian and Soviet archaeology; and issues of identity, heritage, politics, and research ethics. His recent research has focused on early modern colonial history and its implications today in Sápmi (the Sámi areas), the exploitation of natural resources in Sápmi, and the collecting of Sámi material culture in the seventeenth and eighteenth centuries. Ojala is the author of *Sámi Prehistories: The Politics of Archaeology and Identity in Northernmost Europe* (Uppsala University 2009) and coeditor of *Archaeologies of "Us" and "Them": Debating History, Heritage and Indigeneity* (with Charlotta Hillerdal and Anna Karlström, Routledge 2017).

References

Åhrén, Christina. 2008. Är jag en riktig same? En etnologisk studie av unga samers identitetsarbete. Umeå: Umeå universitet.

Atalay, Sonya. 2006. "Indigenous Archaeology as Decolonizing Practice." *American Indian Quarterly* 30(3–4): 280–310.

———. 2012. *Community-Based Archaeology: Research with, by, and for Indigenous and Local Communities.* Berkeley and Los Angeles: University of California Press.

Atalay, Sonya, Lee Rains Clauss, Randall H. McGuire, and John R. Welch, eds. 2014. *Transforming Archaeology: Activist Practices and Prospects.* Walnut Creek, CA: Left Coast Press.

Barlindhaug, Stine. 2013. *Cultural Sites, Traditional Knowledge and Participatory Mapping: Long-Term Land Use in a Sámi Community in Coastal Norway.* Tromsø: University of Tromsø.

Beach, Hugh. 2007. "Self-determining the Self: Aspects of Saami Identity Management in Sweden." *Acta Borealia* 24(1): 1–25.

Berg-Nordlie, Mikkel. 2015. "Two Centuries of Russian Sámi Policy: Arrangements for Autonomy and Participation Seen in Light of Imperial, Soviet and Federal Indigenous Minority Policy 1822–2014." *Acta Borealia* 32(1): 40–67.

Bruchac, Margaret M., Siobhan M. Hart, and H. Martin Wobst, eds. 2010. *Indigenous Archaeologies: A Reader on Decolonization.* Walnut Creek, CA: Left Coast Press.

Byrd, Jodi A., and Michael Rothberg. 2011. "Between Subalternity and Indigeneity: Critical Categories for Postcolonial Studies." *Interventions: International Journal of Postcolonial Studies* 13(1): 1–12.

Cipolla, Craig N., and Katherine Howlett Hayes, eds. 2015. *Rethinking Colonialism: Comparative Archaeological Approaches.* Gainesville: University Press of Florida.

Colwell, Chip. 2016. "Collaborative Archaeologies and Descendant Communities." *Annual Review of Anthropology* 45: 113–27.

———. 2017. *Plundered Skulls and Stolen Spirits: Inside the Fight to Reclaim Native America's Culture.* Chicago and London: University of Chicago Press.

Donahoe, Brian, Joachim Otto Habeck, Agnieszka Halemba, and István Sántha. 2008. "Size and Place in the Construction of Indigeneity in the Russian Federation." *Current Anthropology* 49(6): 993–1020.

Ferris, Neal, Rodney Harrison, and Matthew A. Beaudoin. 2014. "Introduction: Rethinking Colonial Pasts through the Archaeologies of the Colonized." In *Rethinking Colonial Pasts through Archaeology,* ed. Neal Ferris, Rodney Harrison, and Michael V. Wilcox, 1–34. Oxford: Oxford University Press.

Ferris, Neal, Rodney Harrison, and Michael V. Wilcox, eds. 2014. *Rethinking Colonial Pasts through Archaeology.* Oxford: Oxford University Press.

Fforde, Cressida, Jane Hubert, and Paul Turnbull, eds. 2002. *The Dead and their Possessions: Repatriation in Principle, Policy and Practice.* London and New York: Routledge.

Fur, Gunlög. 2013. "Colonialism and Swedish History: Unthinkable Connections?" In *Scandinavian Colonialism and the Rise of Modernity: Small Time Agents in a Global Arena,* ed. Magdalena Naum and Jonas M. Nordin, 17–36. New York: Springer.

Gabriel, Mille, and Jens Dahl, eds. 2008. *Utimut. Past Heritage—Future Partnerships. Discussions on Repatriation in the 21st Century*. Copenhagen: International Work Group for Indigenous Affairs (IWGIA).

Gärdebo, Johan, May-Britt Öhman, and Hiroshi Maruyama, eds. 2014. *RE:MINDINGS: Co-Constituting Indigenous / Academic / Artistic Knowledges*. Uppsala: Uppsala University.

Hansson, Staffan. 2015. *Malmens land: Gruvnäringen i Norrbotten under 400 år*. Tornedalica 63. Luleå: Tornedalica.

Harlin, Eeva-Kristiina. 2008. *Recalling Ancestral Voices: Repatriation of Sámi Cultural Heritage*. Inari: Siida Sámi Museum.

Harrison, Rodney. 2014. "Shared Histories: Rethinking 'Colonized' and 'Colonizer' in the Archaeology of Colonialism." In *Rethinking Colonial Pasts through Archaeology*, ed. Neal Ferris, Rodney Harrison, and Michael V. Wilcox, 37–56. Oxford: Oxford University Press.

Hayes, Katherine H., and Craig N. Cipolla. 2015. "Introduction: Re-Imagining Colonial Pasts, Influencing Colonial Futures." In *Rethinking Colonialism: Comparative Archaeological Approaches*, ed. Craig N. Cipolla and Katherine Howlett Hayes, 1–13. Gainesville: University Press of Florida.

Hillerdal, Charlotta, Anna Karlström, and Carl-Gösta Ojala, eds. 2017. *Archaeologies of "Us" and "Them": Debating History, Heritage and Indigeneity*. London and New York: Routledge.

Holand, Ingegerd, and Ingrid Sommerseth. 2013. "Ethical Issues in the Semi-Darkness: Skeletal Remains and Sámi Graves from Arctic Northern Norway." In *More than Just Bones: Ethics and Research on Human Remains*, ed. Hallvard Fossheim, 21–47. Oslo: The Norwegian National Research Ethics Committees.

Horning, Audrey. 2007. "Cultures of Contact, Cultures of Conflict? Identity Construction, Colonialist Discourse, and the Ethics of Archaeological Practice in Northern Ireland." *Stanford Journal of Archaeology* 5: 107–33.

Lawrence, Bonita. 2004. *"Real" Indians and Others: Mixed-Blood Urban Native Peoples and Indigenous Nationhood*. Lincoln and London: University of Nebraska Press.

Lawrence, Rebecca. 2014. "Internal Colonisation and Indigenous Resource Sovereignty: Wind Power Developments on Traditional Saami Lands." *Environment and Planning D: Society and Space* 32: 1036–53.

Lightfoot, Kent G. 2005. *Indians, Missionaries, and Merchants: The Legacy of Colonial Encounters on the California Frontiers*. Berkeley and Los Angeles: University of California Press.

Liliequist, Marianne, and Coppélie Cocq, eds. 2017. *Samisk kamp: kulturförmedling och rättviserörelse*. Umeå: H:ström.

Ljungdahl, Ewa, and Erik Norberg, eds. 2012. *Ett steg till på vägen: Resultat och reflexioner kring ett dokumentationsprojekt på sydsamiskt område under åren 2008–2011*. Östersund: Gaaltije—sydsamiskt kulturcentrum.

Lundmark, Bo. 2016. "Medeltida vittnesbörd om samerna och den katolska kyrkan." In *De historiska relationerna mellan Svenska kyrkan och samerna*, ed. Daniel Lindmark and Olle Sundström, 221–40. Skellefteå: Artos & Norma.

McGuire, Randall H. 2008. *Archaeology as Political Action*. Berkeley and Los Angeles: University of California Press.

McNiven, Ian J. 2016. "Theoretical Challenges of Indigenous Archaeology: Setting an Agenda." *American Antiquity* 81(1): 27–41.

Naum, Magdalena, and Fredrik Ekengren, eds. 2018. *Facing Otherness in Early Modern Sweden: Travel, Migration and Material Transformations, 1500–1800.* Woodbridge: Boydell Press.

Naum, Magdalena, and Jonas M. Nordin, eds. 2013a. *Scandinavian Colonialism and the Rise of Modernity: Small Time Agents in a Global Arena.* New York: Springer.

Naum, Magdalena, and Jonas M. Nordin. 2013b. "Introduction: Situating Scandinavian Colonialism." In *Scandinavian Colonialism and the Rise of Modernity: Small Time Agents in a Global Arena,* ed. Magdalena Naum and Jonas M. Nordin, 3–16. New York: Springer.

Nicholas, George P. 2010. "Seeking the End of Indigenous Archaeology." In *Bridging the Divide: Indigenous Communities and Archaeology into the 21st Century,* ed. Caroline Phillips and Harry Allen, 233–52. Walnut Creek, CA: Left Coast Press.

———. 2017. "Culture, Rights, Indigenity and Intervention: Addressing Inequality in Indigenous Heritage Protection and Control." In *Archaeologies of "Us" and "Them": Debating History, Heritage and Indigeneity,* ed. Charlotta Hillerdal, Anna Karlström, and Carl-Gösta Ojala, 199–217. London and New York: Routledge.

———, ed. 2011. *Being and Becoming Indigenous Archaeologists.* Walnut Creek, CA: Left Coast Press.

Niezen, Ronald. 2003. *The Origins of Indigenism: Human Rights and the Politics of Identity.* Berkeley and Los Angeles: University of California Press.

Norberg, Erik, and Birgitta Fossum. 2011. "Traditional Knowledge and Cultural Landscape." In *Working with Traditional Knowledge: Communities, Institutions, Information systems, Law and Ethics,* ed. Jelena Porsanger and Gunvor Guttorm, 193–223. Kautokeino: Sámi allaskuvla.

Norberg, Erik, and Ulf Stefan Winka, eds. 2014. *Sydsamer—landskap och historia: ett dokumentationsprojekt på sydsamiskt område under åren 2012–2014.* Östersund: Gaaltije—sydsamiskt kulturcentrum.

Nordin, Jonas M. 2015. "Metals of Metabolism: The Construction of Industrial Space and the Commodification of Early Modern Sápmi." In *Historical Archaeologies of Capitalism,* Rev. ed., ed. Mark P. Leone and Jocelyn E. Knauf, 249–72. New York: Springer.

Nordin, Jonas M., and Carl-Gösta Ojala. 2015. "Collecting Sápmi: Early Modern Collecting of Sámi Material Culture." *Nordisk museologi* 2015(2): 114–22.

———. 2017. "Copper Worlds: A Historical Archaeology of Abraham and Jakob Momma-Reenstierna and Their Industrial Enterprise in the Torne River Valley, c. 1650–1680." *Acta Borealia* 34(2): 103–33.

———. 2018. "Collecting, Connecting, Constructing: Early Modern Commodification and Globalization of Sámi Material Culture." *Journal of Material Culture* 23(1): 58–82.

Ojala, Carl-Gösta. 2009. *Sámi Prehistories: The Politics of Archaeology and Identity in Northernmost Europe.* Uppsala: Uppsala University.

———. 2016. "Svenska kyrkan och samiska mänskliga kvarlevor." In *De historiska relationerna mellan Svenska kyrkan och samerna,* ed. Daniel Lindmark and Olle Sundström, 983–1018. Skellefteå: Artos & Norma bokförlag.

——. 2017. "Contested Colonial History and Heritage in Sápmi: Archaeology, Indigeneity and Local Communities in Northern Sweden." In *Archaeologies of "Us" and "Them": Debating History, Heritage and Indigeneity*, ed. Charlotta Hilldal, Anna Karlström, and Carl-Gösta Ojala, 258–71. London and New York: Routledge.

——. 2018. "Encountering 'the Other' in the North: Colonial Histories in Early Modern Northern Sweden." In *Facing Otherness in Early Modern Sweden: Travel, migration and material transformations, 1500–1800*, ed. Magdalena Naum and Fredrik Ekengren, 209–28. Woodbridge: Boydell Press.

Ojala, Carl-Gösta, and Jonas M. Nordin. 2015. "Mining Sápmi: Colonial Histories, Sámi Archaeology, and the Exploitation of Natural Resources in Northern Sweden." *Arctic Anthropology* 52(2): 6–21.

Össbo, Åsa. 2014. *Nya vatten, dunkla speglingar: Industriell kolonialism genom svensk vattenkraftutbyggnad i renskötselområdet 1910–1968*. Umeå: Umeå universitet.

Phillips, Caroline, and Harry Allen, eds. 2010. *Bridging the Divide: Indigenous Communities and Archaeology into the 21st Century*. Walnut Creek, CA: Left Coast Press.

Preucel, Robert W., and Craig N. Cipolla. 2010. "Indigenous and Postcolonial Archaeologies." In *Archaeology and the Postcolonial Critique*, ed. Matthew Liebmann and Uzma Z. Rizvi, 129–40. Lanham, MD: AltaMira Press.

Rasmussen, Siv. 2016a. *Samisk integrering i norsk og svensk kirke i tidlig nytid: En komparasjon mellom Finnmark og Torne lappmark*. Tromsø: Universitetet i Tromsø.

——. 2016b. "Samiske prester i den svenske kirka i tidlig nytid." In *De historiska relationerna mellan Svenska kyrkan och samerna: En vetenskaplig antologi*, ed. Daniel Lindmark and Olle Sundström, 283–314. Skellefteå: Artos & Norma.

Rydving, Håkan. 1995. *The End of Drum-Time: Religious Change among the Lule Saami, 1670s–1740s*, 2nd ed. Uppsala: Uppsala University.

——. 2010. "Samiska överhetspersoner i Sverige-Finland under 1600-talet." In *Samer som "de andra," samer om "de andra": Identitet och etnicitet i nordiska kulturmöten*, ed. Else Mundal and Håkan Rydving, 259–65. Umeå: Umeå universitet.

Sehlin MacNeil, Kristina. 2017. *Extractive Violence on Indigenous Country: Sami and Aboriginal Views on Conflicts and Power Relations with Extractive Industries*. Umeå: University of Umeå.

Silliman, Stephen. 2005. "Culture Contact or Colonialism? Challenges in the Archaeology of Native North America." *American Antiquity* 70(1): 55–74.

——. 2010. "Indigenous Traces in Colonial Spaces: Archaeologies of Ambiguity, Origin, and Practice." *Journal of Social Archaeology* 10(1): 25–58.

Smith, Claire, and H. Martin Wobst, eds. 2005. *Indigenous Archaeologies: Decolonizing Theory and Practice*. Oxon & New York: Routledge.

Smith, Linda Tuhiwai. 2012. *Decolonizing Methodologies: Research and Indigenous Peoples*, 2nd ed. London and New York: Zed books.

Spangen, Marte, Anna-Kaisa Salmi, and Tiina Äikäs. 2015. "Sámi Archaeology and Postcolonial Theory: An Introduction." *Arctic Anthropology* 52(2): 1–5.

Stottman, M. Jay. 2010. *Archaeologists as Activists: Can Archaeologists Change the World?* Tuscaloosa: The University of Alabama Press.

Svestad, Asgeir. 2013. "What Happened in Neiden? On the Question of Reburial Ethics." *Norwegian Archaeological Review* 46(2): 194–242.

Tarlow, Sarah, and Liv Nilsson Stutz. 2013. "Can an Archaeologist Be a Public Intellectual?" *Archaeological dialogues* 20(1): 1–5.

Tythacott, Louise, and Kostas Arvanitis, eds. 2014. *Museums and Restitution: New Practices, New Approaches*. Farnham: Ashgate.

Wallerström, Thomas, Ulf Segerström, and Eva-Maria Nordström. 2017. *Kunglig makt och samiska bosättningsmönster: Studier kring Väinö Tanners vinterbyteori*. Oslo: Novus.

Watkins, Joe. 2005. "Through Wary Eyes: Indigenous Perspectives on Archaeology." *Annual Review of Anthropology* 34: 429–49.

Xanthaki, Alexandra, Sanna Valkonen, Leena Heinämäki, and Piia Nuorgam, eds. 2017. Indigenous Peoples' Cultural heritage: Rights, Debates and Challenges. Leiden: Brill Nijhoff.

Perspectives on Indigenous Voices and Historical Archaeology

Alistair Paterson and Shino Konishi

Introduction

This volume has presented a range of accounts detailing instances of the presence of Indigenous perspectives on the historical archaeology of colonialism. Our invitation from the editors was to reflect on these chapters, viewing them from our experience of Australian history and archaeology. We are respectively an historical archaeologist (Paterson) and Indigenous historian (Konishi), and we share an interest in the history of Australia focused on the experiences of Indigenous people and, in particular, the colonial world and the ways of knowing various forms of cross-cultural encounters.

In the first part of this concluding chapter, we introduce the reader to a brief consideration of the involvement and significance of Indigenous histories and archaeology on understandings of colonialism in Australia. We then turn to the chapters to generate some broader themes to explore, namely landscapes, materiality, and the methodological dimensions and challenges to accessing forms of Indigenous "voice," given the impasse of knowing colonial pasts where Indigenous voices were largely silent or silenced.

This book admirably seeks to reinstate Indigenous voices and perspectives in the study of colonial historical archaeology. Through a series of particular case studies, centred primarily on Sámi and Native American lands, with one additional Australian example, this book provides fascinating deep histories of local sites. It often illustrates that these locations of colonial encounter between Indigenous peoples and various "incomers," be they amicable, transactional, interventionist, or violent, reflect not just colonial or settler surface histories, but in many instances, deeper histories of Indigenous experience and connections to place. These studies reveal the ways in which historical archaeology can seek to overcome the limitations of historical documentary evidence, which as the editors Tiina Äikäs and Anna-Kaisa Salmi (Introduction) note, often privileges the perspectives of the elites who left the written records and silences Indigenous points of view. As a whole, they acknowledge and model a way in which historical archaeologists can deepen and enrich traditional archaeological approaches in which the material artifacts are interpreted solely by the modern archaeologist, often removed ethnically and temporally from the Indigenous sites they research. Instead, the contributors in the book complement the historical and archaeological data by drawing on Indigenous oral history testimonies as well as present-day Indigenous perspectives on cultural practices and historical legacies.

The Recognition of Indigenous Voices in Australian Archaeology

The relationships that emerge between Indigenous people and archaeologists are contingent on the time and place they occur. In Australia during the 1980s, the politics of Indigenous history was highlighted by the Bicentennial commemoration of British settlement—or invasion—of the continent in 1788 at Botany Bay (Sydney). Archaeology had in previous decades begun to deploy absolute dating techniques to push back Aboriginal history (at that time termed "prehistory," a now largely abandoned term in Australian discourse). Historical archaeology was a very young discipline in the 1980s, and largely focused on "white" European Australian and overseas Chinese sites. However, the 1980s also saw important historical archaeological projects on Aboriginal historical sites, such as the work on First Government House in Sydney by Annie Bickford and Isabel McBryde which highlighted the presence of Eora people at the heart of British colonial administration in the earliest decades of white history in Australia (McBryde 1989). In Tasmania, Judy Birmingham's excavations at Wybalenna, a station on Flinders Island where Aboriginal people from Tasmania had been removed to following Tasmania's "Black War," were particularly important for highlighting the grim treatment of Palawa (Tasmanian) Aboriginal people in the colonial world. Birmingham's work followed that of James Deetz in the Americas, and Carmel Schrire and Martin Hall in South Africa (Birmingham 1992).

The recognition of the presence of Aboriginal people in historical/ colonial Australia and their role within their traditional "country" on settler "frontiers" was part of a wider revisionist history driven by Henry Reynolds and others (e.g., Reynolds 1982), which in many respects answered the 1968 call from noted anthropologist W. E. H. Stanner to shatter "the Great Australian silence" and include Aboriginal people and perspectives in our national history (Stanner 2011). However, for contemporary Aboriginal and Torres Strait Islander Australians there was limited "voice" in archaeological discourse. In 1983 R. F. Langford, on behalf of the Tasmanian Aboriginal Centre, wrote an angry essay, "Our Heritage—Your Playground," about the contemporary conflict between Indigenous people and archaeologists. In summing up the conflict, Langford observed that "archaeologists feel unfairly criticised and feel hurt because they say they are doing their best to develop an understanding of our culture, and we are angry because we are treated to token moves to obtain our approval and consent to what you are doing" (Langford 1983, 2). Here Langford illustrated the important role of emotions in heritage debates, as Indigenous anger was fueled not only by issues of control but also by the painful memory of the nineteenth-century collection of Indigenous human remains. This was a practice in Tasmania, driven by the fantasy that the Palawa people were the world's most primitive people and on the verge of extinction; a practice which had an enduring emotional legacy for Indigenous people. The anger expressed in Langford's seminal essay was particularly acute in Tasmania, since the body of Trugernanner (Truganini) (ca.1812–1876), erroneously believed to be the last Aboriginal Tasmanian, had been displayed at the Hobart Museum until 1947 following sustained protest from Indigenous and non-Indigenous people. Trugernanner was then held in storage until 1976, when Palawa people were finally allowed to reclaim and cremate her, as was custom, and scatter her ashes near her homeland (Florek 2017).

In the decades since the Bicentenary in Australia there has been a fluorescence of historical archaeology of Aboriginal Australia (Murray 1988; Colley and Bickford 1996; Lydon 2006). This has included work on Australian Aboriginal people in missions (e.g., Birmingham and Wilson 2000; Lydon 2009; Ash, Manash, and Bosun 2010; Fowler, Roberts, and Rigney 2016) and other forms of colonial institutions (Lydon 2005a, 2005b) across colonial Australia (e.g., Harrison and Williamson 2004; Harrison 2004a, 2004b; Paterson 2018).

Part of the shift in Australia has been towards archaeologies that variously consult and, on occasion, actively engage with Aboriginal people as collaborators and holders of forms of knowledge that are equally valid as scientific forms of knowledge generated through archaeology. Indigenous archaeologists now have a professional association, and Aboriginal people are regular contributors at the national archaeology meetings. However, there understandably exists much work to be done to better align contemporary Aboriginal people and researchers with archaeology, alongside Aboriginal responses not only to colonial sites but also the more ancient sites extending into over fifty thousand years of ancestral history. Thus, archaeologists and Indigenous communities have now come a long way towards overcoming past emotional conflicts over Indigenous heritage.

The emotional impact of past archaeological practices is palpable in Andre Pike and Ann McGrath's 2014 documentary *Message from Mungo*. This film is about Mungo Lady, a woman who was cremated approximately forty thousand years ago, discovered in 1969 in the eroding sand dunes of Lake Mungo by archaeologist Jim Bowler. It focuses on the reactions of local Paakantji, Muthi Muthi, and Ngiyampaa groups, led in particular by Alice Kelly, a spokesperson for the Indigenous people from the Willandra Lakes area, and their fight to have her remains returned to their community. This film highlights the differing emotional responses to Aboriginal heritage sites. While archaeologists were excited to find that Mungo Lady represents the oldest modern human discovered in Australia, and the world's oldest cremation site, elder Lottie Williams dryly observed that "me and the rest of us know we were here all the time, so that wasn't news to us" (Pike and McGrath 2014). Instead, many of the local Aboriginal people saw Mungo Lady as an ancestor, and felt sadness and empathy, imagining her "crying because she's been taken out of country." In 1992, after much agitation, and similar to Trugernanner fifteen years earlier, Mungo Lady was returned to her country in an equally emotional ceremony. Badger Bates, from the NSW Parks and Wildlife Services, recollected that everybody "had tears in their eyes" and that "it was a moment that moved everybody." Such cases reveal not just the ongoing emotional connections between Aboriginal people and their ancestors, irrespective of whether they passed away a hundred or forty thousand years ago, and the growing political assertions and claims of Aboriginal people over their heritage, but also the growing understanding for these Indigenous sentiments that archaeologists now respect and heed. This collection reveals that this shift in archaeological politics and practice is not unique to Australia.

In Search of Indigenous Voices in Other Parts of the World

In their Introduction, "In Search of Indigenous Voices in the Historical Archaeology of Colonial Encounters," Tiina Äikäs and Anna-Kaisa Salmi remind us that there is a firmly established body of work exploring the colonial encounters between Indigenous peoples and Europeans, and we can assume that this is now an established tenet of historical archaeological inquiry. The timing and character of this form of collaborative archaeology varies for different geographical settings. In North America a longer tradition of historical archaeology research can be in part explained by an interest in historical sites as early as the Depression and the academic development of historical archaeology from the 1960s onwards, while in South America historical archaeology is more recent. In Europe, there is a less distinct tradition of historical archaeology, given the various areas of specialization into the archaeology of literate societies — Classical, Medieval, Industrial, etc. — and a less dedicated focus on "local" colonialism than demonstrated elsewhere in the world. This edited volume then makes an interesting departure and an invitation to consider the historical archaeology of Indigenous people in a different frame, by having chapters from both northern Europe and North America, as well as Australia.

Äikäs and Salmi raise several themes that overarch the various geographies of these chapters, namely that all forms of colonialism produce unequal human relations, and they acknowledge that Indigenous identity is fluid, contingent, and multiple — building on important work into the archaeology of colonialism (e.g., Gosden 2004; Lawrence and Shepherd 2006; Jordan 2009; Panich 2013).

The editors' ambition is for the book to explore "comparative indigenism," that is, its approach compares different Indigenous case studies from northern Europe, north America, and Australia, in order to highlight common and distinct historical experiences of colonization, as well as identify common challenges and solutions in recovering and interpreting these histories. Yet the editors observe that the comparative indigenism approach must be careful not to homogenize or essentialize Indigenous experiences of colonialism, and remain sensitive to the differences in historic experience as well as differences in the conception and articulation of Indigenous identity, as evident, for example, in Inga-Maria Mulk and Tim Bayliss-Smith's chapter (Chapter 2) on Sámi religious syncretism, which is attentive to the fluid and nuanced identities of different Sámi individuals and groups, who adopted Christianity over long periods of Scandinavian-Sámi interaction.

Many of the chapters focus on material culture, and how Indigenous people modify, create, and syncretize material objects in culture contact studies. Foreign objects operated in Indigenous contexts, sometimes replacing traditional objects, sometimes complementing existing practices, and for example, some foreign objects moved from a domestic to ritual purposes (see also Thomas 1991; McBryde 2000). This is a well-established aspect of historical archaeology, and best suited to settings where a landscape multi-site perspective is adopted, a point we return to below. Objects are increasingly recognized as having the potential to reflect past agency, the various multiple meanings objects may have according to different cultural perspectives. As Äikäs and Salmi (Introduction) remind us, material culture has forms of agency in colonial encounters, as well as in the present, where Indigenous sites, objects, symbols, and knowledge can play significant roles in representing forms of history, or indeed reflect the ongoing appropriation of Indigenous culture when, for example, Indigenous objects become symbols for advertising. This ongoing culture of appropriation and misuse, for example by artists, reflects an enduring colonial tradition.

Äikäs and Salmi rightfully acknowledge the challenges of locating Indigenous voices in historical documents, even if read strategically, as written texts usually reflect the perspectives and interests of the elites and exclude marginalized voices. This dilemma has been at the heart of historical archaeological work, which has long argued that the archaeological record potentially provides a counterpoint to such biases by privileging "hidden histories"—referring to Deborah Bird Rose's *Hidden Histories: Black Stories from Victoria River Downs, Humbert River and Wave Hill Stations* (1991), her influential attempt to situate Australian Aboriginal history alongside documentary history.

Material culture, in contrast to documentary accounts, was created and left by everyone, so in principle, represents a broader cross section of perspectives and voices. Yet, material culture is often read by non-Indigenous archaeologists, so Indigenous meanings can be opaque. Consequently, this book draws on scholars who combine data from archaeology, historical evidence, and Indigenous oral histories as well as contemporary Indigenous perspectives and practices, in order to try best recover Indigenous meanings. By including a series of local case studies, this book allows authors to stress local histories and interpretations, and provide alternative stories of colonial histories which are more varied.

The Sounds of Bells and Quiet Narrungga Agency

In their chapter, "The Sounds of Colonization: An Examination of Bells at Point Pearce Aboriginal Mission Station/Burgiyana, South Australia"

(Chapter 1), Madeline Fowler, Amy Roberts, and Lester-Irabinna Rigney focus on church bells at the Point Pearce mission, examining the different historical contexts and sonic registers of the mission's bells. They begin by tracing how the earliest cross-cultural encounters with the Narrungga people were with maritime ships, mainly those of sealers and whalers in the 1830s. Following this the Narrungga encountered graziers and pastoralists, and then the mission in 1868. Thus, by the time the mission was established by Moravians Narrungga people had already come to know the ways and interests of Europeans and were familiar with the sound of the bell.

The Mission's church bell was first described in detail by the Moravian missionary Reverend Julius Kühn, who outlined the use of the bell to signal not just religious services, but perhaps more invasively, the different chores and duties that marked the daily routine of the Aboriginal residents. Thus, the sound of the bell regulated the Narrungga people's Christian life on the mission, reflecting the Moravian church's prioritizing of teaching the gospel over broader "civilizing," or acculturating, efforts, the subject of much scholarship on mission histories.

Yet, while the Moravian missionaries may have been less preoccupied with instilling the markers of "civilization" on Aboriginal bodies, be it through imposed dietary, hygienic, and social regimes, Fowler, Roberts, and Rigney point out that the missionaries sought to interrupt Narrungga practices and inculcate a European sense of time and measured labor, regulated by the sound of the bell.

This history of control and segregation continued after the mission was turned into a government station, and the peel of the bell still used to mark the enforced daily routine and rules. Fowler, Roberts, and Rigney describe this as a "bell hegemony," or a sonic control exerted through the imposition of rules. It also reflects the institutionalization of time and the imposition of a timetable on the daily life of the mission residents. Thus, in a Foucauldian sense this bell hegemony contributed to the remaking of the Narrungga people as "docile bodies" through internalized psychological self-monitoring and control.

The fascinating chapter also explores the bells' tangible connection to maritime history. This not only deepens the cross-cultural history of the Point Pearce mission beyond its incarnation as a mission and reserve but also integrates maritime and Indigenous histories, two spheres which are often treated separately. As Fowler, Roberts, and Rigney argue, maritime history often elides Aboriginal experience, even though the Narrungga were a coastal people and renowned fishermen during the colonial period. Moreover, Point Pearce was located close to Port Victoria, a bustling international maritime port. Consequently, the sound of bells would have contributed to the local Narrungga soundscape since at least the 1830s, many decades before the mission was established. The interconnections between the maritime and mission history is tangibly manifested in the history of two of the mission's bells, which were in fact salvaged from two ship wrecks: the *Songvaar*, wrecked in 1912 and the *Notre Dame d'Avoir*, wrecked in 1920. These bells may have even been salvaged by the mission residents for reuse. The mission bells represented the wider "acoustic ecology of the mission," its connections to the maritime history, and Indigenous memory of mission life after self-management introduced in 1960s.

This chapter also contributes to spatial studies of missions, which focus on the imposition of European sense of spatial order, via a grid pattern and fenced boundaries. But the authors argue that spatial histories are not marked only by physical boundaries, and that such colonial spatial orders were not as fixed and impregnable as historians have suggested. They contend that the boundaries remained permeable, as Aboriginal residents were able to engage in different employments beyond the borders of the missions, as well as maritime subsistence. More specifically, the mission residents also engaged in work on Wardang Island, which was often used for grazing, and the residents there recalled that they had complete autonomy from the authorities while residing on the island, outside of the sonic range of the bell. These examples highlight the complexity of colonial contexts, reiterating the editors' points that Indigenous experience was often contingent.

The chapter concludes by exploring the post-mission history of the sound of the bells, and how the meaning associated with the sound transformed over time in the new context of autonomous self-management. Through oral histories and memories, Narrungga residents recall the role of the bell in contributing to community cohesion, for example, by signaling funerals, so in recent decades, the residents requested a new bell. Thus, the bells represent at once a multitude of concepts and emotions.

In Search of Early-Modern Sámi Voices

The three chapters that deal with Sámi and northern Scandinavia together illustrate the significant work underway there. In Chapter 4, "A Clockwork Porridge: An Archaeological Analysis of Everyday Life in the Seventeenth Century Early Mining Communities in Swedish Lapland," Risto Nurmi focuses on Swedish mining in northern Lapland in the seventeenth century and the contribution of Sámi people to the industry, focusing on material objects related to food, ethnic markers, and industrialization. Risto Nurmi argues that this history is one of integration, as mining produced a shared space between Sámi and southern "incomers." This chapter reminds us that cross-cultural interactions often occurred as a result of resource-driven colonization, and thus sets northern Scandinavia in comparison to, for example: the vast fur processing industries of North America, the Spanish colonization of the Americas, and the colonization of Australia by pastoral industries. Importantly, the settlers (or invaders) were made up of different ethnicities and formed new cultural fusions in these settings, against which indigeneity is sometimes profiled. As Kent Lightfoot's (Lightfoot, Wake, and Schiff 1993; Lightfoot, Martinez, and Schiff 1998) work in California has shown, the archaeological record offers both the potential to reveal the boundedness of ethnic groups, as well as the ways these are cross-cut and transformed by mobile agents, gender, and labor.

Mining in Lapland began in 1635, and the region was regarded as a harsh environment, even though it had been inhabited by Sámi for millennia. Archaeological digs recovered over two thousand finds, most related to everyday household items such as pots, bowls, and spoons, as well as evidence of Sámi slaughtering and butchery practices. These faunal remains suggest that the Sámi were highly involved in food preparation during the site's mining history. It is evident that local game was hunted, and that the miners were self-sufficient. Historical records reveal that local Sámi were employed as cooks, supported by the preponderance of bowls and spoons found throughout the site, which would have been used for Sámi soups, stews, and a gruel flavored and thickened with reindeer blood.

Other archaeological materials found included Sámi handcrafts, and their even distribution suggests that these were used not only by the Sámi but also by the incomers. Moreover, this transference of objects went both ways, as Sámi also appeared to adapt southern material culture. Thus, throughout the life of the mine site, the archaeological evidence suggests that its occupants—Sámi and incomers alike—lived closely, and that there was transcultural adaptation as incomers learned from the locals, and all shared in the intimacies of daily activities.

Further, the evidence of clocks and timepieces, used some three centuries before they were widely adopted in northern societies, offers tantalizing counter-readings to the prevalent contemporary Scandinavian discourse of Sámi laziness, exemplified by the early modern ethnographic accounts. Although, Nurmi acknowledges that the presence of the timepieces may have instead represented a "tool of power," akin to the "bell hegemony" proposed by Fowler, Roberts, and Rigney (Chapter 2), intended to transform and assimilate the Sámi.

In the Chapter 5, "'Not on Bread but on Fish and by Hunting': Food Culture in Early Modern Sápmi," Ritva Kylli, Anna-Kaisa Salmi, Tiina Äikäs, and Sirpa Aalto investigate Sámi food cultures and how they were hybridized when Sámi encountered Scandinavian and Finnic culture in the sixteenth and seventeenth centuries when both the Crown and the clergy were in contact with the Sámi.

Sámi food cultures show complicated power relations and cultural negotiations that took place between the Sámi and Scandinavians. Archaeological data includes faunal assemblages, and the historical evidence comprises early ethnographies and travel accounts, as well as the Bailiff's Accounts of taxes collected. The historical accounts show that fish were important to Sámi, as the Sámi were renowned as fishermen, but they also traded furs and paid taxes in furs. Bailiff's Accounts show the changing fashions in fur over time, and the Sámi moved to collecting more beaver furs as European demand increased during the reign of Elizabeth I. However, Bailiff's Accounts also show that they traded dried pike, and also used it in their tax parcels. Archaeological evidence suggests that pike was primarily used for export and taxes and not locally consumed by Sámi. An inevitable result of the reliance on such rich documentary sources is a focus on the historical period, while when considering archaeological sites other wider and different time periods become available. Reconciling these different time frames into one analysis is often difficult; this chapter reveals how foodways and human-animal relationships, building on Ingold (1988), provide rich opportunities for historical archaeology.

The analysis of tax parcels also sheds some light on cross-cultural interactions, given that Sámi could decide how to parcel their tax commodities. In addition, when Sámi changed items used, this reflects their cultural negotiations with Scandinavians as they recognized which items were more useful and desirable to the Scandinavians.

In the late sixteenth century reindeer became increasingly important, not only because it was consumed by Sámi, but it was also increasingly featured in their tax parcels. Further, the consumption of reindeer shows the influence of Sámi food practices on Scandinavian cultures, as the Sámi method, splitting bones in order to access the marrow, became more widely adopted among non-Sámi. Sámi also bought root crops from neighbors and made milk and cheese to trade. Thus, the archaeological evidence counters the historical narratives, which ethnocentrically dismiss Sámi food cultures as exclusively focused on fish and meat. Pollen analysis also reveals that Sámi from the interior of northern Sweden also cultivated cereals, and other plants such as pine inner bark and angelica which was used for medicinal purposes to fight the plague.

Archaeological data provides an important supplement and corrective to
the historical evidence, for example in the case of the reindeer offerings,
and the diversity of the diet. The importance of reindeer to the Sámi was
also evident in their ceremonial practices as reindeer was used as offerings, usually the antler and crania.

This chapter raises some interesting prospects for future inquiry. The
interface between mobile hunters and more sedentary non-Indigenous
others is a focus for research around the world, such as southern Africa
(Sadr 2005), Australia (Paterson 2017), and elsewhere. The question of
how Sámi perceived animals compared to how others perceived them,
is an interesting issue, especially as the documentary sources are generated from an agriculturalist's perspective, set against the lifeway of Sámi
hunting. The usefulness of zooarchaeological data is demonstrated very
clearly in this study, with the documentary sources providing evidence
of animal use to supplant the biases in archaeological records towards
larger species over, say, smaller boned animal like fish.

In "Colonization, Sámi Sacred Sites, and Religious Syncretism, ca.
AD 500–1800" (Chapter 2), Inga-Maria Mulk and Tim Bayliss-Smith
highlight the diversity of Sámi cultures, economies, and connections to
other Sámi and non-Sámi peoples, contributing to the book's aims to
not homogenize Indigenous histories and identities. It also reveals the
extent to which Sámi maintained Indigenous cultural practices, irrespective of the degree to which they had formally and informally acculturated
to Christianity. The chapter demonstrates that the adoption of external
religious beliefs and cultural practices occurred in a staged way, and not
suddenly, and that different Sámi groups and individuals had differing
contexts and motivations for adopting Christianity over the Medieval
and Early Modern period. This was a highly complex and negotiated
process, as identification with Christianity did not prove to be mutually
exclusive with ongoing Sámi practices and traditions.

Listening to Native American Voices

The set of three chapters from North America highlight the powerful
contemporary issues that arise from troubled colonial histories, and how
such histories resound through generations to the present day. Here
we start to get a different, perhaps firmer, sense of how recent generations view Indigenous history, particularly when compared to the
Scandinavian studies.

In "Landscapes of Resilience at the Cut Bank Boarding School, Montana"
(Chapter 6), William A. White III and Brandi E. Bethke examine the deep

history of the Cut Bank Boarding School from prehistory, when the location served as a bison processing site for the Blackfeet people, through the historic period before the school's establishment, when Blackfeet used the place to slaughter cattle, in an emulation of previous practices. They also trace the school era, when the residential school was established as a governmental means of assimilating Native American children into Euro-American language and ways. It is in this last incarnation of the site that seems most significant, but the authors, drawing on oral history and Indigenous memory, demonstrate that the school remains a site of continued Indigenous connections and evidence of Indigenous resilience in the face of assimilationist endeavors. The authors argue that even during the school era, rather than being assimilated into the dominant culture and ostensibly having their their Indigenous identity erased, the Indigenous students instead learned the ways of the colonizers in order to better manage them. Through their analysis of the school site's deep history, spanning two millennia, and not just the twentieth century history of the school, the authors reveal that the location remains an important site of ongoing cultural learning for the Indigenous people.

In "Conflicts in Memory and Heritage: Dakota Perspectives on Historic Fort Snelling, Minnesota" (Chapter 7), Katherine Hayes deploys settler colonial theory, specifically Patrick Wolfe's (2006) argument on the elimination of the native, to explore the history of the Historic Fort Snelling heritage site. Hayes argues that the interpretation of the site, which seeks to focus on the Fort's original architecture rather than later constructions, serves as a nostalgic reconstruction celebrating the area's settler origins. She argues that this interpretation ignores the emotional impact of this particular point in history for Dakota peoples, as it reminds them of the nineteenth century war and conflict which resulted in a mass execution of thirty-six Dakota warriors, and the removal of the remaining Dakota people from the area. This site is subject to an archaeological study, as befits a significant part of Dakotan history. Yet the one-sided interpretation and focus on the heritage site's settler history reflects the unacknowledged privilege of the archaeologists and heritage workers involved. In an attempt to grapple with the more complex shared history of conflict, and the traumatic history of the exiled Dakota people, the Walker Art Center in Minneapolis commissioned a new sculpture garden, including a provocative sculpture called *Scaffold* (2012), by non-Indigenous artist Sam Durant. This wood and metal construction was intended to comment on capital punishment, and reflect a series of historic executions, including the mass hanging of the thirty-eight Dakota men in 1862. This work sparked significant protests from Dakota people and sympathizers, incensed by the work's seemingly facile and insensitive commentary on

Dakota history, and constituted, for Hayes, another form of settler-colonial appropriation, in which the history and voice of the Dakota people were erased.

To illustrate her argument about the Historic Fort Snelling's ongoing "elimination" of the Dakota, Hayes contrasts the way in which the heritage is commemorated here with the neighboring Fort Snelling State Park. Significantly, at that site there is no reconstruction, and instead the history is commemorated through a monument symbolizing the fort, which contains a "circular carved slab of pipestone, considered sacred material, inscribed with the names of the incarcerated and exiled bands of Dakota." This piece was commissioned and made by Dakota descendants, thus rendering the Fort Snelling State Park a shared space, commemorating both Indigenous and non-Indigenous histories, and a heritage design more sensitive to the intergenerational trauma experienced by Dakota descendants.

Finally, LisaMarie Maliscke's chapter, "Seeking the Indigenous Perspective: Colonial Interactions Fort Saint Pierre, French Colonial Louisiana (1719–29)" (Chapter 3), faces the challenge of a contact history where little is known of the Yazoo, Koroa, and Ofo traditional people who were swept up in the shifting alliances and violence of the colonial world of the early eighteenth century. The attempt to "understand the Indigenous viewpoint by applying a postcolonial ethnohistorical approach to the written and material record" is challenging given the eventual histories of local depopulation, a story familiar in many parts of North America. The documentary record cited in the chapter provides insights into historical events, particularly into events related to violence or attempts to avoid violence, such as French and English understandings of treaties and alliances. The daily record of cross-cultural exchange, largely absent from the historical sources, is better captured in the material record, which reveals the movement of resources from the local residential communities into the fort. However, can such records reveal "viewpoints" from the local population, given the French perspective captured in the sources?

Conclusion

Taken as an assemblage this book provides new insights into the historical archaeology of Indigenous people and illustrates the methodological and historical barriers to generating an Indigenous voice or perspective. Self-evidently, an Indigenous perspective is often different from an archaeologist trying to write *from an* Indigenous perspective or using sources to generate an Indigenous voice. This is an area that has been developing in archaeology—it was only just over two decades ago that Janet Spector's 1993 *What This Awl Means: Feminist Archaeology at a Wahpeton Dakota Village* was a radical attempt to move from archaeological forms of writing to forms that imbedded indigeneity.

Another point highlighted in this volume is the usefulness of mobilizing a variety of sources—historical archaeology, memory, oral history— in integrated reflexive syntheses, as much as to illustrate the biases in sources, as well as to generate new perspectives on the past and to allow "hidden" voices to emerge. This is not always rewarding, and in some cases we imagine people of the past remain largely obscured despite our best intentions—as Maliscke's chapter suggests.

The use of spatial scales is another means of obtaining a broader perspective on the past. If we chose to excavate only the centers of European historical action, such as a fort on a frontier, we are unlikely to gain meaningful evidence of those people who were active across the whole landscape. This has only become more evident in archaeological studies, following seminal work by Kent Lightfoot (e.g., Lightfoot, Wake, and Schiff 1993; Lightfoot, Martinez, and Schiff 1998), Susan Kent (e.g., 1990, 2002), and others. Landscapes have long been noted as "usefully ambiguous" (Gosden and Head 1994) providing spatial and temporal frames that allow us to evade Eurocentric perspectives and extend interpretation into the periods prior to the arrival of Europeans. Even urban archaeology, requiring analysis at a city and neighborhood scale, is tackling the issues of Indigenous people's experiences, for example in Sydney where Eora people suffered the devastating impact of white settlement and increased government intervention (Karskens 2010; Irish 2017).

Over recent years Indigenous voices are entering archaeological writing, at least from our Australian perspective. Archaeologists in the New South Wales National Parks and Wildlife Service worked with local communities to create "shared histories" of heritage sites, which were published in *Shared Landscapes: Archaeologies of Attachment and the Pastoral Industry in New South Wales* (Harrison 2004b) and *Mapping Attachment: A Spatial Approach to Aboriginal Post-Contact Heritage* (Byrne and Nugent 2004). The idea of shared landscapes and shared heritage is increasingly common, and forms of heritage that have often been marginalized are now being better recognized (Smith and Beck 2003). Such work reflects the shift from informing Aboriginal people (talking to), to consultation (talking with), to collaboration (working with). Collaboration involves many elements, not all equal. Collaboration from the beginning of a project allows for Indigenous people to opt out, and even deny a project. It can be a powerful way to design research that is informed by the interests of community. Collaborative research also offers the potential to incorporate Indigenous knowledge and worldviews that are different to non-Indigenous researchers and heritage managers. These different views can sometimes work together to create a fusion, or can sit in dissonance, such as the differences between Australian Aboriginal people's perspectives on their origins compared with archaeological explanations of migration and colonization sometime over fifty thousand years ago. It is more common now for both forms of explanation to sit together. Forms of collaboration are being advocated for in archaeology, with some of the most rewarding experience coming through doing fieldwork: what Silliman titled *Collaborating at the Trowel's Edge* (2008).

To conclude we briefly explore "two-way learning" within a current project titled *Murujuga: Dynamics of the Dreaming*, led by Professor Jo McDonald and including one of us (Paterson) as the historical archaeologist.[1] This three-year project was funded by the Australian Research Council under a national scheme designed to support collaboration with industry. In this case our industry partner was Rio Tinto (a mining company) and the Murujuga Aboriginal Corporation (MAC) was the collaborating partner. Murujuga is a very significant heritage landscape, in particular recognized for its rock engravings (petroglyphs) which are listed on the National Heritage List of Australia's most significant natural and cultural places. There is now a commitment to nominate Murujuga for World Heritage Listing, and the *Murujuga: Dynamics of the Dreaming* has provided significant new evidence regarding the deep-time human occupation when the now coastal islands were located well inland from the Pleistocene coast. The islands were formed in the Holocene by rising seas and remained a significant Indigenous landscape focus into the colonial period when the life of Aboriginal people in the islands was shattered with a massacre of men, women, and children, possible as many as sixty, in 1868. In recent decades Murujuga was developed by the state government as a deep-sea port for mining and gas resource companies, which led to the destruction of rock art sites.

Developing the *Murujuga: Dynamics of the Dreaming* project involved consultation with the Murujuga Aboriginal Corporation for an extended period of time during the application process. We had to determine together what questions the project would ask, which islands would be targeted, how the fieldwork would proceed, what collaboration would look like, how the Murujuga Land & Sea Unit and their Rangers would contribute, where post-excavation analysis would be conducted, and how knowledge would be shared and communicated. The Murujuga Land & Sea Unit provided essential logistical support to the project, especially though the provision of their boat to facilitate travel to the islands. The researchers reported regularly to Circle of Elders meetings, to ensure that cultural protocols and concerns were integrated into the work. The research collaboration developed during the life of the project, and was enhanced by moments of working together, either during fieldwork, or on country, or at the university when Elders and Rangers came to the University of Western Australia to profile the project during the university's annual Research Week. During these visits we have all worked together in the archaeology laboratories on the excavated materials, ensuring that the community can see how the excavated materials are treated and the different forms of archaeological expertise used in their interpretation. At the end of the project the excavated materials are to return to Murujuga to be managed by the community.

The idea of "two-way learning" developed during the project, as we all learned ways of listening and talking. The "two-way" also reflects the fact that important Indigenous knowledge sits alongside archaeological knowledge, something we have now presented on at several national archaeology conferences together. Although it is difficult and expensive to fly from northwest Australia to the cities where large conferences are held, by coming and presenting on the project the Murujuga Rangers and Elders have become familiar with the ways that archaeologists work and think. While this is just one project, the idea of a future archaeology where Indigenous perspectives are valued and contribute to the knowledge generation is an important step.

Professor Alistair Paterson is an ARC Future Fellow in archaeology at the University of Western Australia. His research examines the historical archaeology of colonial coastal contact and settlement in Australia's Northwest and the Indian Ocean. His key interests are Western Australia and Indian Ocean history, Aboriginal Australia, the Dutch East India Company, colonialism and exploration, rock art, and the history of collecting in Western Australia in collaboration with the Western Australian Museum, State Library, Art Gallery, and the British Museum.

Dr. Shino Konishi is an historian based in the School of Humanities and School of Indigenous Studies at the University of Western Australia. She specializes in Indigenous history, focusing on early encounters between Aboriginal people and European explorers, as well as the history of broader Western representations of Aboriginal people, cultures, and gender relations. She is the author of *The Aboriginal Male in the Enlightenment World* (2012) and she has coedited two recent collections on Indigenous intermediaries. She is Aboriginal, and identifies with the Yawuru people of Broome, Western Australia.

Note

1. ARC Linkage Project LP140100393. Administering Organization: The University of Western Australia (UWA). Investigators Prof Josephine McDonald, Prof Peter Veth, Prof Alistair Paterson, Dr. Jamie Hampson, Dr. Katie Glaskin, Dr. Thomas Whitley, A/ Prof Paul Bourke, and Dr. Kenneth Mulvaney.

References

Ash, Jeremy, Louise Manash, and David Bosun. 2010. "Lining the Path: A Seascape Perspective of Two Torres Strait Missions, Northeast Australia." *International Journal of Historical Archaeology* 14: 56–85.

Birmingham, Judy. 1992. *Wybalenna: The Archaeology of Cultural Accommodation in Nineteenth Century Tasmania.* Sydney: Australian Society for Historical Archaeology.

Birmingham, Judy, and Andrew Wilson. 2010. "Archaeologies of Cultural Interaction: Wybalenna Settlement and Killalpaninna Mission." *International Journal of Historical Archaeology* 14(1): 15–38.

Byrne, Denis R., and Maria Nugent. 2004. *Mapping Attachment: A Spatial Approach to Aboriginal Post-Contact Heritage.* Hurstville: Department of Environment and Conservation.

Colley, Sarah M., and Anne Bickford. 1996. "'Real' Aborigines and 'Real' Archaeology: Aboriginal Places and Australian Historical Archaeology." *World Archaeological Bulletin* 7: 5–21.

Florek, Stan. 2016. "Our Global Neighbours: Remembering Truganini." Australian Museum. Retrieved 28 March 2019 from https://australianmuseum.net.au/ blog-archive/science/our-global-neighbours-remembering-truganini/.

Fowler, Madeline, Amy Roberts, and Lester-Irabinna Rigney. 2016. "The 'Very Stillness of Things': Object Biographies of Sailcloth and Fishing Net from the Point Pearce Aboriginal Mission (Burgiyana) Colonial Archive, South Australia." *World Archaeology* 48(2): 210–25.

Gosden, Chris. 2004. *Archaeology and Colonialism: Cultural Contact from 5000 B.C. to the Present.* Cambridge: Cambridge University Press.

Gosden, Chris, and Lesley Head. 1994. "Landscape—A Usefully Ambiguous Concept." *Archaeology in Oceania* 29(3): 113–16.

Harrison, Rodney. 2004a. "Contact Archaeology and the Landscapes of Pastoralism in the North-West of Australia." In *The Archaeology of Contact in Settler Societies,* ed. Tim Murray, 109–43. Cambridge: Cambridge University Press.

———. 2004b. *Shared Landscapes: Archaeologies of Attachment and the Pastoral Industry in New South Wales.* Sydney: UNSW Press.

Harrison, Rodney, and Christine Williamson. 2004. *After Captain Cook: The Archaeology of the Recent Indigenous Past in Australia.* Walnut Creek, CA: AltaMira Press.

Ingold, Tim. 1988. *What Is an Animal?* One World Archaeology 1. London and Boston: Unwin Hyman.

Irish, Paul. 2017. *Hidden in Plain View: The Aboriginal People of Coastal Sydney.* Sydney: NewSouth.

Jordan, Kurt A. 2009. "Colonies, Colonialism, and Cultural Entanglement: The Archaeology of Postcolumbian Intercultural Relations." In *International Handbook of Historical Archaeology*, ed. Teresita Majewski and David Gaimster, 31–49. New York: Springer.

Karskens, Grace. 2010. *The Colony: A History of Early Sydney.* Crows Nest, NSW: Allen & Unwin.

Kent, Susan, ed. 1990. *Domestic Architecture and the Use of Space: An Interdisciplinary Cross-Cultural Study.* Cambridge: Cambridge University Press.

_____, ed. 2002. *Ethnicity, Hunter-Gatherers, and the "Other": Association or Assimilation in Africa.* Washington, DC: Smithsonian Institution Press.

Langford, R. F. 1983. "Our Heritage—Your Playground." *Australian Archaeology* 16: 1–6.

Lawrence, Susan, and Nick Shepherd. 2006. "Historical Archaeology and Colonialism." In *The Cambridge Companion to Historical Archaeology*, ed. Dan Hicks and Mary C. Beaudry, 69–86. Cambridge: Cambridge University Press.

Lightfoot, Kent G., Antoinette Martinez, and Ann M. Schiff. 1998. "Daily Practice and Material Culture in Pluralistic Social Settings: An Archaeological Study of Culture Change and Persistence from Fort Ross, California." *American Antiquity* 63(2): 199–222.

Lightfoot, Kent G., Thomas A. Wake, and Ann M. Schiff. 1993. "Native Responses to the Russian Mercantile Colony of Fort Ross, Northern California." *Journal of Field Archaeology* 20: 159–75.

Lydon, Jane. 2005a. "'Our Sense of Beauty': Visuality, Space and Gender on Victoria's Aboriginal Reserves, South-Eastern Australia." *History and Anthropology* 16(2): 211–33.

_____. 2005b. "'Men in Black': The Blacktown Native Institution and the Origins of the 'Stolen Generation.'" In *Object Lessons: Archaeology and Heritage in Australia*, ed. Jane Lydon and Tracy Ireland, 201–24. Melbourne: Australian Scholarly Publishing.

_____. 2006. "Pacific Encounters, or Beyond the Islands of History." In *Historical Archaeology*, ed. Martin Hall and Stephen Silliman, 293–312. Studies in Global Archaeology. Oxford: Blackwell.

_____. 2009. *Fantastic Dreaming: The Archaeology of an Aboriginal Mission.* Lanham, MD: AltaMira Press.

McBryde, Isabel. 1989. *Guests of the Governor—Aboriginal Residents of the First Government House.* Sydney: The Friends of the First Government House Site.

_____. 2000. "'Barter … immediately commenced to the satisfaction of both parties': Cross-Cultural Exchange at Port Jackson, 1788–1828." In *The Archaeology of Difference: Negotiating Cross-Cultural Engagements in Oceania*, ed. Anna Clarke and Robin Torrance, 245–84. London: Routledge.

Murray, Tim. 1998. "The Changing Contexts of the Archaeology of Aboriginal Australia." *Archaeology of Aboriginal Australia: a Reader*, ed. Tim Murray, 1–6. St Leonards: Allen & Unwin.

Panich, Lee M. 2013. "Archaeologies of Persistence: Reconsidering the Legacies of Colonialism in Native North America." *American Antiquity* 78: 105–22.

Paterson, Alistair G. 2017. "Once Were Foragers: The Archaeology of Agrarian Australia and the Fate of Aboriginal Land Management." *Quaternary International* 489: 4–16.

———. 2018. "Historical Archaeology of Pearling in the Indian Ocean: Through the Lens of North West Australia." In *Connecting Continents: Archaeology and History in the Indian Ocean World*, ed. Kris Seetah, 171–203. Athens, OH: University of Ohio Press.

Pike, Andrew, and Ann McGrath. 2014. *Message from Mungo*. Australia: Ronin Films.

Reynolds, Henry. 1982. *The Other Side of the Frontier: Aboriginal Resistance to the European Invasion of Australia*. Ringwood: Penguin.

Rose, Deborah Bird. 1991. *Hidden Histories: Black Stories from Victoria River Downs, Humbert River and Wave Hill Stations*. Canberra: Aboriginal Studies Press.

Sadr, Karim. 2005. "Hunter-Gatherers and Herders of the Kalahari During the Late Holocene." In *Desert Peoples: Archaeological Perspectives*, ed. Peter Veth, Mike Smith, and Peter Hiscock, 206–21. Malden, MA: Blackwell Publishing.

Silliman, Stephen W. 2008. *Collaborating at the Trowel's Edge: Teaching and Learning in Indigenous Archaeology*. Tucson: University of Arizona Press.

Smith, Anita, and Wendy Beck. 2003. "The Archaeology of No Man's Land: Indigenous Camps at Corindi Beach, Mid-North Coast New South Wales." *Archaeology in Oceania* 38(2): 66–77.

Spector, Janet D. 1993. *What This Awl Means: Feminist Archaeology at a Wahpeton Dakota Village*. St. Paul: Minnesota Historical Society Press.

Stanner, W. E. H. 2011. *The Dreaming & Other Essays*. Melbourne: Schwartz Publishing.

Thomas, Nicholas. 1991. *Entangled Objects: Exchange, Material Culture, and Colonialism in the Pacific*. Cambridge, MA: Harvard University Press.

Wolfe, Patrick. 2006. "Settler colonialism and the elimination of the Native." *Journal of Genocide Research* 8(4): 387–409.

Index

www.ingramcontent.com/pod-product-compliance
Lightning Source LLC
Chambersburg PA
CBHW070923030426
42336CB00014BA/2511